urban
life styles

urban
life styles

Natalie Allon
Philadelphia College of Textiles and Science

wcb

Wm. C. Brown Company Publishers
Dubuque, Iowa

PRINCIPAL THEMES IN SOCIOLOGY

Consulting Editor

Peter Manning
Michigan State University

Copyright © 1979 by Wm. C. Brown Company Publishers

Library of Congress Catalog Card Number: 78—74488

ISBN 0—697—07558—3

Printed in the United States of America

To my parents
and to H. J. L.
in love, courage, and peace

Contents

CHAPTER FOUR SINGLES BARS, with Diane Fishel

CHAPTER FIVE CONCLUSIONS

APPENDIX SOME PERSONAL REACTIONS TO MY RESEARCH

REFERENCES 197

INDEX 205

LIST OF FIGURES

Foreword

It is said that the wars fought by England were won on the playing fields of the grammar schools Eton and Harrow. Late in the afternoon, in the waning light, little men properly dressed, played the rugby and cricket of their fathers, and replicated the orderliness of English life. In the highly complex rules, the nuances of progession, momentum and respect of others' moves and counter moves, the English games, such as cricket and rugby, displayed, on the surface, the underlying code of a highly ritualized and stratified order. It was the assigning of roles, the movements between them, the accepting of outcomes often hopelessly weighted at the beginning, the good fight and the honor of victory, that bespoke the competitive, but finely tuned, nature of late Victorian civility that is only now beginning to crumble. Shadows fell on that life, as on the games in fall afternoons. The shadow and the act are mirrored in F. Madox Ford's *Parade's End*, where the protracted game of English life of the late Victorian period was played out long after the meaning had been drained from the form. In leisure, surfaced work. As the child's play was playing at work, so work was a replication of the play of the English gentleman. They mirrored each other in transformed symmetry. To play one was to play the other while to work at one was to make the other work. There is, of course, something sensible about all this, for sensibility inheres in form in well-articulated cultural systems. The transformations made from leisure to work and back are made mindlessly, that is to say, in the proper frame of mind. That there was a proper frame of mind was a felicitous consequence of the close connection between the sensibilities of the strata involved and the technological infrastructure of the society.

In modern, post-industrial society, the contradictions of feeling and production are no longer rooted. The productive order produces more goods than can be easily consumed, so that consumption must be learned. Not only must consumption be learned, but *elastic* consumption is required; one must want more than one has, endlessly. Our work becomes, as it were (and as it is), the work of doing leisure, of doing fun, of being happy. This alteration in the relationship between work and play in industrial societies has often been remarked on. Perceptive observers have noted that while an industrializing society is rooted in a folk culture of eroding traditional meanings, a fully industrialized social order takes its "traditions" from its industrialized forms—from its forms of production and work. The symmetry between work and leisure is not reversed in the sense that people now work in order to play, or that work is a transformation of play, but play becomes an artifice demanded because work no longer either replicated play or indeed replicates anything but itself.

Leisure, conversely, becomes an independently justified entity in whose content one finds more and more isolated, individualistic, status-seeking and maintaining self-centered phenomena. Take, for example, the "jogging" fad, with its associated panoply of expensive "suits," imported shoes, and underthings. Its aim, if justified culturally, is "self-improvement" or "health" while its symbolic dimensions are, as Veblen wrote, those of conspicuous consumption and conspicuous leisure. Endurance, strength, persistence, and refined musculature no longer have any centrality in most work, and certainly not in the lives of joggers of the effete middle and upper middle classes. Skills relevant to work are those of "style," appearances, polished "lines" and "raps," "put-offs" and "put-downs" and gamesmanship. Ironically, it would appear, we now work at our play, and the play has less and less to do with anything and more to do with any person.

The settings within the urban world studied here would appear to be mediating structures that stand between the work world with its patterned emptiness and the world of individual leisure with its self-created empty patterns. If we conceive of individualistic preoccupations on one side and the fully submerged work world on the other, then settings such as these are opportunities for group-articulated self-expression, where the code is implicit and person-centered. We do not have an urban sociology that deals with such developments. The Chicago school, once so sensitive, now seems to somehow overlook these matters of individual style in structures almost set by self-service. The Chicago version of urban sociology, to which Allon refers in the introductory essay, was a theory for industrialized society in which economic relations produced the structure of city life. The Chicago school, Park, Burgess, and McKenzie in particular, were enough populists and infused with German idealism (most especially Park who studied with Simmel), to retain a modicum of cultural determinism in their theories of urban life. Thus paired with the determinism of the economic i.e., in this case land values and related movements to seek functionally appropriate territory, was the determinism of meanings associated with the special cultural areas of the city. These were ecological niches in which life styles of a certain kind flourished—the Gold Coast, the slum, the area of transients, the ethnic enclaves. There is a tension, of course, in this view which is unresolved—which came first, and which determines the other in cases of conflict between sets of determinants? Park and Burgess were equivocal on this issue and maintained *both* a social psychological view of the city taken from Simmel and Weber, and a view adopted from economists and ecologists. The self seemed to be worked out in such theories.

As with the English scene above, work and play could be seen to reflect each other, but in Chicago in the twenties, the scene began to show the strain. Vaguely articulated forms of leisure began to appear, only marginally related to the productive order, and indeed seemed to be negating it as in the gang boys' activities studied by Thrasher. Their working seemed to be the most likely to be integrated into the social order, whether they be Polish immigrants, the young, or newly arrived rural migrants. But the contradictions of urban leisure remained in the taxi-dance halls, where the cultural forms of nations merged.

In the leisure scenes described by Allon, the new frame of mind of the middle-class urbanite is revealed. In these mediating structures where work and leisure do not so much *replicate* each other structurally, but merge and sub-merge each other, the contrary nature of much of this kind of life is manifested. First, note that the self-absorption Allon found and so humanely illustrates is a kind of structurally rooted narcissism lying somewhere between play as work and work as play. Is one preparing for work by dieting, so that one's clothes look good, and one "gets ahead?" Or is one doing it for fun, to be with other people in a sociable setting? Or is it just "good for me" "I like it?" Note also that conflicting commitments locate people between obligations to self and to other, playing on their structurally induced ambivalences. The third theme, authenticating and validating a self, is more problematic as it becomes more and more important to carve out a unique self. Finally, careers within such settings become not "alternative life styles," but life styles in themselves. That is, they become ways of life with independent rationales standing apart from work as something from which one "gets away from," and take place in transitional settings in which freedom to actualize a new self is socially conferred.

There is a desperate quality to the little dramas that are here reported, quite apart from the developments I have used to contextualize them. They seem so fragile, delicate and so much spidery elaborations of selves only partially validated by networks of situated others. Unlike the little games of school boys where the meanings of the games were perfectly obvious (of course they were perfectly obvious because the meanings were buried deep in a shared implicit code that need not be verbalized), these games seem to float on their own air.

Much of the sociological work done by Allon on the following pages is a very neat way of asking us to consider if it really is this way for all of us. Do we all have something of these superficial gamelike tendencies, and avail ourselves of them only unself-consciously? Are we in the liminal position without roots in work or in leisure in the conventional meanings of those terms? The flickering of lights on the pool, off the scales at Trim-Down meetings, and from the faces of eager conversationalists in "singles bars" may foreshadow a post-industrial structural form.

Peter K. Manning
Michigan State University

Preface

This book of essays of ethnographic sketches, based upon the research methodologies of participant observation and open-ended interviewing, examines processes and structures of three settings of supportive social networks: dieting groups, health spas, and singles bars. It focuses upon how mutual support in coping with stigmas is developed through group rituals which manifest sociability and alienation, play and work, after providing brief backgrounds of each setting. Nurturance and mutual aid in empathetic atmospheres of self-degradation and self-elevation were processed through four basic dimensions of each setting: (1) basic commonalities evidenced in self- and body-absorption; (2) the sharing of some ambivalent and contradictory commitments, in terms of attitudes, feelings, and behaviors; (3) common processes involved in authenticating or validating the self; and (4) a sharing of constructive behavioral performances and careers fostered by the settings.

The essays discuss some of the searching and discovery processes of finding, locating, maintaining, and validating a self in complex urban America in the sixties and seventies. Many of the people studied in this book desired to conform to the urban societal image of what white middle-class mass media and advertising preach to us is a happy, healthy, attractive, and morally good person. The three environments of group dieting, health spas, and singles bars worked on both reinforcing and changing aspects of the individual to fit into *status quo* urban America, rather than stressing macrosocietal changes of institutions.

Participants voluntarily conformed to the settings which emphasized cooperation, competition, and achievement, as people often examined themselves in relation to others and sought social approval in atmospheres of sociability. The three settings studied proposed individualistically-oriented socio-psychological ways of coping with the world more smoothly and effectively. Because participants established rapport with each other on the basis of a common interest or problem, as weight losing, physical fitness or meeting others, they often took for granted the notion that they had much in common with each other beside the formal purpose of gathering together.

These essays offer an in-depth look at three settings of supportive social networks that have been rarely investigated by sociologists. They weave together empirical details of the settings with some basic sociological insights. By discussing the unique as well as the common characteristics of the settings, readers may gain analytic and descriptive insights into settings of self-help and mutual support. The essays examine common preoccupations in urban life styles in contemporary America—in particular, perceptions, feelings and judgments about self and body images, and interpersonal relationships. Students in the social sciences as well as others who read this book may learn about prevalent contemporary American life styles which are sources of serious concerns as well as diverting pastimes.

I have collaborated with Hannah Wartenberg on the chapter on health spas. I have worked with Diane Fishel on the chapter on singles bars. Diane Fishel and I presented some of our ideas about singles bars in a paper presented at the American Sociological Association meeting in August 1973, and we subsequently published some of our ideas. (Allon and Fishel, 1977, pp. 8–26)

Suggested topics for thought and projects on group dieting, health spas, and singles bars follow each chapter.

Acknowledgments

Many people have encouraged my research and writing over the past few years, and have provided me with valuable intellectual insights as well as support for my work. I am very grateful for their guidance and encouragements. Some very special people who have really extended themselves to me include: Hilde Bruch, Werner Cahnman, Arlene Kaplan Daniels, Renee Fox, Everett Hughes, Rachel Kahn-Hut, David Kallen, Nora Scott Kinzer, Arthur Shostak, and Samuel Wallace. A very special mention of gratitude goes to Peter Manning, who encouraged me to write this book. My colleagues in the Sociology Department of Hofstra University who have provided me with valuable insights and much understanding include: Meyer Barash, Regina Davis, Hyman Enzer, Tadeusz Krauze, Warren Mintz, Joseph O'Donoghue, and John Wildeman. Two former colleagues in my department have also been quite helpful: Gloria Evans and Joan Miele.

I want to thank others for their multifaceted help, including: Aldebaran, Sally Hillsman Baker, Edith Berman, Platon Collipp, Lewis Coser, Rose Laub Coser, Deborah David, Lynne Davidson, Dawn Day, Allan Eister, Sonja Eiteljorg, Robert Emerson, William Fabrey, Lisbeth Fisher, Vivian Fromberg, Sanford Gifford, Judith Gordon, Ignacio Gotz, Marci Greenwood, Kirsten Gronjberg, Harriet Gross, Marvin Grosswirth, Sally Guttmacher, Richard N. Harris, Richard Hessler, Lynda Lytle Holmstrom, Irving Louis Horowitz, Louisa Howe, Dorothy J. Jessop, Jack Kamerman, Corinne Kirschner, Paula Krauss, Shirley Langer, Lauren Langman, Lois Lindauer, Lora Liss, Judith Lorber, Teresa Marciano, Rita Seiden Miller, Peter New, Carol Poll, Gary Rosenberg, Ruth Rubenstein, Roberta Satow, Yaffa Schlesinger, Lenore Monello Schloming, Philip Slater, Peter Stein, Judith Stern, Thomas Szasz, Athena Theodore, Gaye Tuchman, Ethel Weiss, and Robert S. Weiss.

I would like to thank many members of the New York Metropolitan and National Sociologists for Women in Society for their insights and support. A special word of thanks goes to Elaine Misko, who helped me invaluably in completing footnote and bibliographic references. Additionally, I am very appreciative to Bob Nash, Sociology Editor of William C. Brown

Company Publishers, for his initial interest and encouragement of the book. I am very grateful to Jean Pascual, Assistant Editor, for her helpful and clear-cut editorial suggestions, as well as encouragement of my work. I am very thankful to Suzanne Satnick and Lennie Adelman for typing pages of the manuscript. A special thanks goes to Randy Cooper for all kinds of help.

My dear parents, Frances Allon and Samuel Allon, have provided me with much technical assistance as well as emotional support in the preparation of this book. I would like to thank my good friend Harvey Levin for his many kinds of help.

I cannot really express enough gratitude to the many generous and insightful people whom I met in dieting groups, health spas, and singles bars. Quite a few of these people were indeed collaborators in the development of some of my ideas.

Most recently, I would like to thank my colleagues in the Department of Humanities and Social Sciences, Philadelphia College of Textiles and Science, for their support of my work.

Natalie Allon
Philadelphia
December 1978

Introduction

1

THE MODERN URBAN LIFE SETTING

These essays discuss the searching and discovery processes of finding, locating, maintaining, and validating a self in complex urban America in the sixties and seventies. Looking to define and clarify a sense of self is contingent upon putting oneself into situations and interactions so that relationships between self and others pattern out basic aspects of the self. This book examines the three diverse life styles of: dieting groups, health spas, and singles bars. Ethnographies of these three distinct arenas show a basic similarity in that they all direct and crystallize cognitive and affective patterns. The three settings reinforce membership views by focusing and articulating preexisting feelings, attitudes, and behavior. Participants entered each setting out of their own sense of responsibility or choice, or because they felt called to the setting, or because of pressures from others. The people studied reflect some basic themes of modern urban culture.

During the 1920s and 1930s, a number of sociologists at the University of Chicago believed that urban land specialization could be explained by analogy to the ecological model in biology. These sociologists saw the urban environment as a product of competition and natural selection; they were concerned with symbiotic relations—the unplanned interdependence of city-dwelling humans. Some sociologists studied how geographical areas became characterized by the cultural characteristics of people who lived in them. (Park, Burgess, and McKenzie, eds., 1925; Park and Burgess, 1969)

The growing complexity and specialization of land use along with the increasingly heterogeneous life styles in the city have led some sociologists to see the city as the prototype of mass society. Urban culture in contemporary America has been described as future-oriented, undergoing rapid change, with the consequent breakdown of traditional values and practices. Social structures in the city are loosely articulated, composed of a welter of conflicting, competing groups and ideologies. Mores have been weakened and folkways redefined in the city. Legal norms and laws have supplanted unwritten codes. There are few universally accepted beliefs, values, and standards of behavior. The mass movement of heterogeneous mixtures of peoples to cities weakened or even obliterated the control formerly exerted by family and neighbors. Complex formal agencies of control, as the police, have arisen in the cities.*

In the city, relations with others are often transitory, impersonal, superficial, and anonymous, with people careful to expose only segments of their total selves in everyday interaction. Indifferences toward strangers has replaced rural hospitality or hostility. The city life exemplifies a proliferation of social roles and an intricate division of labor. There are few fixed, ascribed positions; individuals must seek out and compete for positions. In the complex social structures of cities, individuals occupy many statuses and play many different and unrelated roles. There is a tendency for sex and age roles to converge and become more alike; yet these roles are more ill-defined.

In the city, there is much communal dissensus rather than consensus. Social organization becomes increasingly atomistic and ill-defined. There are soaring rates of social disorganization with the value orientations of various subcultures automatically clashing. Many of these uncertainties beget anomie and marginality. Within this atmosphere of contradictory norms and even apparent normlessness, the philosophy of "rugged individualism" takes hold with much individualistic experimentation. Self-centered progress becomes the goal. With this emphasis upon individual achievement, there is a universalistic stress on the idea that the same norms apply to all. The city fosters an open, permeable social class system, with a consequent emergence of class-consciousness, status striving and conspicuous consumption. Rags-to-riches themes, whether in wishes, theory or practice, are part of the fiber of city life.

The city has a complex economic system with an elaborate division of labor and a quick transfer of goods and services. There has been a gradual demise of individual enterprise and an increasing potency of big business in cities. Specialization and competition continue to prevail. More "sophisticated" (as well as synthetic and manufactured) entertainment fare has arisen, along with a growth of "spectatoritis"—the mushrooming of competitive spectator sports. The mass media have grown increasingly potent and pervasive.

In the city, many children and wives have broken free of father-husband domination. Life has become decreasingly familistic and increasingly individualistic, with the family losing its central role. Divorce rates soar and families become smaller. Mass education has emerged in the city and has become increasingly democratic and available to many. Working toward and achieving various "diplomas" have become goals for many people.

As a scholarly synthesizer, Wirth has succinctly discussed some basic themes of urban life—depersonalization, impersonalism, anonymity, utilitarianism, and indifference. (Wirth, 1938, pp. 1-24) One of the most

___

*My description about contemporary American urban culture in the next few pages has been informed by the overview in: Harold M. Hodges, Jr., *Conflict and Consensus: An Introduction to Sociology,* 2nd. ed. (New York: Harper & Row Publishers, Inc., 1974), pp. 152-55.

brilliant analyses of such themes was written by Simmel in the very beginning of the twentieth century, and is still relevant today. Simmel discussed the psychological basis of the metropolitan type of individuality, which he viewed as consisting of the intensification of nervous stimulation which resulted from the swift and uninterrupted change of outer and inner stimuli. The metropolis created psychological conditions which used up much consciousness in focusing on nonlasting, highly differentiated impressions which were not regular and not habitual. Uneven, irregular, fast-paced urban life consisted of the rapid crowding of changing images, a sharp discontinuity in the grasping of a single glance as well as the unexpectedness of onrushing impressions. (Simmel, 1962, p. 152)

Simmel believed that the metropolis fostered a blasé attitude, in which participants often seemed to carry on the motions of interaction in acting *to* and *at* each other, not always *with* each other. The blasé attitude resulted from the rapidly changing and closely contrasting stimulation of the nerves. One became blasé in the boundless pursuit of pleasure in the city because one agitated one's nerves to their strongest reactivity for such a long time that one's nerves finally ceased to react at all. The blasé attitude essentially consisted of the blunting of discrimination. Objects were in fact perceived, but the meaning and differing value of things, and thereby the things themselves, were experienced as insubstantial. Things appeared to the blasé person in an evenly flat and gray tone; no one object deserved preference over any other. (Simmel, 1962, pp. 156–57)

Simmel discussed how the city's money economy with its dominance of the intellect over feelings reduced all quality and individuality to the question: How much? Urban dwellers' precise weighing and calculating with a plethora of numerical determinations reduced qualitative values to quantitative ones. The city's stress on anonymity and matter-of-factness led to indifference—even a slight aversion, and mutual strangeness and repulsion between people. The city did enable people to be free from close scrutiny by others. Still, so as to avoid getting lonely and lost in the metropolitan crowd, city dwellers exaggerated their unique particularities in order to remain audible to themselves. A person in the city often sought to distinguish and elaborate upon her/his irreplaceable individuality, which set her/him apart from others. People fought pressures which transformed the individual into a mere cog in an enormous organization of things and persons. (Simmel, 1962, pp. 157–65)

This book is about the many ambivalences and nuances in the struggles of individuals to find and *authenticate* a sense of self on the one hand, while on the other hand, their confronting of pressures to conform to some white upper-middle-class values of city life. Many of us feel the tensions of the people discussed in this book. Indeed, the people whom we studied have articulated most insightfully many of our joys and sorrows. The people with whom we talked and observed were searching for their own viable standards of morality, health, and beauty, very much aware of the definitions of such standards given by others. They chose to look for their standards in mutual help groups where their behavior was regulated by firm customs, with informal community pressures, as the threat of gossip or ostracism. The people chose to abide by the quite clear-cut rules as well as to break such rules of groups which they joined voluntarily.

Most importantly, many people with whom we talked were searching for some aspects of a folk culture, which was unified by specific norms for appropriate and inappropriate behavior, and which offered intimate, personal, and sometimes long-lasting primary relationships. (Hodges, 1974, pp. 152–55) In the limited time and place settings of the protective enclaves of the self-help groups, people showed dependence upon others for approval and affection in the midst of anonymous, impersonal, and heterogeneous urban life. In the midst of anomic cities, people welcomed the groups' definite strategies and tactics which, in a straightforward manner, educated people about what to do, and how and why to carry out certain life styles. Many were seeking to be active participants in shaping their own destinies, rather than be mere passive victims to urban powers which depersonalized them. This book is about many of us who have many wishes and fears about fighting for as well as losing our independent individuality and our powers of empathy in contemporary urban society. Like many of us, many people we talked with felt alone and alienated in modern, impersonal urban life, not sure if anyone really cared about each other. Many came to the three settings which we studied in order to be cared for and to care for others, to express, cope with, and try to solve some of their problems of aloneness and alienation.

OVERVIEW OF THE BOOK

Most of the people studied in this book desired to conform to the urban societal image of what white middle- and upper-middle-class mass media and advertising preach to us is a happy, healthy, beautiful/handsome, morally good person. (Kinzer, 1974, pp. 2–9) Some were a bit ambivalent about such goals, but they did voluntarily process themselves through social institutions which stressed conformity to some traditional ideals of a desirable, attractive, and well-adjusted person. The essays in this book discuss people who basically want to fit into and make it in *status quo* contemporary urban America as it is—who are not strong advocates of social and political change. The three environments worked on both reinforcing and changing aspects of the individual to fit into *status quo* urban America, rather than stressing macro-societal change.

This book points out the many vocabularies used to capture and interpret the experiences of self and body in contemporary America, as suggested by Manning and Zucker.

> . . . a moral language of sin; a behavioristic language of mechanical action; a legal language of social culpability; a biological language of physicalistic

determinism; a psychoanalytic deterministic language and a psychoanalytic language of rehabilitation and justification; an everyday language of practical necessity; a computer-derived language of machinelike functioning of the mind and body . . . Man is no longer the center of his universe, an agent who sees the world unfolding with himself as *subject,* but sees himself instead as an *object* . . . . man sees himself in terms of the external world rather than seeing the external world as a reflection of himself . . . . (Manning and Zucker, 1976, pp. 76–77)

In these settings, people groped to define and clarify themselves, to improve parts of their persons which they deemed perfectible, to support each other as equals as well as to differentiate themselves from others. (Simmel, 1904, pp. 130–55) Many members in the three settings described themselves as being in the process of becoming, in some ways, better people. They stressed their efforts at self-knowledge, self-growth, and self-improvement, carried out alone in their own minds and hearts as well as in interactions with others. They underlined the means and process of perfecting themselves—many claiming that they neither desired nor could reach the final goal of self-satisfied perfection. All three settings pointed to aspects of sociological and psychological ambivalence in that they both reinforced and mitigated against negative and positive aspects of varieties of stigma attached to the selves, bodies, and clothes of participants.

All three settings were sponsored by more or less profit-making voluntary organizations which encouraged a relative freedom to choose alternative life styles within the context of some basic norms and rules. Voluntary conformity to the settings with much consensus between formally defined leaders and followers was clear in visible and in invisible attitudes and behaviors. The management of the body in face-to-face interaction was stressed in all the settings. The constant examination of oneself in relation to others was apparent in all settings, with processes of competition and antagonistic cooperation viewed as basic to improving oneself. (Sumner, 1940, pp. 30–32, 58, 297)

Persons often searched for social approval in the settings. Supportive consolation and solidarity emerged in each setting as people groped to gain a greater sense of themselves through others as positive and negative reference individuals and groups. (Hyman and Singer, eds., 1968) Ambivalently alone and alienated, self-contained and contemplative, as well as together and sociable, outgoing and gregarious, people seriously worked hard and played in fun in the three environments. Empathetic comfort as well as competitive achievement anxieties and restlessness pervaded the atmosphere of the three settings.

Some members showed full and deep internal commitment to the ways of life advocated in the settings. Vociferous or very visible minorities showed mere external conformity to the rules of the game of the settings— they were not so committed to the ideologies and practices of the environments as total life styles. Various types of Believers, Doubting

Thomases, and Devil's Advocates with reference to prescribed and preferred ways of life emerged.

Genuine empathetic as well as *pseudo-gemeinschaft*—feigned sincere and caring—relationships occurred in the restless search for self-discovery. The three settings combined *gemeinschaft* qualities of warm and affectionate close-knit familylike ties stressing diffuse, unspecified, unlimited, and particularistic relationships with *gesellschaft*-type activities which were oriented to gain specified and limited goals. (Tönnies, 1957; Cahnman, ed., 1973) Sociability for its own sake emerged in all the settings, where people made friends with each other as people and enjoyed the delights of social intercourse above and beyond motivations and goals set forth in the settings. (Simmel, 1964, pp. 40–57)

Participants developed and displayed a definite sense of the sacred and profane in quasi-religious rituals which emphasized guilt-atonement as well as confessional-testimonal-redemption cycles. (Durkheim, 1961; Pruyser, 1968). Degradation, elevation, and purification ceremonies of self emerged, where the process of perfecting oneself was the ultimatum. (Garfinkel, 1956, pp. 420–24) Ideologies in the settings refused to acknowledge the final achievement of the goal of final perfection: saints-in-the-making arose from some basis of sinning. The castelike and secret society nature of the settings as kinds of sects with the exclusiveness of privileged elects came out in the esoteric language and behavior of in-group members, as distinct from out-group others. (Simmel, 1964, pp. 345–76; Wilson, 1961)

Four main themes captured many of the feelings, attitudes, ideologies, and behaviors which arose in the three settings. The first concerned the direction of attention and involvement, focused on the self, labeled *self-absorption*. Many participants were engrossed in themselves, "soaked" in themselves, as an end or as a means to a higher involvement with superempirical or ideal reference points. Often the self and one's body occupied one's full attention, interest, and time. Such a focus on self often consisted of mental and physical concentration.

The second theme involved some conflicts about holding in and giving out parts of the self, urges to gratify as well as suppress or repress feelings, thoughts, and actions. The existence of mutually conflicting feelings or thoughts, such as control and release together, about some person, object, or idea led to some controversy about to whom or what a participant was committed. People wavered with regard to whom they had confidence in and to what positions on issues they would pledge themselves. Such ambivalent vacillations pointed to the idea of *conflicting and contradictory commitments.*

The third theme stressed the means by which participants sought to *authenticate or validate themselves,* primarily through certain attitudes and feelings of themselves and others. The groping for *authenticity* involved means by which people tried to establish or prove that they were trustworthy or genuine—worthy to be liked and respected. Being genuine presupposed evidence that the people were what they claimed to be. By producing desired results, often on their bodies, people would *validate* their well-grounded, sound selves. *Valid* referred to qualities that gave inner strength and the capacity to resist challenge or attack. Participants sought to support and strengthen their self-esteem by means of substantial or tangible concrete evidence. *Validating* oneself meant that one found a sense of oneself through others and that one could conclude at the very least that one was an "O.K. person."

The fourth theme was the actual *construction of performances* in the settings, stressing behavior. Such behavior involved deliberate contriving and planning of distinctive routines and rituals. Self and bodily *careers* were processed through the three settings, with varying degrees and kinds of successes and failures and leadership and followership.

RESEARCH STRATEGIES

I was a participant observer in 90 Trim-Down (pseudonym) group dieting meetings located in the northeastern United States from 1967 through 1970. I received permission to carry out my study from Trim-Down executives, and was not required to pay the weekly fee. I met 31 different lecturers and observed about 1,400 members in these meetings which lasted between 45 minutes and two and one-half hours. About 95 percent of the members were women, and about five percent were men. I conducted about 350 informal interviews with Trim-Down members and promoters and I had about 20 formal interviews with promoters.

My colleague, Hannah Wartenberg, and I were regular, paying members of a spa with different branches, located in the urban and suburban northeastern United States. We each went separately to the spa to carry out our research. Focusing mainly on women, we observed over 600 different spa participants in 1976–1977. Each of us attended the spa over 100 times, between one and one-half and four hours each time. We carried out our observations and conducted open-ended interviews with people in the actual physical processes of partaking in spa activities, telling some members and employees that we were doing research on physical fitness.

I joined in the research project of one of my undergraduate students, Diane Fishel, on singles bars in a large northeastern metropolitan area in the United States. Diane Fishel and I were both participant observers and open-ended interviewers in eight singles bars, often telling people that we were doing research. We interviewed 150 women and men between 1972 and 1974. Our interviews varied in length from 15 minutes to four hours, and took place in the bars between 8:00 P.M. and 2:00 A.M. Diane and I visited the different bars a total of over 250 times for purposes of our study.

All three studies were undertaken to discover and generate ideas and hypotheses which we hope can be more systematically investigated in future research.

SELF-ABSORPTION

The dimension of *self-absorption* showed that in group dieting, health spas, and singles bars, participants focused inwardly on themselves—selves which included feelings and thoughts sometimes centering on the body. The focus upon oneself enabled some to keep away from or keep their distance from others as they lived in their own little worlds. Such self-concentration enabled others to get a grip on themselves so that they would be able to extend themselves more effectively outwardly to others. This preoccupation with self, this self-centeredness, took much time, energy, and money as is true for many of our self-preoccupations. This involvement with self, sometimes labeled a "new consciousness," has itself become a commodity according to Schur.

> It is being heavily promoted, packaged, and marketed, much like any other commercial item. While the movement provides middle-class consumers with an attractive new product, attention is diverted from the more serious social problems that plague our society—poverty, racism, environmental decay, crime, widespread corporate and governmental fraud. (Schur, 1976, p. 7)

So most often the focus on self in group dieting, health spas, and singles bars meant a stress on accepting, reinforcing, and changing the individual, not society. Such institutions invited a participant to become preoccupied and even "possessed" with oneself and one's sensations, thus diluting already weak feelings of social responsibility. Group dieting, health spas, and singles bars all emphasized care of the beauty and health of the body, graceful movements, and shaping/keeping up one's fitness as a *raison d'être* of their existence, especially for women. Schur has commented:

> . . . it is striking that in these regimes women end up doing essentially what they have done before: trying to conform to the movie-star image of what will be pleasing to men, indirectly upholding the idea that how women look and feel is more important than what they do. (Schur, 1976, p. 133)

Such settings stressed that people could and should be in the company of other like-minded individuals, and even openly used such others for the sake of self-learning and self-development. Sometimes they encouraged separation of oneself from others.

Could group dieters, health spa participants, and singles bars attenders who were out to maximize their own sensory experiences still be able to care about others? Members of the three settings often talked about attempts to be good to themselves; they often legitimated their self-indulgence, self-pampering, and self-mothering. They stressed that they were always so self-sacrificing with others that they deserved to come to the settings and focus upon themselves, often leading to feelings of skin and muscle eroticism by self-massaging.

Quite a few participants in the three settings acknowledged that their self-focusing was not always pleasure-ridden, but often quite masochistic. In their self-concentration, they realized big and small things that were wrong with themselves, their bodies, and their lives. Self-focusing could mean self-destructiveness as well as self-constructiveness, as is true for many of us.

For many, *self-absorption* led to multiple reactions of what it meant to be alone or lonely. (Moustakas, 1961, Weiss, ed., 1973) Many stated that they were quite content and even happy in isolation; some said that they chose to impose physical isolation upon themselves so as not to be distracted by others. Those who talked about being lonely in *self-absorption* stressed the painful consequences of being by themselves; they longed for companionship to pick up their sad spirits. Many indicated that they felt legitimated and even congratulated by others for their self-focusing. They needed others to give a stamp of approval to their *self-absorption* so as to gain ego strength for themselves. They sought applause from others for taking on the initiative and responsibility of taking charge of themselves and their bodies—a responsibility which was an outcome of their self-preoccupation. Congratulating a kindred spirit on her/his insights and expertise demonstrated in taking control of oneself was also a process of self-congratulation. By *self-absorption,* one could become a kind of an expert about oneself as a human guinea pig, testing out and proving oneself—be it in dieting, exercising, or in interpersonal communication skills.

Self-absorption also involved ambiguities about prescribed social roles and one's definition of oneself. Some complained that they were continually at the mercy of definitions of self which others had given them and that they were seeking a sense of unique, personal wholeness beyond such definitions. (Goffman, 1974, pp. 269–86; 573–75) So being absorbed in losing inches or pounds to some meant that they were taking charge of their own bodies—moving beyond pressures toward certain eating styles by families and friends. *Self-absorption* in one's body could be a key to independence from others. Some stressed that they were social conformers and they knew that they would fit in better with others and gain others' approval if they lost weight and inches. Some singles bar participants said that they enjoyed playing different roles with different people—such playing was a kind of game. Others lamented this game-playing, stressing that many were anxious and phony in carefully managing their impressions for others; contrived moves to score with others meant that some were afraid to be just plain, genuine people beyond affected roles. (Goffman, 1959, pp. 208–37)

Such *self-absorption* did involve role embracement as well as role distance for participants in the settings and for many of us. Goffman has described three features of role embracement:

. . . an admitted or expressed attachment to the role; a demonstration of qualifications and capacities for performing it; an active *engagement* or spontaneous involvement in the role activity at hand, that is, a visible investment of attention and muscular effort. (Goffman, 1961, p. 106)

When there is a wedge between the individual and her/his role, between doing and being, there is role distance according to Goffman, which is an ". . . 'effectively' expressed pointed separateness between the individual and his putative role . . . ." (Goffman, 1961, p. 108) In such instances, the individual does not actually deny the role but the virtual self that is implied in the role for all accepting performers. In showing role distance, the actor may have some measure of disaffection from and resistance against the role. (Goffman, 1961, p. 108)

In group dieting and health spas, privatized, loner responses by which one moved away from others in the situation showed a kind of *self-absorption* that removed one in some ways from the concrete interactions at hand. Singles bar participants often seemed to be role embraced and role distant at the same time with particular others. They might be playing up to one person in words, seemingly involved, but be seeking out another with their eyes. For participants in all the settings, *self-absorption* meant a moving away from immediate others. In turning oneself away from others, one gave oneself up for a time to a world in which she/he alone participated—a world involving a reliving of past experiences or a rehearsing of future ones. (Goffman, 1966, pp. 69-70) Goffman has stated:

At such times the individual may demonstrate his absence from the current situation by a preoccupied, faraway look in his eyes, or by a sleeplike stillness of his limbs, or by the special class of side involvements that can be sustained in an utterly 'unconscious' abstracted manner—humming, doodling, drumming the fingers on a table, hair twisting, nose picking, scratching. (Goffman, 1966, p. 70)

The settings often prescribed, preferred, permitted, and tolerated self-consciousness as a meaningful involvement obligation of self in self. Such self-consciousness has been described by Goffman—but in the settings was quite an appropriate focus and not a kind of alienation from interaction as Goffman has suggested:

Self-consciousness. At the cost of his involvement in the prescribed focus of attention, the individual may focus his attention more than he ought upon himself—himself as someone who is faring well or badly, as someone calling forth a desirable or undesirable response from others . . . . Self-consciousness for the individual does not, it seems, result from his deep interest in the topic of conversation, which may happen to be himself, but rather from his giving attention to himself as an interactant at a time when he ought to be free to involve himself in the content of the conversation. (Goffman, 1967, p. 118)

Such self-consciousness often included auto-involvements—the individual's own body or an object directly associated with her/his body, such as clothing. (Goffman, 1966, pp. 64-69) Such a self-directed focus upon one's physical being was a most appropriate main and dominating involvement in group dieting, health spas, and singles bars. Attention paid to one's body was not merely a subordinate and side involvement. (Goffman, 1966, pp. 43–44) In many public settings, such attention to personal appearance often is viewed as an improper distraction from dominating involvements. Goffman has defined such involvements:

> A main involvement is one that absorbs the major part of an individual's attention and interest, visibly forming the principal current determinant of his actions. A side involvement is an activity that an individual can carry on in an abstracted fashion without threatening or confusing simultaneous maintenance of a main involvement . . . A dominating involvement is one whose claims upon an individual the social occasion obliges him to be ready to recognize: a subordinate involvement is one he is allowed to sustain only to the degree, and during the time, that his attention is patently not required by the involvement that dominates him. Subordinate involvements are sustained in a muted, modulated, and intermittent fashion, expressing in their style a continuous regard and deference for the official, dominating activity at hand. (Goffman, 1966, pp. 43–44)

Varying degrees of a focus on oneself and on one's body as major or peripheral involvements in the settings exemplified aspects of an embodied and unembodied self as Laing has described. Some participants did feel their bodies to be alive, real, and substantial—so they felt themselves to be alive, real, and substantial. Such people felt themselves as inextricably bound up with or in their bodies. Such people experienced themselves as embodied. (Laing, 1965, p. 66) Yet many experienced themselves as unembodied—as being more or less divorced or detached from their bodies.

> *The body is felt more as one object among other objects in the world than as the core of the individual's own being.* Instead of being the core of his true self, the body is felt as the core of a *false self,* which a detached, disembodied, 'inner,' 'true' self looks on at with tenderness, amusement, or hatred as the case may be . . . The unembodied self, as onlooker at all the body does, engages in nothing directly. Its functions come to be observation, control, and criticism *vis-a-vis* what the body is experiencing and doing, and those operations which are usually spoken of as purely 'mental.' (Laing, 1965, p. 69)

Group dieters, health spa participants, and singles bar attenders often viewed their bodies as objective geography, as marketplace commodities which were worth more or less depending on shape and size—sometimes depending upon the kind of clothing that their bodies could fit into. They judged their bodies according to pounds weighed, inches measured, and clothing or ornaments displayed. Do we share such views?

Members of the three settings often seemed to be slaves to their bodies, catering to multiple beauty and health dimensions of their bodies. They were successes or failures, good or bad, attractive or unattractive, had a high degree or low degree of self-esteem and peace of mind depending upon their judgments of their bodies. Taking time out from their everyday routines in order to put time into and cater to their bodily selves, these people wanted to strengthen and control their bodies so as to fight decay, illness, the inevitable aging process, and death. Pushing youth, health, and attractiveness, they sought immortality and eternity, in some ways to rise above the human race in beating the fates of aging and dying. The idea was to work for immortality in their everyday lives of the here-and-now present time.

Members of the three settings required external, behavioral evidence in their immediate worlds that they were succeeding in self-improvement. Bodily changes and interpersonal skills could make such people part of a secular elect. Very *self-absorbed,* these people worked on bodily manifestations to prove that they themselves were worthwhile human beings, perhaps capable of saving their own souls. Group dieters, health spa participants, and singles bars' attenders purified themselves by accentuating the materialism of bodily achievements.

Acquisitiveness, possession, and achievement of bodily goals were stressed by group dieters, health spa participants, and singles bar members. The three groups of participants often viewed the body as a valuable or not so valuable piece of merchandise, sometimes as a machine when it was turned on to exercise. Indeed, increasing and decreasing the value of the body in terms of bodily changes was stressed in group dieting and health spas. Buying and selling of the body sometimes occurred in singles bar "meat markets" (a term used by participants themselves) where certain sizes and shapes of bodies were worth more than other bodies.

In their strategies and tactics of *self-absorption,* participants in all three settings had varying orientations in facing up to, coming to grips with, or escaping, avoiding "reality," as they perceived such reality. For some, "core reality" was their overweight, disproportioned bodies which they had almost forgotten about or tried to minimize for quite a while. For others, "core reality" included pressures and difficulties in one's personal life; therefore, people sought to lay aside or escape such realities and "make merry," "shoot the breeze," or "forget their troubles" and let themselves go emotionally, mentally, and physically in group dieting, health spas, and singles bars.

All three settings stressed practical measures of success—could and would one's *self-absorption* "pay off" and lead to successful results? Would a concentration upon oneself lead one to reap the rewards prized by the various institutions—in such varied forms as pounds and inches lost, better interpersonal relationships, inner peace? There had to be external and often quite reductionistic and oversimplified signs to indicate that *self-absorption* was working, was getting someone somewhere, as is the case for many of us. Such signs could include reducing the body to a marketplace commodity and judging its value as on the increase as its size was on the decrease in group dieting and health spas. Another sign would be an accumulation of potential or actual heterosexual dates or qualitatively meaningful relationships in the singles bars.

The more concrete and tangible were the signs of payoff for *self-absorption,* the easier they were to measure in quantitative terms, as pounds and inches. The more abstract and intangible were the signs of payoff for *self-absorption,* such as interpersonal skills, the harder they were to measure in even qualitative terms. Sometimes singles bar participants were more restless and searching in testing and trying to improve themselves than were group dieting and health spa participants. The standards of proving oneself to be a success or failure were much simpler and clear-cut in terms of bodily changes for group dieters and health spa participants than the interpersonal standards set for singles bar participants.

For participants in all the three settings, *self-absorption* had one common denominator: people could achieve in some limited ways in the environments if they kept trying hard enough, even if they were having trouble achieving in the bigger world outside the particular setting. In their restricted, time-bound and space-bound setting with some degree of clarity of standards for achievement, people could measure their *self-absorbing* efforts more easily than in big, amorphous, anomic America at large. Participants in all three settings practiced one basic strategy of *self-absorption:* doing things to themselves on the outside, acting-out behavior led to knowledge about their inner selves.

CONFLICTING AND CONTRADICTORY COMMITMENTS

The dimension of *conflicting and contradictory commitments* sensitized us to see that in the three settings, participants vacillated between holding in or concealing parts of themselves, being closed, and giving out or revealing parts of themselves, being open. They fluctuated between ascetic and hedonistic displays. On the one hand, they showed tendencies to tighten up, put controls on, and suppress/repress parts of themselves. On the other hand, they showed an openness to give into, indulge in, and gratify certain feelings, thoughts, and behavior. (Bates, 1971) Many of us show such fluctuations. Sometimes they fiercely guarded the private territory of themselves; at other times, they wanted to expose themselves most publicly.

Members of the three environments showed intra- and inter-role sociological ambivalence in terms of role conflict and status inconsistency. The sociological theory of ambivalence refers to the social structure, not to the personality, as Merton and Barber have suggested:

> *In its most extended sense,* sociological ambivalence refers to incompatible normative expectations of attitudes, beliefs, and behavior assigned to a status or to a set of statuses in a society. *In its most restricted sense*, sociological ambivalence refers to incompatible normative expectations incorporated in a *single* role of a *single* social status. (Merton and Barber, 1967, pp. 94–95)

In these extended and restricted senses, this ambivalence is based in the social definition of roles and statuses, not in the feeling-state of one or another type of personality. Indeed, sociological ambivalence may be one major source of psychological ambivalence—people in a status or status-set which has a large measure of incompatibility with its social definition will tend to develop personal tendencies in the direction of contradictory feelings, beliefs, and behavior. (Merton and Barber, 1967, p. 95; Room, 1976, pp. 1047–65)

Such conflict meant that participants had mixed orientations about being alone, alienated from others, or being together, sociable with others, as many of us do. Sometimes they wanted to be separate from others; at other times they wanted to be merged with others. At times, members wanted to be on the same level or on equal terms with others in the settings; at other times, they wanted to differentiate themselves out as distinct individuals. They showed pushes and pulls toward being dependent on others as well as independent from others. On some occasions, participants wanted to engage playfully in leisure, have fun, and enjoy themselves. On other occasions, they wanted to be serious and work hard with much diligence and sobriety. They held traditional and experimental views about their life styles.

Conflicting commitments were shown in efforts to suppress/repress and or gratify/indulge one's desired feelings, attitudes, or behavior. Group dieters and health spa participants talked about how they hated to feel like martyrs and restrict their eating. Sometimes they enjoyed being bad and cheating on their diets—giving into every food which they loved. Then they would feel guilty about their self-indulgence and go on a very strict diet or do vigorous exercises to make up for the errors of their ways. After being a saint for a while, it was time to allow oneself to be a sinner again. In terms of their bodily conduct, such participants showed constant cycles of the saint-sinner phenomena, expressing continuous patterns of guilt and atonement as do many of us in parts of our lives. Singles bar participants fluctuated between playing up parts of themselves which they knew would attract some, and being quite genuine and sincere with others. They swung, pendulumlike, between putting on a happy face, acting most courteous and interested in another, and letting out their many mixed feelings, often including fear and anger, with others. One bar participant would put on a show of being attracted to someone he/she was not attracted to; another would be quite open in saying that he/she was not so interested in another, and about to move on to somebody else. Participants fluctuated in their desires for control and release of parts of themselves.

Along with gratification-suppression tendencies, members of all settings showed mixed feelings about how private and closed off from others they wanted to be as well as how open and public they wanted to be with others as do many of us. Sometimes some were quite self-contained and alone in settings; they minimized verbal and nonverbal communications with others as they carried out the routines of the setting, whether weighing in, exercising, or drinking. Others wanted to share their feelings about their immediate or not-so-immediate life experiences with others as they carried out the tasks of the setting. Some said that they wanted to be open in a certain setting because everybody there was equal and "in the same boat," sharing some common interest or problem. Yet, others emphasized that they really were in a setting for individual, private reasons—they resented being forced to be open to certain strangers whom they hardly knew. The latter types of participants often tried to distinguish themselves as separate from others. Many participants did struggle with their mixed feelings about being similar to as well as different from others with whom they at least appeared or more actively joined in activities in the settings.

Participants expressed much ambivalence about how alone/single or coupled/with/together they wanted to be or in fact were—in their feelings, attitudes, and behavior. The four settings exemplified aspects of both *alienation* and *sociability.* Seeman has presented one useful analytic framework with which to understand *alienation,* pointing to five significant aspects of *alienation.*

> *Powerlessness* as one variant of alienation can be viewed as: . . . *the expectancy or probability held by the individual that his own behavior cannot determine the occurence of the outcome, or reinforcements, he seeks.* (Seeman, 1964, p. 527)

Second, *alienation* as *meaninglessness* implies that the individual is unclear as to what he/she ought to believe. In *meaninglessness,* a person's minimal standards for clarity in making a decision are not met. With such *meaninglessness* comes the ". . . *low expectancy that satisfactory predictions about future outcomes of behavior can be made.*" (Seeman, 1964, p. 530)

Third, *alienation* as *normlessness* involves the idea of anomie—a situation in which social norms which regulate individual conduct have broken down or are no longer effective to control behavior. From an individual viewpoint, such *normlessness* means that there is a ". . . *high expectancy that socially unapproved behaviors are required to achieve given goals.*" (Seeman, 1964, p. 532)

Fourth, people who are *alienated* in the *isolation* sense are those who ". . . *assign low reward value to goals or beliefs that are typically highly valued in the given society.*" (Seeman, 1964, p. 533)

In *self-estrangement,* the fifth kind of *alienation,* the person experiences him/herself as a stranger, as distant, and even foreign to the self. *Self-estrangement* refers basically to the inability of the individual to find self-rewarding or self-consummatory activities which engage him/her. *Self-estranged* connotes the loss of intrinsic meaning or pride in work for its own sake. "Other-directed" *self-estranged* people are given to appearances, placing values on aspects of life according to impressions and effects made on others. *Alienation* in *self-estrangement* involves ". . . *the degree of dependence of the given behavior upon anticipated future rewards,* that is upon rewards that lie outside the activity itself." (Seeman, 1964, p. 535)

Seeman has stressed that reward value, behavior, and expectancy are key elements in the five basic types of alienation which he has described. (Seeman, 1964, p. 536) These three concepts are also important in Weiss's five categories of relational functions—approaches that people use to make some contact or connections with others. *Sociability* along with *alienation* were highlighted in the three settings.

Weiss has characterized *intimacy* as the ". . . provision of an effective emotional integration in which individuals can express their feelings freely and without self-consciousness." (Weiss, 1971, p. 200) *Intimacy* seems to prevent the individual from experiencing the sense of emotional isolation which is expressed in the idea of loneliness. Thus, trust, effective under-standing, and ready access are part of *intimacy.* (Weiss, 1971, p. 200-1)

Second, *social integration* connotes relationships which allow for much sharing of experience, information, and ideas. Exchange of favors and help are involved. The absence of a relationship of social integration may be perceived and felt as social isolation and often boredom. (Weiss, 1971, p. 201)

> *Social integration* is provided by relationships in which participants share con-cerns, either because of similar situations ('we are in the same boat') or because they are striving for similar objectives (as in relationships among col-leagues) (Weiss, 1971, p. 201)

The third category of relational functions is the *opportunity for nur-turant behavior,* where an adult takes responsibility for the well-being of a child, which perhaps could be extended to various types of protective, caretaking roles. The absence of this function for some people may mean that their lives are unfulfilled, meaningless, and empty of purpose. (Weiss, 1971, p. 201)

Fourth, there exist *reassurance of worth* relationships. Such relation-ships ". . . attest to an individual's competence in some role." (Weiss, 1971, p. 201) The lack of recognition of one's work, one's value, or one's ability may result in decreased self-esteem. (Weiss, 1971, pp. 201-2)

The fifth kind of relationship is that of *assistance,* through which ser-vices are provided and resources are made available. Kin, friends, and neighbors may provide *assistance.* Without the assurance of *assistance* if needed, there will be a sense of anxiety and vulnerability. Perhaps emo-tional and/or mental assistance as provided by mental health professionals may be a special kind of assistance called *guidance.* (Weiss, 1971, p. 202)

Beside shifting commitments to *sociability* and *alienation,* there was a constant interplay between *playfulness* and *seriousness* which exemplified complementariness as well as conflict in the settings, as in various settings of our daily lives. The settings showed four basic characteristics of the *playful-serious* continuum, drawing upon some of Huizinga and Riezler's ideas about *play* and *seriousness,* and adding some more thoughts, especially about *seriousness.*

1. *Play* as voluntary; *seriousness* as deliberate and compulsory. *Play* is freedom and superfluous. The enjoyment of *play* makes it a need. *Play* always can be deferred or suspended—it is not imposed by physical necessity or moral duty. *Play* is done at leisure, during free time. One is free to choose to enter or leave *play. Seriousness* connotes compulsoriness—something one must be or do. *Seriousness* involves basic necessities and cannot be put off or eliminated. *Seriousness* is bound up with notions of obligation and duty. *Seriousness* involves shoulds and should nots; *play* stresses wishes and desires. *Play* involves spontaneity of the moment, of the immediate present; *seriousness* means the deliberate planning for future goals. Settings of *play* offer wide latitudes of permissible behavior which encourage self-indulgence and very often improper acts, acts considered improper outside the setting of the *play.* In *play,* one can invent and change the rules and conventions of the "regular" world. Settings of *seriousness* have formal and informal rather strict rules and regulations for prescribed, preferred, permitted, tolerated, and prescribed attitudes and behavior. In the *serious* world, all things are connected with all things; every effect is a cause, every end a means. Ascetic self-denial and impulse control with clearly defined norms for proper viewpoints are encouraged in many contexts of *seriousness.* (Huizinga, 1955, pp. 7–8; Riezler, 1941, pp. 506–7)

2. *Play* as out of the ordinary; *seriousness* as real life. *Play* can involve a "let's pretend" world—doing things only for fun. Even in fun, however, *play* can involve much intense absorption of the self. *Play* is a temporary sphere of activity. *Play* is separated from the real world. The rules of *play* are not the rules of the real world or of ordinary life. *Play* is disinterested—it is an activity that is satisfying in itself and it ends there. *Play* is detached from the demands of the real world. In the self-made play-world of one's own mood, with one's own rules and goals, one can enjoy his/her activities as the maker or breaker of rules, the master of his/her own means and ends. *Play* is an interlude in daily life. Yet as a regularly recurring relaxation, *play* can be an integral part of life. People *play* for the sake of diversion from the real world—one who *plays* often forgets the "real world." *Play* as stepping out of reality adorns and amplifies life. (Huizinga, 1955, pp. 8–9; Riezler, 1941, pp. 505–6, 509, 511, 513–14)

Seriousness involves a steady and enduring commitment to the realities of life—doing things because they matter and they have important consequences for real life. *Seriousness* involves sometimes passionate vested interests encompassing past, present, and future motivations and goals. *Seriousness* entails a devotion and dedication to the real world. *Seriousness* means putting time into hard work; *seriousness* is the core of life, not a mere embellishment. *Seriousness* involves some tension and lack of ease, some rigor. *Seriousness* is a concern for that which really matters rather than for that which merely amuses. *Seriousness* can involve the pressures of weighty interests and responsibilities. *Seriousness* negates the volatility and frivolity of *playful* "let's pretend" worlds. *Seriousness* often is involved with material interests and with the gaining of profits. (Huizinga, 1955, pp. 8–9; Riezler, 1941, pp. 505–6, 509, 511, 513–14)

3. *Play* as limited in time and place; *seriousness* as having no such fixed boundaries, and extending over much time and many places. *Play* is limited and secluded—it contains its own course and meaning. *Play* begins and is over—play is self-limiting. In the play-world, chains of causes and effects are thought of as having limits. *Play* is separated out from other concerns and is not connected with more total concerns. A sovereign whim or human-made agreement isolates an area of *playing*. *Playing* is not a means to a goal, but one's activity in *playing* is its own end. (Huizinga, 1955, pp. 9–10; Riezler, 1941, pp. 506, 511–12, 517)

Play has a distinct spatial playground, often marked off materially and deliberately. The playground is isolated, hedged in, hallowed—within which special rules obtain. *Play* space is a temporary world within the ordinary world, dedicated to the performance of an act apart. *Seriousness* is a perpetual and pervasive process and flow of life—it has no self-contained beginning, middle, and end. *Seriousness* is the basic fiber of life—it does not start and stop. *Seriousness* extends throughout all time and space arenas. *Seriousness* is everywhere and at all times—permeating all of life. *Play* is clear-cut, narrow order; *seriousness* involves complicated networks of means and ends, causes and effects, which can mean chaos and confusion. Rules and criteria for success are unclear in *seriousness*. (Huizinga, 1955, pp. 10–12; Riezler, 1941, pp. 505–17)

4. *Play* as a special secret; *seriousness* as part and parcel of everyday, ordinary life. *Play* involves the distinction between an esoteric, special group of "us insiders" as distinct from "those others out there, the outsiders." *Play* is for us, not for the others. What the others do outside is no concern of ours at the moment. In the *play*, there are special modes of being and doing—the laws and customs of ordinary life no longer count. People dress differently in *play*, with costumes, disguises, and masks. He/she becomes another being by *playing* another part. *Seriousness* is embedded in prosaic everyday life—it is not exotic and separated from the fabric of daily routines. In *seriousness*, "we's" and "they's" intermingle and merge. *Seriousness* is everyday routine and regularity, not something special. (Huizinga, 1955, pp. 12–13; Riezler 1941, pp. 505–17)

Members of the three settings sometimes were *playful* and sometimes were *serious*. They had multiple and sometimes contradictory orientations to traditional and changing life styles as do some of us. Group dieters and health spa participants were in large part sold on white upper-middle-class standards of beauty and health perpetuated by the mass media, clothing and cosmetic advertising, and by many Western medical doctors. They wanted to conform to such traditional standards by shaping up their bodies. Yet quite a few were open to many variations of dieting and exercising—they were trying every new plan or idea which they heard of or read about. A vociferous minority were beginning to question why they need conform to traditional standards of beautiful thinness. Why could not some degree of overweight be attractive? (Grosswirth, 1971; Louderback, 1970; Reichman, 1977)

Singles bar participants were most eager to perpetuate live examples of traditional sex role stereotypes—men actively took the initiative to start and continue acquaintanceships and relationships; smiling, fairly, soft-spoken women often were on the receiving end, not expected to appear too aggressive or domineering. Yet the singles bar scene challenged some traditional norms of behavior in many public places—norms stressing not looking at or not touching others. Over-staring and over-touching were expected behaviors in the bars.

The three group settings latently and ambivalently both reinforced and mitigated against negative self-feelings and images. The three group atmospheres permitted and even prescribed discussions about insecurity, personal anguish, self-doubts, and even self-hatred. Some group participants dwelled on their unhappy lot in life as they focused on self-degradation. Yet one latent function of the sociability in the settings was the opening up of philosophical and practical possibilities for the participants to make their lives happier and more meaningful with an improvement of self-esteem. The atmosphere in the settings allowed for the expression of actual despair as well as potential hope about positive self and body images. The groups therefore encouraged self-uplifting and self-elevation so as to make oneself rise above the depths of self-dissatisfaction. The settings often encouraged a stripping down of self in order to raise oneself up; a good self had to arise from the depths of a bad self.

AUTHENTICATING AND VALIDATING ONESELF

The three settings showed both processes and goals of *authenticating* and *validating* the self. Strategies and tactics of bodily movement, bodily changes, and bodily self-control were used by participants as means to learn more about oneself, often with the aid of others. Participants wanted to both affirm and change aspects of themselves which existed before they came to the settings. Some were eager to be, and in fact were, converted and resocialized to orientations in the settings.

Quite a few participants were restless and dissatisfied with at least part of themselves and they wanted to change. They looked for cues that they were changing for the better, such as acceptance and approval by others and bodily improvements. They wanted to put into practice their ideal images of a better self—sometimes bodily changes indicated a more attractive and healthier person, which were clues to a morally better self. (Szasz, 1975, pp. 96–113) Getting along with others, fitting in comfortably with others, praise and compliments by others were ways of *self-validation* for members of all three settings.

Searching for *self-validation,* people tried to prove that they were reliable, trustworthy, sincere persons who deserved to be well-liked and respected, as do many of us. They would gain even more inner strength and more positive self images if they showed others evidence of self-scrutiny and behavior leading them to become physically, mentally, and morally better people. Self-examination went hand-in-hand with others' responses to and evaluations of them. For participants in the three settings, *authenticating* the self was based upon an intense sensitivity to responses of others, summarized by Cooley as the looking-glass self.

A self-idea of this sort has three principal elements:

> . . . the imagination of our appearance to the other person; the imagination of his judgment of that appearance, and some sort of self-feeling, such as pride or mortification. The comparison with a looking-glass hardly suggests the second element, the imagined judgment, which is quite essential. The thing that moves us to pride or shame is not the mere mechanical reflection of ourselves, but an imputed sentiment, the imagined effect of this reflection upon another's mind. (Cooley, 1964, p. 184)

All the three settings studied encouraged and even prescribed a heightened sensitivity to others' responses to oneself and a concern about others' judgments of oneself as do some settings in our daily lives. The idea of other-consciousness which Goffman has discussed as an indicator of alienation from interaction seemed to be a meaningful involvement obligation in dieting groups, health spas, and singles bars.

> During interaction, the individual may become distracted by another participant as an object of attention . . . .
> If the individual finds that whenever he is in the conversational presence of specific others they cause him to be overly conscious of them at the expense of the prescribed involvement in the topic of conversation, then they may acquire the reputation in his eyes of being faulty interactants, especially if he feels he is not alone in the trouble he has with them . . .
> If the speaker's communication apparatus itself conveys additional information all during the time that transmission is occurring, then the listener is likely to be distracted by competing sources of stimuli, becoming over-aware of the speaker at the expense of what is being said. The sources of this distraction are well known: the speaker may be very ugly or very beautiful . . . . (Goffman, 1967, pp. 120–21; 123)

Goffman's distinction between the terms "affectation" and "insincerity" is relevant in this context. Affected individuals are mainly concerned about controlling the evaluation which an observer will make of them, and they appear to be partly taken in by their own pose. Insincere individuals are quite concerned about controlling the impression which the observer will form about their attitude toward certain people or things, especially toward the observer, and they do not seem to be taken in by their own pose.

(Goffman, 1967, p. 121) Quite a few people in the three settings worked hard at their poses of insincerity and affectation.

Group dieters, health spa patrons, and singles bar participants often showed another meaningful involvement obligation with regard to sensitivity to others' responses which Goffman has commented on as an indicator of alienation from interaction. It was a sign of good manners in the three settings for participants to take on the responsibility for interaction going well, to keep "small talk" going, to avoid or cleverly manage "painful silences." They were to be interaction-conscious. They were to become consciously concerned with the way in which the interaction, *qua* interaction, was proceeding, rather than becoming spontaneously involved in the official topic of the conversation. While Goffman has suggested that this interaction-consciousness is often an improper distraction from the ongoing conversation, people in the three settings studied in this book often showed care and support for each other by a careful utilization of interaction-consciousness. (Goffman, 1967, pp. 119-20)

In their searches for *self-validation,* participants in all three settings had to come to grips with the fact that they often were *stigmatized* by many in the society: whether they had inferior or inadequate bodies, or were psychologically disturbed, or morally loose characters as singles. Group dieters and health spa participants were often held responsible for their bodily problems; they were blameworthy for not showing enough self-control and willpower. (Aubert and Messinger, 1972, pp. 288-308; Freidson, 1970, pp. 224-43)

Some singles were *stigmatized* as being too free and easy sexually—always "on the make." Many people lowered participants in all these settings ". . . from a whole and usual person to a tainted, discounted one" and so increased their own feelings of well-being, safety, and superiority. (Goffman, 1963, p. 3)

The *stigmatization* of these people involved the rejection and disgrace which were connected with conditions viewed both as physical deformities/abnormalities and as behavioral aberrations. Those who communicated with such people did not grant them the:

> . . . respect and regard which the uncontaminated aspects of his social identity have led them to anticipate extending, and have led him to anticipate receiving; he echoes this denial by finding that some of his attributes warrant it. (Goffman, 1963, pp. 8-9)

Participants in all three settings believed that their stigmatizing characteristics became exclusive focal points of interaction—the particularities of their *stigmas* called forth some concentrated attention to themselves. Others were viewed as not really oriented to the totality of the participants, but rather to that which was uppermost in their awareness—the marks of *stigma.* (Davis, 1972, pp. 134-35. Allon, 1976, pp. 14-15, 18-23)

These *stigmatized* people felt that they had the potential to overwhelm expressive boundaries. People in all three settings might evoke in a "normal" person various inner feelings, such as pity, fear, repugnance, and avoidance—so they believed. They felt that the marked dissonance of such emotions of the "normal" with the outward expressions considered most salient for the occasion, as pleasure, warm interest, identification with the other would result in overwhelming multiple feelings for the "normal." Many different and contrasting feelings would weaken the expressive controls of the "normal"—so that the "normal" would blurt out situationally inappropriate expressions. Such statements included: "Sorry to make you bend—I do hope it is not too much trouble for you to get into the back seat of my car;" "I hope you do not feel too out of place at the party as a single person." (Davis, 1972, pp. 135–36)

Those branded with various *stigmas* in all three settings said that often "normal" others viewed their *stigmas* as discordant with other attributes of themselves. Such "normals" could only resolve the seeming incongruence by assimilating or subsuming the other attributes to that of the *stigmatized* attribute—often in a patronizing or condescending way. "Normals" often said, "You have such a beautiful face and you are so well-coordinated even though you're a bit heavy;" or "You have a most exciting and interesting life even though you're single." Participants often felt reduced to their particular *stigmatizing* features. (Davis, 1972, pp. 136–37)

Many noted that their *stigmas* were ambiguous predictors of joint activity. The "normal" was not always so sure if an overweight person would want to engage in physical exercise or go out to eat. Even if the overweight person did not want to engage in the projected activity, would she want to come along for the sake of company? How could coupled people gauge the single person's preference to come to a party with all married people, without making a thing out of the initiation of joint activity, or without conveying the impression that the single person's needs and wishes were not being sufficiently considered? If singles refused a social invitation, was it a genuine refusal or were they merely offering their hosts and hostesses polite, though half-hearted, outs? Did others really want the "different" single to come along, or were they merely being polite? In spite of the open invitation, would the single's acceptance and presence somehow lessen many people's enjoyment of the activity? (Davis, 1972, pp. 137–38)

The self-help offered in the three settings counteracted the isolation and alienation that resulted from being different, by creating a place in which a member could belong. The self-help in the settings provided a world within a world where the person labeled in some ways "deviant" was given a voice that could be heard and was accepted as part of the collectivity. In all three settings, people got the security of being one of a majority, rather than being in isolation. (Killilea, 1976, p. 61) Participants sought association with others like themselves to assist in the handling of their problems and conditions *stigmatized* by the larger community. Members of the three settings had to face up to, accept, and perhaps try to fight or change such everyday *stigmatization* processes. The three settings encouraged some to manage or live with their *stigmas*; they incited others to try to overcome their *stigmas*. Dieting groups and health spas heightened the sense of bodily *stigmas,* while singles bars attempted to lessen the *stigma* attached to being alone or single.

In confronting their *stigmas,* group dieters, health spa, and singles bar patrons *validated* themselves through sharing common experiences which meant that the members of each setting had a common base of mutuality of problems. In offering each other support, quite a few participants *validated* themselves by becoming helpers; they increased their sense of interpersonal competence as they received social approval from those whom they helped. In an atmosphere of collective willpower and belief, participants *authenticated* themselves by telling and showing each other that many of the ideologies and programs of each setting worked. As participants shared information and suggestions for action, they also carried out constructive actions toward shared goals which increased their self-esteem. *Self-validation* for some included constant self-reexaminations and attempts to change oneself. (Killilea, 1976, pp. 37–93) Quite a few were testing themselves out; they often took on bodily, soul-searching, and interpersonal challenges and wanted to succeed in a spirit of conquest in *authenticating* themselves. Some were tentative and uncertain about their sense of self; they were in transitional phases in discovering and finding out parts of themselves. Participants scrutinized, questioned, doubted, and affirmed parts of themselves as they acknowledged their weaknesses and strengths in *validating* themselves.

Besides *validating* themselves by coping with their *stigmas,* group dieters, health spa, and singles bar patrons *authenticated* themselves through *sociability for its own sake,* which existed beyond formal group goals. Watson has stressed that *sociable* interaction offers the individual the chance to stress her/his unique personal qualities, allows a person to dramatize that part of oneself which overlaps with the culture of the group which she/he is in, stresses the novelty and entertainment values of topics discussed, and provides for conversations which center around nonroutine and special interests of individuals. (Watson, 1958, pp. 269–280) Riesman, Potter and Watson have stressed that *sociability* brings forth a product for which the producers are also the consumers and the performers are also the audience. These authors have also discussed how *sociability* is the kind of interaction which occurs between people who come together to enjoy each other's company, or between people who are trying to enjoy each other's company because they have been brought together. (Riesman, Potter and Watson, 1966, pp. 323–40)

The nature of *sociability* has been astutely analyzed by Simmel. Simmel viewed *sociability* as autonomous, existing for its own sake outside of reality. He stated that pure *sociability* has no objective purpose or aim beyond the success of the momentary, immediate present. Through *sociability,* concrete interactions are freed from reality, and they come to move in themselves and recognize no purpose extraneous to them. *Sociable* talk is it own legitimate purpose, and so its nature includes the ability to change topics rapidly and with ease. The purpose of the conversation is not the content, and the *sociable* conversation must not pursue an objective result. (Simmel 1964, pp. 46–47, 52–55)

Simmel has said that *sociability* has no content, and it entirely depends on the personalities among who it occurs. The conditions and results of the process of *sociability* are exclusively the persons who find themselves at a social gathering. The character of *sociability* is determined by such personal qualities as amiability, refinement, cordiality, and many other sources of attraction. Yet precisely because everything depends upon their personalities, participants are not allowed to stress their personalities too conspicuously. Objective attributes which are centered outside the particular gathering in question must not enter the setting. *Sociability* minimizes if it does not eliminate a concern for wealth, social position, erudition, fame, and exceptional capabilities and merits. Also *sociability* does not focus upon the purely and deeply personal traits of one's life, character, mood, and fate. In *sociability,* it is tactless to display merely personal moods of depression, excitement, and despondency—that is, the light and the darkness of one's intimate life—because such a display militates against interaction, which monopolizes *sociability.* The axiom for the principle of *sociability* is that each individual should *offer* the maximum of *sociable* values, such as joy, relief, and liveliness, that is compatible with the maximum of values which he/she him/herself *receives.* (Simmel, 1964, pp. 45–47)

Simmel stressed that the world of *sociability* was the only world in which a democracy of the equally privileged was possible without frictions, and, as such, was an artificial world. It was composed of individuals who had only the one desire to create wholly pure interaction with others which was not disbalanced by a stress of anything material. In the three settings, many participants stated that they enjoyed being with each other just for the sake of company. (Simmel, 1964, p. 48)

CONSTRUCTION OF PERFORMANCES: THE PROCESSING OF CAREERS THROUGH SOCIAL SETTINGS

Group dieters, health spa, and singles bar patrons consciously and deliberately planned certain routines and rituals which they undertook as means to affirm, clarify, and improve parts of themselves. Self and bodily *careers* were processed through the three settings. Hughes has viewed *career* in a broad perspective as an example of one's ambitions and accomplishments which involves some sequence of relations to organized life. In a rigidly structured society, a *career* consists of a series of statuses and clearly defined offices, with standardized duties and privileges. In a freer society, an individual has more latitude for creating her/his *career,* or choosing from a number of existing *careers*—such a person also has less certainty of achieving any given position. (Hughes, 1958, p. 63) The three settings appeared to contain characteristics of the less structured and the more structured society in relation to *career.*

Careers in Hughes' terms may be occupational and avocational. A *career* demonstrates how an individual's life intersects with the social order through various avenues of social accomplishments, be they business and professional achievements, or the social processes of influence, responsibility, and recognition. (Hughes, 1958, p. 64) Using Hughes' perspective, many group dieters, health spa attenders, and singles bar participants could be viewed as being very absorbed in *careers* of their bodies.

> Subjectively, a career is the moving perspective in which the person sees his life as a whole and interprets the meaning of his various attributes, actions, and the things which happen to him. This perspective is not absolutely fixed either as to points of view, direction or destination . . . . a study of careers—of the moving perspective in which persons orient themselves with reference to the social order, and of the typical sequences and concatenations of office—may be expected to reveal the nature and 'working constitution' of a society. Institutions are but the forms in which the collective action of people go on. In the course of a career the person finds his place within these forms, carries on his active life with reference to other people, and interprets the meaning of the one life he has to live. (Hughes, 1958, pp. 63; 67)

Whether stressing *careers* of the body, *careers* of self-discovery, or *careers* of interpersonal communications skills, participants in the three settings developed a strong sense of identification with their *careers* as do some of us with various *careers.* Many invested an irreplaceable quantum of time in their particular *careers*; in various ways, they would lose their investment if they would not continue to follow their chosen fields. (Becker and Carper, 1956, p. 296) Participants developed certain rhetoric, titles, and ideologies which itemized the qualities, interests and capabilities of those identified with their *careers.* Others approached or avoided participants on the bases of their language and ideologies. (Becker and Carper, 1956a, pp. 342–43)

Participants continued to develop various interests and skills in regard to their *careers.* They learned specialized techniques by watching superordinates and peers at work. They took pride in their skills as they became committed to their tasks and interested in specialized problems. (Becker and Carper, 1956, pp. 296–97) Their self-confidence increased as they viewed themselves as generalists in some areas, and specialists in others. (Becker and Carper, 1956a, p. 343)

Many delved into their sense of commitment to various aspects of their *careers.* Some did raise questions about the worth of their activities. Why were they leading their kind of life rather than another kind? (Becker and

Carper, 1956, p. 297) They found general and specific answers for why they were and should be interested in their *careers* as they sought to define success for themselves, sometimes viewed in relationship to others. (Becker and Carper, 1956a, pp. 344–45)

Formally and informally in their relationships in small groups and apprenticeships, the participants developed emotional and intellectual rationales for pursuing their various *careers*. They understood their choices and could explain them to others. They translated their impulses about their life styles into socialized actions. (Becker and Carper, 1956, p. 297) Many participants were highly motivated to achieve in their *careers* and they had high levels of aspiration. All the *careers* stressed aspects of willpower and strength as goals, be they attractiveness, health, or moral potencies.

Careers in each setting showed social assistance and mutual aid in various support systems. Dieting groups, health spas, and singles bars as types of social movements aimed to produce changes mainly within their members rather than in society. Aspects of *careers* in the settings exemplified inspirational, spiritual movements, and secular religions, which stressed the primary goal of the good life here and now. There was a sense of an esoteric exclusiveness of a privileged elect in the settings, where insiders in a kind of secret society with their own special ways of thinking, talking, and behaving could be quite distinguished from outsiders. (Simmel, 1964, pp. 345–76) As kinds of *sects,* the settings did recruit people for whom they could fulfill specific social functions. With sectlike qualities, the contexts served as small and "deviant" reference groups in which individuals could seek status and prestige, and in terms of whose standards they could measure their talents and accomplishments in more favorable terms than were generally available in the wider society. Group ideologies and cohesion among members provided environments of emotional security for group dieters, health spa, and singles bar patrons. (Wilson, 1961, p. 354) *Careers* of participants showed that the settings were agencies of social control which used various strategies of resocialization which focused upon the self-interest and satisfaction of members. In their *careers* in their therapeutic environments, members developed strategies for coping with short-term and long-term problems as well as with life cycle transitions, as marriage, childbearing, divorce, and widowhood. (Killilea, 1976, pp. 37–93)

CONCLUSIONS

The three settings fostered interaction and mutual assistance between peers, often encouraging much self-revelation. In non-therapy oriented milieus, as church rooms, community centers, hotel rooms, exercise rooms, locker rooms, and bars, peers in the three self-help settings could identify with each other since they were similarly affected by a trouble. Peers were role models who set examples for each other; peers were active, judgmental, supportive, critical, and talkative. Peers shared disclosures. They received and gave support with others in a reciprocal fashion. They urged appropriate behavior as defined by the settings, even if underlying causes for problems and dissatisfactions were not removed. Some aspects of the settings sometimes were "no-therapy" in the sense that they suppressed symptoms and problems and encouraged conformity. (Zusman, 1969, pp. 482–85) They did not always deal directly with inner life—the thoughts and feelings of an individual. (Killilea, 1976, pp. 65–66)

The settings put a premium upon holding the participant individually responsible for her/his behavior, attitudes, and feelings. The settings emphasized faith, willpower, and self-control as peers aimed to reach each other at a "gut level." Continuing support was available with a primary emphasis on day-to-day victories. (Killilea, 1976, pp. 66) The line between independent leaders and dependent followers was blurred as patients were also therapists, students were also teachers, laity were also secular religious leaders, those who were being healed were also healers, and those who were childlike at times were parentlike at other times.

All three settings proposed individualistically-oriented socio-psychological ways of coping with the world more smoothly and effectively. Because participants established rapport with each other on the basis of a common interest or problem, they often took for granted the notion that they had much in common with each other beside the formal purpose of gathering together. A major latent function of all three settings, that of empathetic sharing of life's vicissitudes, led to the sharing of some general socio-psychological goals of increased self-worth and self-improvement. All the settings had the latent function of prescribing the ingredients for increased self-respect, discussed as a proximal and realizable goal. Often such self-respect was not encouraged by outsiders to the settings who spurred on self doubts by chastising participants for their problems and shortcomings. The unintended and informal services of mutual support were just as basic if not more basic to all the settings than were the more intended and formal goals of the settings—such as to lose weight or to succeed in a relationship with another. (Allon, 1975, pp. 66–68)

Such nurturance and self-support, often leading to a reconciled or peaceful state of mind, was processed through four basic dimensions of each setting: (1) basic commonalities evidenced in *self-* and *body-absorption*; (2) sharing of some *ambivalent* and *contradictory cognitive, cathectic,* and *evaluative commitments;* (3) common processes involved in *authenticating* or *validating* the self; and (4) a sharing of constructive *behavioral performances* and *careers* which were processed through the three settings.

These dimensions of each setting were demonstrated in the multiple conversations of gestures in the settings. Participants often talked with one person, looked at another person, and had some physical contact with a third person. In such complex communication patterns, participants were both involved with and distanced from particular others. Sometimes their overt behavior reflected their inner feelings and attitudes; at other times, their minds and hearts were far from their external behavior.

In terms of avoiding larger social concerns of the day, participants partly victimized themselves by their own versions of awareness-traps. (Schur, 1976) In their supportive networks, often members of the settings were caught up in *troubles* of their own little worlds, and were oblivious to or minimized aspects of larger problems as *issues*—as Mills has discussed. Are we caught up in our *troubles*?

> *Troubles* occur within the character of the individual and within the range of his immediate relations with others; they have to do with his self and with those limited areas of social life of which he is directly and personally aware. Accordingly, the statement and the resolution of troubles properly lie within the scope of his immediate milieu—the social setting that is directly open to his personal experience and to some extent his willful activity. A trouble is a private matter: values cherished by an individual are felt by him to be threatened.
>
> *Issues* have to do with matters that transcend these local environments of the individual and the range of his inner life. They have to do with the organization of many such milieux into the institutions of an historical society as a whole, with the ways in which various milieux overlap and interpenetrate to form the larger structure of social and historical life. An issue is a public matter: some value cherished by publics is felt to be threatened. (Mills, 1961, p. 8)

The three settings did exemplify Lasch's view:

> It is no secret that Americans have lost faith in politics. The retreat to purely personal satisfactions—such as they are—is one of the main themes of the seventies. A growing despair of changing society—even of understanding it—has generated on the one hand a revival of old time religion, on the other a cult of expanded consciousness, health and personal 'growth.' (Lasch, 1976, p. 5)

Members in the three settings often applied their increasing self-awareness to maximizing their focus upon themselves. Consumed by their own *self-absorption,* they did not often have the energy or time to extend outwardly to others in relation to social *issues.* Group dieters, health spa participants, and singles bar attenders often diverted themselves and escaped from parts of their own lives as well as larger social problems by going to their respective settings. All three fairly small, enclosed, and protective settings ambivalently accentuated as well as mitigated against the problems of impersonalism, routinization, and standardization of mass culture. Perhaps by increasing their self-esteem in their nurturing environments, participants were preparing themselves to extend themselves more openly to others. What kinds of nurturing environments do we seek out, and for what reasons?

Group Dieting

2

INTRODUCTION

Historically and cross-culturally, people have had different values about thinness and fatness. (Beller, 1977) In different times and in different places, people who have struggled to achieve the rewards of food, for whom the acquisition of food has been a problem, tend to praise fatness more than thinness. When food is not a taken-for-granted part of the natural order of things, overweight is often valued as a sign of prestige and success. Success in this context is equated with beauty. One has become sufficiently rich in goods so as to acquire enough food to make one beautifully fat. The fat body is often considered to be a strong body. (Allon, 1973a, p. 95: Bruch, 1957; Bruch, 1973; Powdermaker, 1960, pp. 286–95; Rudofsky, 1971, pp. 99–111)

In contrast to the prestige of fatness in some societies, people who take for granted economic abundance in general, and food in particular, as a way of life tend to praise thinness more than fatness. With the opportunity for the overconsumption of abundances, one literally can afford to worry about "too-muchisms," including overweight. Obesity as a widespread condition of poor people usually occurs only when there is ample and relatively inexpensive food for everybody, combined with more leisure and release from toil and effort through mechanization. Obesity exists on a large scale in present-day affluent countries like the United States and some European countries, with almost nonexistent physical activity in many occupations and passive leisure time activities. (Allon, 1973a, p. 96; Bruch, 1957; Bruch, 1973; Powdermaker, 1969, pp. 288–91, Wagner, 1970, pp. 311–15)

In a recent sample of over 10,000 persons, obesity, as measured by triceps skinfold thickness, was found to be most prevalent in women, particularly black women in the older age group (45–74 years) who had a prevalence of 32.4 percent. White men had a higher prevalence of obesity than black men; the lowest prevalence of obesity, 7.7 percent, was found in black men, 45–74 years old. Men did have lower percentages of obesity than women did. Percentages for men ranged from 7.7 percent for black men 45–74 years old, to 16.0 percent for white men 20–44 years old. For women the ranges were from 18.9 percent for white women 20–44 years old, to 32.4 percent for black women 45–74 years old. (Abraham, 1975, p. 28)

Lower income levels were associated with a higher prevalence of obesity for both white and black women. In fact, black women, regardless of income, had a higher prevalence of obesity than white women did.

In the younger age group, 20–44 years, higher income level was associated with a higher prevalence for white men. This association was also true for black men although the magnitude of the difference of the percentage of obesity was small. In the older age groups, income level was less consistently associated with the prevalence of obesity. In the older age group, regardless of income level, white men had a higher prevalence of obesity than black men did. Such an association was not evident in the younger age group. (Abraham, 1975, p. 28)

Writers, citing public health reports, have stated that in contemporary America over 79 million overweight, sometimes calorie-conscious eaters are part of a $10 billion diet industry which promotes thinness through the restriction of food intake, specialized foods and drugs, physical exercise, prayer, hypnosis, individual and group therapy, health spas, and books on dieting. More than 42 million people are concerned about their waistlines; 9.5 million are on specific diets. (Wyden and Wyden, 1968, p. 11; Lichtenstein, 1973, p. 94; Wyden, 1966, p. 1)

Life insurance companies, cosmetic and clothing industries, and mass media advertising mark out contemporary American overweight as a central target for puritanical fervor and vindictiveness. Fat people, chastised for their lack of self-control, are held responsible for their voluntary, self-inflicted stigma and disability. (Cahnman, 1968, pp. 283–99) Thinness, as symbolizing youthfulness and sexiness, is an ideal which people, especially women, of all ages and sizes should work hard to achieve. There is some snobbery in this ideology advocating the Ideal of Thinness since many diet and low calorie foods are expensive. American society's negative views about overweight are seriously reflected in its attempted denial of fat. Clothing for fat women is advertised by models who wear sizes 10 and 12; on television, weight reduction ads always talk about the successes, never the failures. (Craft, 1972, p. 679)

Many American overweight people are considered immoral because they are held blameworthy and responsible for their excess weight. Responsibility involves the final outcome or end of fatness, which the overweight person is believed to bring upon him/herself. Responsibility also involves the means by which the end of fatness has been obtained—usually, assumed overeating and/or under-exercise.[1] What lies behind the viewpoint of overweight as a sin, with the corollary that with willpower, one can put oneself on the straight and narrow road to salvation?

> . . . even if the reputed association between leanness and longevity were demonstrably false . . . fatness would still be assessed negatively as unaesthetic and as an indication of self indulgence. In a society which has

historically been suffused with a Protestant Ethic, one characteristic of which is a strong emphasis on impulse control, fatness suggests a kind of immorality which invites retribution. Correspondingly, the reduction of overweight and the avoidance of the contagion of gluttony implies self-denial, which ought to bring appropriate rewards, including good health. This moral orientation is, in turn, reinforced by aesthetic considerations. . . . physicians, and most middle-class individuals, consider extreme overweight unsightly. (Maddox, Back and Liederman, 1968, p. 288)

Dieters play out a basic *moral* scenario—the dramatic cycle of *pollution* and *purification*. Food and eating are prominent in this script. The most universal ceremonial of purification is fasting; the most common ceremonial of self-indulgence or pollution is feasting. Szasz has discussed how medicine replaced religion as a new kind of religion to treat and correct traits viewed as bad habits. So dieting has replaced fasting and the treatment of obesity has replaced the absolution for the sin of gluttony. Such replacements are but one facet of the pervasive *medicalization of morals* which has taken place during the last three centuries. Fasting formerly served and dieting now serves the important ceremonial function of self-purification; this function is now concealed by the technical arguments in favor of weight reduction. (Szasz, 1975, pp. 96–97; 56–69)

Szasz has described historically the ancient presumption, the masculine fear and the feminine acceptance of, woman as a particularly "polluted" person in need of special rites of "purification." He related contemporary women's excessive preoccupation with being overweight and dieting to the ancient belief of women being "unclean." The "overweight woman" is merely one contemporary version of the mythology of feminine pollution. Some earlier versions were menstruation, superior sexual powers, witchery, and "familiarity" with the devil. Each had its appropriate purificatory precaution. (Szasz, 1975, p. 98)

Orbach has underlined the moral dimension in her discussion of fat as a social disease which is a response to the inequality of the sexes. Fat expresses a rebellion against the powerlessness of women, of women having to look and be a certain way, of it not being acceptable for women to be assertive and self-confident. The fat woman may be trying to reject the whole meat market syndrome as she wants to be accepted for who she is, and not what she is supposed to look like on the outside so as to please males. (Orbach, 1978) Advocates of fat liberation, in fact, have stressed the immoral persecution of fat people in thin-crazed America as they have stated that fat people have the right to be fat and eat what they want to eat. In particular, women need to be aware of the sexism in their socialization, which has forced them to regard their bodies as objects to be sacrificed for the ideals of thin beauty. (Aldebaran, 1975, pp. 5–6; Aldebaran, 1977, pp. 34–38)

Using sickness as a label for overweight people may mask some moral and aesthetic biases. One study showed that medical doctors disliked people being fat, a dislike derived from values of white middle-class American society and informal experience rather than from science and formal training. The doctors studied preferred not to manage the overweight patient, and most did not. They did not expect the success of weight reduction if they did treat the overweight. The doctors believed overweight to be unaesthetic and indicative of a lack of personal control. They gave an extremely negative picture of the very overweight person, who was described as weak-willed, ugly, and awkward, through a self-administered questionnaire and a semantic differential procedure. The doctors evaluated the overweight people more harshly than the overweight rated themselves. (Maddox and Liederman, 1969, pp. 214-20)

Although being overweight is judged as immoral, ugly, and a disease in contemporary America, cultural paradoxes reflect wishes and fears about eating, thinness, and overweight. There are conflicts between the need for *repression* and the wish for *gratification* of eating desires. This conflict is clear in the popularity of the mouth-watering substitute products "without calories." This "fake asceticism" of desserts and candies with few or no calories illustrates the American paradoxical cultural value of "having one's cake and eating it too," or "eating one's cake," and not needing to suffer the "bad" fattening consequences. (Bruch, 1957, p, 56)

Other examples of this cultural paradox in the struggle for thinness abound in popular women's magazines, which appear to be "split personalities." Pictures on the covers of these magazines show luscious fattening foods. Women read that they can get their men and keep them if they lure their men with the seductive bait of fattening and exciting recipes. As women read further, however, they find out about the harm which will befall them if they themselves indulge in such fattening delicacies. Overweight is dangerous and ugly; the magazines offer diet suggestions to get and keep women thin and beautiful. (Bruch, 1957, p. 57)

Some case studies suggest the ambivalence of chronically reducing thin parents who envy their fat children, as well as condemn their fat children. These children are viewed as daring to satisfy the same impulses which the parents wish that they could give in to, but which the parents keep under strict control. (Bruch, 1957, p. 56) Perhaps some thin people who severely condemn overweight people are envious of the overweight person's apparent self-indulgence, and the yielding of self-discipline.

There is not a precise, commonly agreed upon definition of the obesity-overweight phenomenon among medical doctors and physical scientists. Overweight is defined as body weight in excess of an ideal weight, based upon height- and sex-specific standards, often with some regard to bone structure and age. Such an ideal is often set by insurance companies. Overweight can result from excesses of bone, muscle, fat or more rarely, fluid. Practically everyone who is more than 20 percent overweight is also overfat, or obese. Yet not all people who are heavy are excessively fat. The relative contributions to overweight of bone, muscle, and fat vary between people—it is often hard to recognize the differences. The component that actually causes weight in excess of normal (the criteria of which are never clearly defined) is less than clear when overweight is in the more moderate range—less than 20 percent over ideal weight. (Dwyer, Feldman and Mayer, 1970, p. 269)

Obesity is defined as body fatness in excess of age- and sex-specific standards, often considering height and bone structure. Body weights grossly in excess of standards are indicative of obesity. Moderate overweight is sometimes but not always due to obesity. Some people whose weights are normal are also obese. Thus, overweight (heaviness) and obesity (excessive fatness) are not necessarily synonymous. Weight deviations can give only imprecise estimates of obesity; football players, for example, may be overweight because of their massive bone and muscle structure, yet not be overfat at all. (Dwyer, Feldman and Mayer, 1970, p. 269) Also, many sedentary persons can be excessively fat but not overweight. (Berland and eds. Consumer Guide, 1977, p. 20; Wohl and Goodhart, 1971, pp. 4–5)

Overweight generally means that one weighs more than one should for one's height and build and sex, according to certain "normal" statistics; obese generally means that one's body carries too much fat. The differences between the sexes in terms of fat become accentuated with maturing during adolescence. Body fat increases in amount among girls as it decreases in boys. "Womanly curves" involve fat accumulation at breast and hips; often boys develop "manly" shapes as a result of the build-up of their muscles, largely through exercise. Because of their actual greater fat accumulation in their bodies, women in general may be more concerned about fatness than men. (Berland and eds. Consumer Guide, 1977, pp. 18–19; Dwyer, 1973, pp. 82–108)

Body types or somatotypes are also significant in the study of overweight and obesity. Variations in outward appearance are due, at least in part, to underlying anatomical differences in the amount, distribution, or conformation of fat, muscle, and bony tissue—all of which are reflected in body form. Sheldon and others have described three basic variations: (1) endomorphy, the display of a soft and round appearance; (2) mesomorphy, appearing as a combination of bone and muscle development; and (3) ectomorphy, distinguished by linearity, fragility, and attenuation of body build. Most obese persons are not just thin persons with an excessive burden of fat; the majority of the obese tend to be somewhat larger in their bone and muscle components as well as fatter than the nonobese. Different weight goals are necessary for persons of different body types to allow for the fact that they vary in the relative contribution of the nonfat components to their weights. (Dwyer, Feldman and Mayer, 1970, pp. 269–70)

There are uncertainties and multiple standards in objective as well as subjective connotations of the supposed "fact" of overweight or obesity. People have their own ideas about how fat or thin they are, based upon complex biographical and reference group factors. Some lower-middle-class Italian and Irish group dieters whom I met thought that they were quite thin if they could squeeze into a size 20; then they would not "spill over" their seats in a theater and they could fasten seat belts on airplanes. These women jokingly told me that I was a "little thing" and that they would need to fatten me up so that I really could understand what I was studying. Some upper-middle-class Jewish dieters whom I met began to feel "panicked" when their size fives started feeling tight. Some pinched their waistlines, saying that they needed to get rid of the flab that would "hang out" in their bikinis. These women looked me up and down with piercing eyes, frowns, and scolding fingers, some being bold enough to suggest that I really should come to the groups to try to lose some weight myself, not just to carry out academic research. I could use my own body as a yardstick to see how variable definitions of overweight were among group dieters. In fact, one study has suggested that the concern about weight is the greatest among the affluent, least obese populations. (Dwyer and Mayer, 1970, p. 513)

Overweight people often have believed that they belong to a minority group—with withdrawal, passivity, the expectation of rejection, and an over-concern with self image as part of their lives. (Monello and Mayer, 1963, pp. 35–39) Some have been made to feel that they deserve discrimination. (Cahnman, 1968, pp. 283–99; Kalisch, 1972, pp. 1124–27) Perhaps in part because some overweight people are so sensitive to others' negative responses to them, some studies have found that such people are over-responsive to external cues; under-responsive to internal visceral cues. (Schachter, 1968, pp. 751–56; Schachter, 1971, pp. 129–44; Schachter and Rodin, 1974) Preoccupied with their obesity, overweight people often have viewed the world in terms of body weight, envying persons thinner than themselves and feeling contempt for those who were fatter. (Stunkard and Mendelson, 1967, pp. 1296–1300) In experimental studies of uniform and variant reactions to physical disabilities, child and adult populations have very often ranked the overweight child as least likable among a group of children with disabilities. (Goodman, Richardson, Dornbusch and Hastorf, 1963, pp. 429–35; Maddox, Back and Liederman, 1968, pp. 287–98; Matthews and Westie, 1966, pp. 851–54; Richardson, Hastorf, Goodman and Dornbusch, 1961, pp. 241–47)[2]

GROUP DIETING: MAIN THEMES

In group dieting, participants focused inwardly on themselves, often centering on their bodies, as they communicated verbally and nonverbally with others. Losing weight symbolized the shaping up of oneself which would lead to more social approval by others and increased self-esteem. Many group dieters were aiming to conform to the contemporary American feminine stereotype of the attractive woman as a thin woman.

What group dieters shared with others was a common interest in self-centeredness, including the working through of feelings and thoughts about oneself symbolized by the processes of eating and dieting. With a focus on one's body as a main and dominating involvement, many viewed their bodies as rather detached from themselves—to be judged by quantities weighed, lost or gained, and by dress sizes which did or did not fit. Such judgments led group dieters to deem themselves as good/bad, successes/failures, attractive/unattractive. For many, losing weight could make one a more worthwhile human being. The body was a valuable (thin) or not so valuable (not so thin) piece of merchandise. The payoff of *self-absorption* for many group dieters could be measured in quantitative terms—pounds on the scale. Some dieters did begin to question why their self-esteem need be so strongly based on becoming thinner.

Expressing *contradictory and conflicting commitments* about dieting, many group dieters vacillated between ascetic and hedonistic eating patterns. At times they wanted to prove to themselves and others how much strict self-control that they could exercise on their diets; at other times, they wanted to let loose and indulge their eating desires—sometimes in elaborate food binges or orgies. They expressed the ambivalence of gratification and suppression of eating urges that are encouraged by much of the mass media and advertising. They fluctuated in wanting to remain private and self-contained about their dieting behavior, as well as desiring to share the joys and sorrows of their dieting with others in a spirit of sociability. Many believed that they were on equal terms with others in the group, but yet they sought to differentiate their eating, dieting, and bodily styles from others. Some were playful and had fun in group dieting as entertaining nights out with female friends in which gossip and laughter were shared. Others were sober and serious about undertaking their dieting assignments as challenging hard work requiring much concentration.

Group dieting ambivalently reinforced and mitigated against the stigma of overweight. Group dieters degraded themselves because of their fatness but then supported each other's dieting efforts and so increased their self-esteem. Perhaps it was not so bad to be fat if one could find satisfying relationships with others who were also fat in the group; fat people could understand and help each other. In a context of sociability, group dieters expressed despair as well as hope about positive self and body images, related or not so related to their weight-losing.

Many group dieters wanted to *validate* themselves by proving to themselves and others that they could change their bodies for the better in terms of weight loss. *Self-validation* comprised the processes of self-examination and self-criticism with an extreme sensitivity to the responses of others. Other-consciousness in group dieting went hand-in-hand with self-consciousness; group dieters were constantly comparing themselves with others in and out of the setting.

Many group dieters felt that they were comfortable with each other and that they belonged together where they would all accept each other, more than in the outside world of thin people. Some described how they felt isolated and alienated around thin people. Overweight people were part of a majority in group dieting, which helped make them feel *authentic,* whether they chose to overcome or live with the stigma of their overweight. Group dieters shared a mutuality of problems as they accepted and supported each other. Some people in the groups formed close-knit primary groups, where people came with friends or made new friends and discussed many parts of their lives with each other, beyond the topics of eating and dieting.[3]

Group dieting encouraged psychological probes of self-awareness as well as good times and many laughs to make people forget their troubles. Increased knowledge from sharing much detailed and technical information about dieting was a basis for *self-validation*. Group dieters *authenticated* themselves by taking action to do something constructive about their overweight.

Group dieters carried out distinct routines and rituals to clarify and improve parts of themselves, as weighing in on the scale, chatting with others, listening hard to the group leaders's message each week, asking questions about dieting in relation to one's own eating styles, learning new diet recipes, and feeling good or not so good about oneself as group leaders read off weight losses and gains. Some directly confronted their bodily selves as they exercised in the groups. The groups structured distinctive group dieting *careers* with clear-cut and discrete segments and emphases. Group dieting exemplified how *careers* of the body could be processed through a social institution. In their *careers* as group dieters, participants developed certain rhetoric, dieting ideologies and skills, as well as strategies to justify nondieting.

Group dieting was part of a general health-weight social movement aimed to collectively promote the individual change of weight loss. Group dieting as an agency of social control to resocialize people into the values and practices of thinness was a microcosm of a more general public concern over excess pounds and flab. Group dieting's social services for consumers paralleled, complemented, and competed with other more professionalized services, especially medical systems, for managing weight-losing.

Revering ideals of thinness showed that group dieting was a kind of spiritual movement and a secular religion with continuing cycles of guilt-atonement. One cheated on fattening foods and felt guilty. One then confessed the errors of one's cheating and engaged in an ascetic eating pattern to make up for one's cheating. Many offered testimonies to the merits of thinness. Group dieters stressed their day-to-day here-and-now existence as they often showed a missionary zeal in proselytizing to others about the goodness of dieting efforts. Initial doubters often became converted to group dieting as a basic part of their life styles. Some Doubting Thomases gathered evidence to become more skeptical about dieting.

Group dieting showed aspects of a therapeutic method where there was a letting off of steam and a catharsis of multiple feelings. Group dieting was a friendly, sociable occasion which provided enough comfort for many to face their general and specific fears and worries. Modest but attainable goals for reducing the body were set on a weekly basis, so that expectations were realistic and not impossible to meet. Increased self-esteem was just as important for many as was weight-losing.

The rituals in group dieting *careers* which I observed were not so strange or eccentric. They were not so different from various interactional routines which many of us perform in everyday life, especially when we are working on a particular problem. Many of us have been conditioned to the goodness, beauty, and health of thinness in white middle-class America and are intensely aware of what we eat. Many feelings, attitudes, and behaviors expressed in group dieting are merely a concentrated intensification within a restricted time and place setting of many of our taken-for-granted orientations toward eating and dieting. Many of us are not so nonchalant and relaxed as we stand on scales weighing ourselves, especially many of us who are women who have been told repeatedly that we must fight the battle of the bulge as a way of life.

TRIM-DOWN DIETING: VALUES AND NORMS

Trim-Down as one of the largest of the privately-owned, profit-making diet clubs which started in the middle 1960s in the northeastern United States, now uses many behavior modification techniques, although such techniques were not in use at the time of my study. Trim-Down has over 35,000 members in 28 states, the District of Columbia, Canada, and Bermuda. Compulsive-eating, fat housewives who were so humiliated about their overweight that they had to do something about it started Trim-Down as a group of a few women in each other's living rooms who provided support and help for each other's weight and dieting problems. Other group weight-losing plans, one in particular, was the inspiration for Trim-Down.[4] Presently 61 franchisers of Trim-Down conduct over 1,250 groups. Ten-week commitment plans are sold for $25.00. Trim-Down stresses the control of eating, and Trim-Down leaders often work closely on dieting with each individual member, offering extra personal attention, more than do other weight-losing organizations. The stress is on never giving up—if dieters drop out before achieving their goal, they are called and encouraged to come back. (Berland and eds., Consumer Guide, 1977, pp. 196–98)

Mechanics need to replace faltering motivation; an apple as a mid-afternoon snack curbs the urge to eat cake. Trim-Down has organized retreats to certain geographical areas so that people can talk about their eating and weight problems and also stick with a diet. For about $75.00 for 10 hour and a half sessions, one may participate in Trim-Down's in-depth seminar program which uses a variety of psychodynamic strategies and tactics for the final achievement of weight control. Members of these seminars are often diet dropouts and are not losing any weight. In these seminars, Trim-Down leaders use more group and individual therapy philosophies and strategies than are used in most other group dieting programs. The Trim-Down diet has been developed by one medical doctor in conjunction with some executives in the organization. Trim-Down has compiled recipes which are sold in booklet form and in a paperback book about Trim-Down. (Berland and eds., Consumer Guide, 1977, pp. 196–98)

At the time of this study in the late 1960s, the main headquarters for the Trim-Down organization were located near a large city in the northeastern United States. The organization sponsored over 125 different weekly meetings in places within a 60 mile radius of this large city. At the time of this study, close to 4,000 people attended these meetings—about 95 percent were women and five percent were men. There were about 125 promoters working for the organization, who consisted of executives, group leaders, clerks, and secretaries. Almost all the employers and employees had lost or were losing excess pounds—weight loss was a major criterion to be a group leader. Less than three years before the start of the study, the Trim-Down organization had consisted of four overweight women sitting around in each other's living rooms trying to help each other lose weight, and devising a plan for others to lose weight as well.

The number of participants in meetings which I attended varied between five and 93. In most meetings, there were 20 to 50 members. The ages of the participants ranged from nine years to 75 plus years. Most members were between 25 and 55 years old. A core group appeared to be those between 35 and 50 years old—over 80 percent of these were married women. In the two groups which I observed for a seven month period, there were about 250 different members. Two hundred and thirty-eight were women and 12 were men. In the 41 other groups which I observed, there were about 1,150 different members; 1,090 were women and 60 were men. Therefore, about 72 out of the 1,400 Trim-Downers, or about five percent I observed, were men; this study refers only to the women.

The Trim-Downers whom I saw had between 0 and 125 plus pounds to lose; most had between 20 and 45 pounds to lose. Many had lost between five and 15 pounds on the Trim-Down diet, and intended to lose more weight.

I did not have any hard and fast statistics, but I could make a few generalizations about many members from what I learned from their names, words, and appearances. I observed no very poor Trim-Downers. Most appeared to be middle-class women, including lower and upper middle classes. More tended to be upper rather than lower middle. Four ethnic-religious groups seemed to make up most of the membership. About 25 percent of the Trim-Downers I met were Jewish. Another 25 percent were Italian and Catholic in background. Ten percent of the Trim-Downers were Irish; another 10 percent were Armenian. The remaining 30 percent of the Trim-Downers were of mixed origins, notably, English, German, and French. In this latter group, there were a number of White-Anglo-Saxon Protestants as well. I had the impression, however, that most Trim-Downers were Jewish or Catholic. I observed only five black female Trim-Downers.

These religious and ethnic differences sometimes seemed to be related to weight-losing "progress." Perhaps people of certain backgrounds shared common attitudes toward many of the dieting leaders and plans which they chose. Italian and Irish Catholics who were accustomed to put their trust in priest-healers for their sins also appeared to put their faith in the external social control force of the Trim-Down dieting system. Many of these members yielded to the authority of Trim-Down leaders; they obeyed these leaders' prescriptions and often lost weight.

In contrast with Catholicism (that is, some kinds of Catholicism until recent times), Judaism has a long history of continual dialectics and running battles between rabbis and laity. Many Jews have not regarded their rabbis as much as the absolute holders of truth as have some Catholics perceived their priests. As Jews have doubted and challenged their rabbi-healers, so they have been skeptical toward their Trim-Down leaders. Some Jewish members seemed to tell their Trim-Down leaders; "I dare you to take the weight off me." Fewer Jews than Catholics lost their excess pounds in the course of my study. I speculate that one reason for this difference may lie in the different religious backgrounds of the members. Women stated:

I go to church and confess all to the priest, and he forgives me and I try to be better the next week. And here is the same thing, but it is the diet leader I tell all my cheating sins to. The priest knows what is best for my soul and the diet leader knows what is best for my body and I put my trust in these leaders. It is easy to follow exactly what the diet leader says—than I lose weight and don't feel guilty about cheating. I guess I'm a good Catholic on the diet!

As a Jew, I have never been sure about the meanings and purposes of God, and I have always debated with rabbis in my temple about the historical destiny of the Jews. I have been in these intellectual discussion groups and you see there are hundreds of interpretations for one little passage in the Bible. Who knows what's right? And the lecturer here seems so sure of herself—she knows that one basic diet will work for all and I am not so sure. I dare her to take the weight off me with her be-all and end-all diet—nobody, and I have been everywhere, has been able to get me to stick to a rigid diet before, but I will give her a try. Rabbis, diet leaders, they all think that they have the answer, but I am never sure their answers are right.

There were some other religious and ethnic differences among members. Italian, Armenian, and Irish middle and lower-middle-class women often stressed the *sociability* functions of Trim-Down meetings. They called the meetings "fun" or "amusing." They enjoyed gossiping and being entertained by lecturers. They often placed the subject of dieting within the context of sociability.

Lower-middle-class Irish woman:

We have a jolly good time here. It is a barrel of laughs. We exchange recipes and confess our cheating sins. Then we gossip about everybody under the sun. I am sure glad that I can fit these meetings into my schedule—I have club meetings every other night of the week. The lecturer here is a real character, and we have a ball. Some of us do lose a little weight for a while, but the main thing is, we have fun and scream and laugh and get lots of our tensions off our chests.

Middle-class Armenian woman:

It feels good to laugh here. We are a bunch of gossips here and we do get catty about people. The lecturer tries to get us for our cheating but then we have fun getting her back, saying something bad about how she looks, like insult humor. We could go on nightclub routines. We gab and get at people, like our morning coffee sessions. So we get a conscience about stuffing ourselves here, but we have great snacks afterward. Besides, there is nothing different here— the subject of dieting is common wherever we go.

Lower-middle-class Jewish women often mentioned this *sociability* function of the dieting groups, along with the purpose of *weight reduction*. They said that the meetings were an enjoyable, friendly, and helpful way to lose weight. They seemed more concerned with the weight-losing functions of the groups than did some Armenian, Irish, and Italian women.

Lower-middle-class Jewish woman:

So you gain a little—so you lose a little—so what, everybody goes up and down. At least you cheat with a conscience when you come here. You can't be so fanatic and serious about it, but the group does help. You come here and learn how everybody is doing. This is good, because you get so busy, that you don't have the chance to see everybody so often. Most of us belong to this temple, and we talk about the temple and our kids. It is a relaxing way to spend a morning and it does encourage you to lose.

Upper-middle-class Jewish women seemed to stress the *weight reduction* functions of the meeting to the exclusion of the sociability functions. They asserted that they came to the group to lose weight—not to be entertained. They had enough sources of fun outside the group. Some rather wealthy Jewish women did not appear to delight in talking about foods and recipes for their own sake, as did the Italians, Armenians, and Irish. Rather, these Jews stressed the pragmatic values of some foods and recipes; such foods were viewed as ''healing agents'' to the end of weight reduction.

Upper-middle-class Jewish woman:

I know that there are lots here who think it is a big club or social party. I don't. My weight is my own business and I don't like to make it the public property of everybody. Usually, I come and weigh in and leave. I only need the scale, not the group therapy part. That part is superficial and amateurish—I know, because I have been in real group therapy. I don't come to play around here; I have plenty of friends outside the group. All I care about is if the recipes will work to make me lose weight; I don't care about how good they taste. I am here to lose weight, and I care about me, myself and I. I don't need the moral support from others. People here are nice, but they really aren't the types I would pick for friends. We all should be coming to the group only for one purpose—to lose weight.

These wealthier Jews seemed to place little value on the sociability aspects of the meetings. They considered the group therapy aspects of the meetings. They considered the group therapy aspects of the dieting sessions "trite" and "ineffective." Some of these Jewish women seemed obsessed with the single purpose of weight reduction. They appeared to recognize only those aspects of the meeting which were directly related to weight-losing, as the scale and diet recipes. Other ethnic and class groups seemed to view the Trim-Down group as more multi-functional. The latter people appeared less tense and more relaxed about their Trim-Down *careers* than were the wealthy Jews; *sociability* in the groups was just as important to them as getting cured from their fatness. (Hughes, 1958, pp. 62–67)

The Trim-Down group dieting plan consisted of a uniform diet for all in most groups to follow, with the exception of those in diet conference groups and mini-losers' groups. This diet contained between about 1,000 to 1,200 calories a day, with a strong emphasis on protein.[5] Group meetings encouraged people to stay on the diet plan.

Many Trim-Downers believed that it took a fatty or at the least an ex-fatty to know a fatty—the empathetic understanding of the complexities of overweight in the groups was more significant than all the doctors' pills for weight reduction. Some asked: Why is the medical doctor better qualified to help people lose weight because he (they did not say she) has had X numbers of years of training and X numbers of degrees than the fat person who has lived through the "school of hard knocks" with overweight? For some, the significantly smaller fee for Trim-Down group dieting treatment than for doctors' prescriptions also made a difference. Trim-Downers prided themselves on being "do-it-yourself" authorities in weight-losing; at a low cost and through social support, they would help each other. Some said that they had more *professional expertise* in dieting than people who had M.D.'s or Ph.D.'s after their names.

Some group dieting plans as Trim-Down highlight the *loss of the general practitioner* doctor in contemporary America, who, in an idealized image, has the capacity to view the whole person and not just specialized body parts. Some Trim-Downers remembered the "good old days" of the family doctor who took time and cared about his (most group dieters did not say "her") patients' feelings and attitudes, as well as about the patients' ills and complaints of the body and mind. Such a general practitioner type seemed to be sorely missed by many Trim-Downers—they felt too "scared" or too "threatened" or too "normal" to pay large amounts of money to psychiatrists or other specialists to help them with their overweight problems. Group dieting filled the "*gemeinschaft gap*" left in many secondary, impersonal relationships of short duration between patient and Western medical doctor.

Some Trim-Downers, rather ironically, more severely condemned the bad habit of overweight than did some doctors. Some Trim-Downers who looked for a way out of such condemnation sought medical doctors who had a more relaxed and open-minded, tolerant attitude toward over-weight—although such doctors were not easy to find. Perhaps some medical people could "afford" to be somewhat relaxed about some degrees of overweight—their business did not rest solely on catering to the overweight market. In contrast, some profit-making dieting groups as Trim-Down depended upon this overweight affliction for their very survival.

In fact, some group dieting promoters as Trim-Downers and medical doctors wanted to work together—group dieting would monitor weight and offer psychological support for some overweight people; medical doctors' time and energy would be confined to periodic assessments of diets and weight goals. Group dieting organizations as Trim-Down had the endorsement of many medical specialists; they had consulting physicians on their staff. Many Trim-Down promoters said that the doctor's advice should always take precedence when one was dieting. Many said that they were not trained as psychiatrists to handle the many emotional problems which an overweight person might have—in fact, they might get hit with a lawsuit if they tried to give too much advice. They were only lay people who could talk about an effective way to lose weight. Some Trim-Down promoters made some rather *uneasy compromises* with medical doctors about who were the "real experts" with regard to overweight.

One of the strongest themes which emerged in Trim-Down group dieting as part of the general health-weight movement in contemporary America was that of *morality*. As part of a spiritual movement, the groups had qualities of a secular religion. Leaders and members of Trim-Down groups constantly used religious terminology. They referred to cheating on the diet as "sinning." Some called themselves "saints" or "angels" if they stuck to the diet and did not cheat. Members talked about how important it was to "confess" cheating or "sinning"; some said that group leaders had the power to grant "absolution" for cheating. Participants referred to the card with the basic diet written on it as the "diet Bible." (Allon, 1972; Allon, 1973, pp. 36–42; Allon, 1975, pp. 59–69)

Sagarin has discussed how groups such as Trim-Down function on group therapy lines with religious or pseudo-religious concepts for reinforcement. Such groups paint members as worthwhile individuals, souls to be saved. They view the condition bringing people to the groups as immoral, sinful, and self-defeating. People with the condition are labeled deviant and are subject to scorn, discrimination, gossip, pity, and punishment because they carry a stigma. Deviance-reducing Trim-Down groups did frown on members who strayed from dieting, and they exerted much pressure to stick to the diet through inner group loyalty. Often Trim-Downers more harshly condemned the deviance of overweight than members of the general population. Trim-Down members as well as promoters feared the enlightened and permissive view that the consequences of the deviance of overweight would be less severe if only social attitudes toward overweight were changed. Such a view was a threat to the Trim-

Down organization and its program, and for the members, a temptation to stray from the straight-and-narrow of the diet. In condemning this view, Trim-Downers stressed the morality of thinness and the immorality of fatness, reinforced by religious orientations. (Sagarin, 1969, pp. 17–22)

Trim-Down group dieting rituals in a quasi-religious service *established and reinforced the stigmatization of the overweight people as sinners.* Trim-Downers used the group as a sounding board for their own badness, and as a hearing board for the badness of others—through showing and discussing their bloated and puffy bodies. The Trim-Downers socialized each other into a collective conscience about the evils of their overweight as they were very *self-absorbed* in their own excess pounds. If, within the confines of her protective group, a Trim-Downer could be brought to see herself as a glutton (gluttony being one of the seven deadly sins), such a distressing stigma might motivate the Trim-Downer to diet. (Sagarin, 1969, p. 72) The stigma of overweight was used to change behavior from deviant to normal. (Laslett and Warren, 1975, pp. 69–80)

Yet, while fat became a "dirty word" in the Trim-Down group dieting experience, the group experience did *mitigate* the stigmatization of fat. Trim-Downers stated: "It is not so bad to be fat because there are a lot of us here in the same boat." A Trim-Downer was not such a bad, even a good fat, in that she lay herself bare before the group, with some vague hope or more determined resolution to shed pounds. The morally good group dieter was one who admitted her sins of the flesh and who attempted to perfect a better and better, thinner body. Such a Trim-Downer wanted to be healed from her excess flesh, and often, for a little while anyway, she showed healing progress in her behavior. She was being healed by losing pounds. Yet, "sinning a little" was only human—one might not always get the cure in a quick and straightforward manner. The final cure of a thin body evolved from a fat body. Indeed, for thinness-healing to be such a supreme good, it must arise from the depths of bad fatness.

The optimum-value in many Trim-Down groups did not seem to be the final thinness-cure, but the process of healing thinner. This process of healing was emphasized more that the final product of healed-thinness. Holiness lay in the act of cleansing the dirty fat body. How much better healed and how much holier was the person who cleansed herself of the sin of fatness and who became a "saintly thin," than she who remained a "*status quo* thin" all along! To become a thin saint, one must start as a fat sinner. Some Trim-Downers did say that it was good to be fat if such fatness led to the continually ameliorating stages of "thinnerness."

The Trim-Down groups stressed "saints-in-the-making," who, by the way, were "monetarily good" paying customers to the profit-making weight-losing organization. Having arrived at thinness was not such a noble *fait accompli,* for, after all, the "cured thin" need no longer pay to get healed. As in many undertakings, "success" was the process of moving toward a final goal, not the achievement of the final goal itself.

That group dieting tended to accentuate as well as lessen the stigma of overweight was shown in its ambivalence about "normal eating." The Trim-Down group dieting plan *normalized deviant patterns of eating,* deviant in the sense that they were different from and more restricted than many people's notions of "normal" or "average" eating. The Trim-Down group dieting plan seemed to normalize the obsession with eating or noneating, especially as it advised members to pay close attention to everything that they put into their mouths and to weigh foods with a postal scale before they ate such foods. Programs as Trim-Down tended to make the concern about food a bigger proportion of a person's total life style than was true for "outsiders" to the group. Sometimes the Trim-Down plan capitalized upon the legitimacy of deviant thought patterns in its stress upon addictive rhetoric. Trim-Down leaders said that there was nothing wrong with an eating compulsion as long as it was channeled into the correct, low-calorie foods. One could cope with the stigma of overweight by getting a weekly "high" or "fix" at the group, which could inspire one to "destigmatize" oneself.

Group dieters underlined their fat stigma by *confessing* to each other the past and present errors of their eating ways. Yet Trim-Downers mitigated against their stigma by the losing of weight and *testifying* on behalf of the goodness of thinness and the Trim-Down diet plan, which had "saved the lives" of some. The sense of normalizing a "deviant" preoccupation with eating, dieting, and weight suggested a sectlike quality of diet groups, which were small reference groups which set up particular standards for in-group members. (Wilson, 1961)

TRIM-DOWN GROUP DIETING SETTING

A group dieter walked in the door of the building where the dieting meeting was held. First she paid her weekly fee at a table most often located near the entrance. Sometimes the dieter waited in a line to pay this fee to either the group leader or a clerk who kept written records of the members' payments. The member then proceeded usually to a different part of the room, or another adjacent room or hallway, to be weighed in by the group leader. Weigh-ins were private transactions between the member and the group leader. The scale was either surrounded by a partition or in a separate room behind a closed door so that others could not witness a person's weigh-in. Sometimes members had to wait in lines to weigh in on the scale. The group leader kept records of each members' weight progress on separate cards. She read weekly and sometimes more long-term progress reports from such records during the formal meeting. The leader usually kept such cards in a box on a table near the front of the room. Members chatted with each other in these weigh-in and pay-in lines; sometimes they stood and chatted in empty free spaces near the back of the meeting rooms.

After members paid and weighed in, they most often sat down in fairly symmetrical rows of chairs, commonly placed in two sections, separated by

FLOOR PLAN OF A GROUP DIETING MEETING ROOM

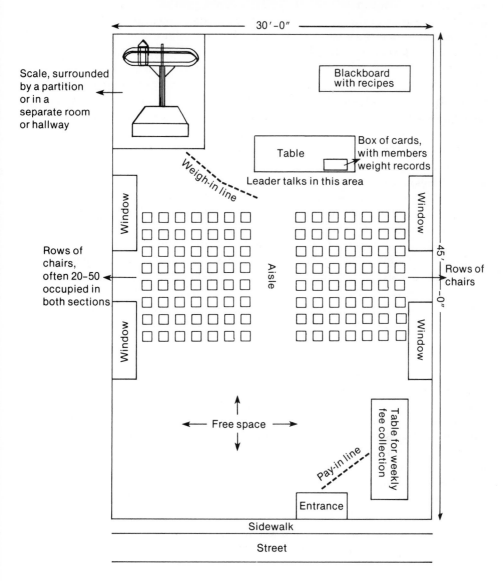

Scale, surrounded by a partition or in a separate room or hallway

30'-0"

Blackboard with recipes

Weigh-in line

Table

Box of cards, with members weight records

Leader talks in this area

Window

Rows of chairs, often 20-50 occupied in both sections

Aisle

Window

45'-0"

Rows of chairs

Window

Window

Free space

Table for weekly fee collection

Pay-in line

Entrance

Sidewalk

Street

an aisle. Sometimes friends came together to the meeting and sat next to each other; sometimes friends saved seats for each other when they did not enter together. Some members struck up a conversation with each other in the weighing-in or paying-in process and then sat down next to each other and chatted. Some members somewhat arbitrarily chose any seat and started up a conversation with someone sitting nearby. Often there were at least 50 to 125 chairs set up in the meeting room; 20 to 50 members sat in these chairs in many meetings. Seating patterns varied in different groups. Generally, women sat near the front of the room in groups of two to six women who talked with each other. There were very few loners in the groups.

After all the members who came to a particular meeting paid and weighed in, leaders and clerks took a few minutes to get their records straight. They figured out if everyone who weighed had paid the correct amount of money (members had to pay varying amounts for the meetings missed); they also calculated group mean-averages of weight losses for the particular group for one week's time or longer. The group leader then began her formal talk. She stood or sat near a table in the front of the room, with members responding to her, raising hands to make comments and ask questions. Quite a few members continued to chat with others sitting near them, either side-to-side, in back or in front of them during the time that the leader was speaking. The dual processes of a formal message by the leader and informal chatter between members went on simultaneously in many dieting groups.

Sometimes a leader used a blackboard which was located near her table in the front of the room to stress a point, to pass on information, and quite often, to write down the ingredients and preparations for diet recipes. Occasionally, leaders and members arranged chairs in a circle formation so as to encourage conversation and eye contact between members and between members and leaders. A few leaders stated that the circle formation was a useful strategy for increasing open communication and rapport among participants, but they continued to talk in the front of the room to women seated in rows of chairs.

As members first came to the group meeting, they paid in a weekly fee of $2.00 after an initial registration fee of $5.00. The paying-in process lasted between five and 45 minutes, usually between 15 and 25 minutes. They were then required to weigh in each week on the group scale, where their weights were recorded by group leaders. The Trim-Down organization kept detailed records of weight losses and gains. The weigh-in process lasted between 10 to 50 minutes, usually between 20 and 30 minutes. Group leaders gave a 10 minute to 50 minute (often 12 to 25 minute) lecture each week stressing the assets of thinness and the liabilities of fatness as well as providing some nutritional and dieting information. Members then asked questions about dieting in general and about specific aspects of the Trim-Down diet for about 10 minutes. Lecturers, taking between five and 20 minutes, read off mouth-watering, low-calorie recipes to members, which members wrote down. Leaders for five to 20 minutes then read off the numbers of pounds each person lost or gained during the time since they attended their last meeting. Lecturers sometimes commented on total losses of individuals since they had started the Trim-Down plan. Lecturers often passed quickly over gains or did not read the gains at all. In some groups, there was mild isotonic exercising at the end of a meeting, usually lasting less than 10 minutes. Newcomers stayed to hear the specific details of the diet explained to them by group leaders.

Fifteen Trim-Down meetings which I attended were held in meeting halls and classrooms of Jewish temples and synagogues. Thirteen meetings were held in assembly rooms of churches which were mainly Protestant denominations. Eight sessions were held in meeting rooms in neighborhood houses and community centers, sponsored by the YMCA and Red Feather agencies. Three sessions were held in the meeting room of the central headquarters of the Trim-Down organization. One meeting was held in the assembly room of a fraternal organization; one, in the conference room of a supermarket; one, in a combined conference-dining room of a hotel; and one, in a conference room of an apartment building.

Most Trim-Down sessions started between 7:00 and 8:00 P.M. and lasted between one and three and one-half hours. Most lasted between one and one-half and two and one-quarter hours. Almost 75 percent of all meetings were held in the early evening hours. The morning meetings began between 9:00 and 10:00 A.M., and usually lasted between one and one and three-quarter hours. The Trim-Down organization did not hold afternoon meetings.

THE RITUALS OF GROUP DIETING

Having chosen Trim-Down group dieting, participants partook of certain group rituals which composed the primary method of operation of the Trim-Down healing system. Some authors have stressed the psychological implications of such religious processes in groups. Others have discussed the structural aspects of religion and ritual in everyday life.[6] These authors have pointed out how ideals and ultimate systems of values believed in by leaders and followers get patterned into routines of day-to-day existence. So *reverence for the Ideal of Thinness* got *patterned* and *regularized* into certain structures and processes of group dieting. The term "religion" in reference to group dieting refers to the idea that people strive toward ideals of thinness as very important and sometimes *ultimate value systems* for themselves on earth. Rituals of group dieting are "this-worldly"—oriented to the secular values of thinness—and have no supernatural or superempirical reference points.

Trim-Downers made *territorial processions* inside the doors of the meetings as rites of entrance. This initial walk might be viewed as a rite of separation from the dieters' previous world, in which they were "unclean" and "unhealed." (van Gennep, 1961, pp. 15–25) This state of "unhealedness" was a legitimate initial stage in the Trim-Down world. Once a member had one foot in the door, literally, she became "sacred" according to group norms, because she was on the road to becoming healed from her fatness. (Durkheim, 1961, pp. 52–53) Walking inside the door was the first initiation rite in the Trim-Down healing system; it usually took between 10 and 35 minutes for all the members to enter. In fact, this territorial passage through the door might be viewed as the beginning of an initiation rite. In this light, group participation and weight loss which occurred inside the door might be seen as an initiation rite into the "culturally preferred" thin American way of life. One woman said:

> You are dirty and a sinner before you walk in this door, but coming in the door is your first step on the way to salvation. You begin to be a saint when you admit that you need to walk in this door. That first step means that you are going to try damned hard to really make it into the mainstream of American life and be thin. You don't want to be a deviant and outcast for the rest of your life, and you are going to try hard to change yourself.

Marching through the door was the *first processional walk* in the Trim-Down group. Participants sought out other "entrance-partners" in their walk inside, on their way to worship the Ideal of Thinness. Such entrance-partners exchanged *pro*-fessions of their goodness and *con*-fessions of their badness in regard to their healing progress. A woman stated:

> You sort of don't like to be alone, you want to be with somebody else when you come in here, so you feel you have got a buddy working for the same thing as you. Sometimes I need to tell somebody how great I've been on the diet even with all the parties, and I want them to congratulate me for not giving into temptation. Sometimes I need to let out on somebody why I did cheat on what kinds of food—that chocolate marshmallow cake last week made me hang my head in shame in front of Sue, because I was being such an angel on the diet before that.

The *second processional march* in the Trim-Downers *careers* took place as members waited in pay-in lines to offer their standardized and required alms to lecturers or clerks. As continuing members, they paid $2.00. The initial registration fee was $5.00. Those who missed meetings paid one dollar for each meeting missed, never to exceed the initial $5.00 fee. Trim-Downers thus made a monetary payment for their healing. Indeed, one means of redemption in gaining possession of "thinnerness" was to pay money to the group, which acknowledged the state of sin and indicated a reciprocity between giver and receiver.[7] There was also a "noncontractual" element of the healing contract. (Durkheim, 1964, pp. 200–29) Healers and potential healers shared a basic trust that those overweight in Trim-Down terms could and would be helped to shed their excess pounds. One member explained:

It really is like you are in church here and you are giving an offering to help you be better. And you get penalized here if you don't come to this church—you pay more. When you pay, you know there is something wrong with you that you can help cure, and it's up to you to get something for your money. If you don't lose, your money is going down the drain. I have got faith that I will lose, and I will put my money where my mouth is, put my money on the line to lose. I trust that they will help me here. I wouldn't have such an incentive to lose if I wasn't sacrificing some money—the money means my weight-losing is a serious thing; I am paying for my sin.

Trim-Downers appeared to speak with their bodies in pay-in lines, as they were very *absorbed* in their own appearances. Some appeared to cope with their embarrassment about their bodies by snuggling in their coats and loose-fitting clothes so as to hide their bodies. (Modigliani, 1968, pp. 313–26; Gross and Stone, 1964, pp.1–15) Others seemed to announce their mixed feelings about their bodies to the world by throwing open their coats and exhibiting their bodies exposed in tightly-fitting clothing. Many engaged in double conversations of eyes sizing up one another and of chatter about the diet and social activities, as many of us do in everyday life. One said:

The body does say everything here and you can tell how embarrassed people are by what they wear here. Like they wear the same big cotton house dress week after week even in the winter so their bulges won't poke out. Some want to make their fat stomachs and rear ends really hang out by wearing skirts that are about to burst open—they are proving to everybody that they are really fat. I do both things myself, because I am so self-conscious about my extra 35 pounds. Then I will be carrying out some stupid conversation about the diet with somebody next to me but my mind and eyes will wander around the room to see if I have the biggest rear end in the room and try to find somebody fatter than me. You keep comparing your body with others here.

The *third processional march* of Trim-Down group dieting *careers* occurred in weigh-in lines. The scale appeared to be the *totemic representation* of the Ideal of Thinness.[8] As Trim-Downers confronted the scale, they praised the Ideal of Thinness and atoned for their cheating sins—they sought out purification of their overweight bodies. Some seemed to pray in the presence of the scale. They cried out in joy or sorrow about their weight-losing progress; they stared straight in front of them in devout silence while on the scale. In their moment of judgment on the scale, some felt cleansed from their sins of cheating, while others felt exalted in their holiness of good eating. On the scale, some felt *uplifted* because their weight was going down; others felt *degraded* because their weight was staying the same or going up. (Garfinkel, 1956, pp. 420–24) Indeed, Trim-Downers labeled themselves good or bad according to the scale's decree of a two or three digit number, as many of us do. A woman reflected:

It is like the scale is some kind of a god and you pray that its judgment of you will be in your favor. I act out a lot on the scale. I yell and laugh if I do well, and cry if I do bad. What the scale says is a great reward for my dieting. But sometimes I say, O.K., the scale has condemned me and I have to wipe the slate clean, my guilt is laid bare, and I'm going to start fresh and new in a new week to be good on the diet again. You can't bribe the scale!

Trim-Downers anthropomorphized the scale, calling it a "kind friend," or a "mean white monster." Many talked to the scale and asked the scale to be "fair," "give me a break," "have a heart," or not be a "devil." As some begged the scale to be good to them, they appeared to disrobe toward a naked innocence. Shoes and heavy jewelry were taken off; sometimes woolen skirts, belts, slips, and girdles were removed. A few women took off their wigs. These women talked about how they were going to give themselves every benefit of the doubt, and they did not want anything unnecessary to be held against them—it was the weight of their body that counted. Some added that they wished that there were facilities in the group so they could take off all their clothes so as to get their "true" body weight. Trim-Downers were quite involved in making their bodies weigh the lowest amount possible.

At this time, some Trim-Downers continued to compare parts of their bodies to those of others, competitively checking out who was thinner or fatter in which body part—as they did in pay-in lines.[9] Others seemed to try to smoothe out or down their unembodied fat, by rubbing their cheeks or stomachs or hips up and down, or pulling down sweaters and skirts, as if to compress their fat. Others were pure socializers who spent time walking around and talking with many members, almost as if they were part of an official greeting committee, asking "how are you?" and "how are you doing?" and "so what's new?" (Goffman, 1967, p. 41) A few were very silent and motionless, and tended to keep to themselves and not talk with others, so displaying distance from their roles as active group participants. (Goffman, 1961, pp. 83–152)

All these different types of Trim-Downers met up with the common leveler of the scale. Leader-healers calculated Ideal weight goals for the Trim-Downers, the point at which the participants would be proclaimed "healed" of their overweight. These who were healed were admonished to work hard to maintain their healed-state; there was no guarantee that the Trim-Down cure was permanent. In Trim-Down lingo, those healed were called "graduates." The Ideal weight goals which they achieved were based upon the edicts of insurance companies, which suggested weights for women and men based upon their height, bone structure, and age.

In a very concrete, quantitative manner, the scale made the *final judgment* of the degree to which each Trim-Downer was healed each week. The leader-healer read this absolute sentence to each member. The scale in no uncertain terms decreed the fates of the Trim-Downers. Pounds shed indicated that healing was taking place. It was very simple to measure healing in Trim-Down terms. Many of us appreciate simple quantitative measures of progress, as grades in school.

In the *sociable chatter-time* of dieting *careers* that followed, healees "responsively read" each other verbally and visually for between 10 and 45 minutes. Ego and alter questioned and answered each other about their dieting efforts; they offered each other pep talks. Some seemed to pray with each other at this time as they asked the Ideal of Thinness to bestow Its omnipotent blessings on them. Many believed that thinness did mean beauty, happiness, and health, and would mean their own greater *self-validation*. *Self-absorbed* Believers discussed their faith in the Trim-Down diet creed. Offering testimonies to the Ideal of Thinness, they stressed how much healthier and happier their lives were becoming as a result of their weight-losing. In contrast, some skeptics challenged the Trim-Down diet creed—they did not like the food on the diet, or they questioned why they needed to be healed from their fatness anyway.

Lecturer-healers were on center stage in the following period of the *lecture-sermon*. These healers exalted the Ideal of Thinness and the Trim-Down diet plan as the best means to reach the Ideal. Many lecturers divulged humorous and sad anecdotes about their own weight-losing *careers*. Some exclaimed how their lives had been saved by the Trim-Down healing method. They described sinfulness—conversion—regeneration cycles. (O'Dea, 1969, pp. 62-63)

Other prophetic healers told of the horrors of fatness and the evil fortunes which befell those who resisted Trim-Down healing. They warned that members must not be tempted to stray from the straight and narrow of the diet and eat tabooed foods. (Radcliffe-Brown, 1952, pp. 133-52; Steiner, 1956) Some lecturers gave elaborate rationales for parts of the Trim-Down creed. They emphasized how and why the Trim-Down healing system was the best of all healing systems for overweight, including pills, doctors' diets, exercising, and other group methods. Lecturers got their points across through jesting, story-telling, and solemn admonitions.

The detailed and technical *question-and-answer period* was the next stage in group dieting *careers*. It followed the *lecture-sermon*. Member-healers and lecturer-healers seemed to engage in "responsive readings" with each other, with members doing most of the asking, and lecturers doing most of the answering. The ideology of thinness was stressed in the *lecture*; the *question-and-answer period* concentrated upon the tactics of Trim-Down thinness-healing—the "how to do it." There was an elaborate exchange of information about the kinds and amounts of food on the diet. Some clarified and elaborated upon the creed for others at this time. Some affirmed and lauded the Trim-Down creed; others challenged it. One woman elaborated:

> You can find out a lot here, like it is better to eat the tuna packed in oil and I learned where to buy the unsweetened frozen fruit juices at this time. I asked and found out which breads are best to eat. You do ask the same questions over and over again so you won't forget and you can really get it into your head what you should eat. I tried to get the lecturer to tell me how much weight to lose each week, but she didn't want to be pinned down, but I think one and one-half to two pounds seems good to her. I asked her what to eat to maintain my weight after I lose it all. And I complain at this time that I am not used to

eating breakfast and my family doesn't like to eat my diet foods. I get gas, constipation, excess urination, and very tired on this diet. The lecturer says it is good if I go a lot because it means that my fat is turning to fluid and leaving my body, and her cure works for constipation—an iced drink followed by very hot coffee. And she tells me here when I get the sweet horrors to eat lots of diet gelatin. I don't come here for depth therapy, but I have specific problems on the diet, and I get short, concrete, and practical answers back from the lecture—here, I want to learn how to eat better—how do women come here and expect the leader to tell them what to do with a cranky husband who makes them go off the diet? That is too big a question for a lecturer here to answer.

Many Trim-Downers wanted to be nurtured as they asked lecturers to repeat over and over again the Trim-Down creed. They seemed to demonstrate a "repetition compulsion," common in children described by Schachtel. People depend upon repeatedly available and constant, unchanged objects. One enjoys knowing and doing over and over again that which one already masters, as compared with the hazards of a new venture. One feels control over oneself in repeatedly exposing oneself to the familiar. Yet one also wants to explore and discover unknown aspects in what may ostensibly impress one as mere repetition. (Schachtel, 1959, p. 265) As children, many Trim-Downers sought to be instructed as to each and every bit of food that they were permitted to put into their mouths, whether or not they followed such instructions. An infantilization process seemed to occur as lecturers spelled out in most detailed ways what and how much members must, might, and should not eat.

The specific healing procedure was articulated in each weekly meeting as the lecturer read the *recipe-scripture passage.*[10] This presentation was similar to the reading of a sacred text, in that many listened devoutly to each and every word, carefully writing down and memorizing every last detail. Healees responded to the healer's prescription of "recipe-medicine" as they became involved in an exegesis of the text. Many spent much time and energy on the particulars of ingredients of recipes which were seductive in their mouth-watering names. For example, there were Trim-Down recipes for lasagna, chicken curry, eggplant kebab, Indonesian egg roll, pink cloud chiffon pie, lemon custard, and upside-down spiced peach cake. Exotic as well as international titles made the recipes sound exciting and appealing— the recipes had universal appeal to all types of people.

As some members' tongues were hanging out at such recipes, they seemed to delight in their own special Trim-Down language:

Cheese dips for us mean using cucumbers or celery, and not potato chips. It is fun to have our own meanings for words. We know that "fry" does not mean to use butter and oil the way most people think, but to use bouillon cubes or tomato juice in a Teflon pan. Our kind of 'sour cream' is made of buttermilk, cottage cheese, horseradish, and lemon juice. It makes you feel important to belong to a group with its own special lingo.

Such special language seemed to demonstrate a secret society aspect of Trim-Down meetings. (Simmel, 1964, pp. 330–76)

It was the Ideal of Thinness which appeared to be worshipped in the giving and receiving of the weekly diet recipe. Trim-Down healers and healees did not worship the recipe-scriptures as perfect. Recipe cures might not be infallible; for example, they might call for too many sweets or spices. Worship of the recipes *per se* would be idolatry—it was the Ideal of Thinness which was revered. The diet recipes were a significant medium through which this Ideal spoke to Trim-Downers by calling them to respond in faith and obedience.

Again, healees and healers appeared to "responsively read" each other verbally and visually as the healers *announced* their individual members' *weight losses and gains* as specific achievements kept on records called "report cards." With these public announcements of individual and group weight loss averages, the worthiness of the Trim-Down healing method was confirmed. Most lecturers mumbled weight gains quickly if they did not completely ignore the existence of gaining. They preferred to minimize the fact that the Trim-Down cure was not working for all; the cure meant that bodies were losing pounds. In terms of pounds shed in a total group, the Trim-Down healing method seemed quite effective. One Trim-Downer commented:

> The lecturers here say these large numbers like the group lost 87 pounds and it makes you think that everybody lost at least 10 pounds until you stop and think that there are close to 70 in this group. It is like getting grades in school, and you feel bad about letting down the group. They sometimes don't bother to use the word 'lost' as they go through the list, but they always use the word 'gain' to show a member she's going in the wrong direction. And it is taboo here to state the total numbers of pounds that anyone weighs—you can only say the changes week by week. The lecturers say that we should all help the backsliders, and people who gain should not be afraid to come to meetings.

In this portion of the meeting, lecturers offered some *legitimate excuses* for why members were not losing much or any weight on the diet. When a lecturer said that a member was on a "plateau," she meant that the member had lost a certain amount of weight and had reached a standstill due to metabolic processes in her body. The second most common legitimate excuse which lecturers gave members for lack of weight progress was that of water retention. The third category of legitimate excuses included commonly-held designations of particular patterns of losers, as "every other week losers," or "big once a month losers." The fourth category of legitimate excuses for poor weight progress included legitimate, situational contingencies. A member might weigh more in the evening than in the morning; clothing and medications might be slowing down weight losses. Trim-Downers learned the ropes of using such legitimate standardized excuses for their "poor" weight progress, whether or not such excuses really applied to them—some enjoyed "passing" or "masquerading" as dieters with legitimate excuses for gains. (Goffman, 1963, pp. 73–91) *Illegitimate excuses* included much cheating on the diet due to lack of willpower, as ''I just could not resist the tempting foods over the holidays,'' and ''I just had to taste my own cooking.''

As leader-healers read off weight losses and gains, they appeared to offer *individualized benedictions* to members as they wished them well on the diet; this portion of the meeting underlined the supreme importance of impersonal numbers in the groups as well as the fleeting personal attention paid by lecturers to members. Lecturers seemed to bless the members in their dieting efforts, and wished that the members would approach nearer and nearer to the Ideal of Thinness in their bodies. Lecturers controlled and directed the dialogues, often a highlight in group dieting *careers*:

'We haven't seen Josephine for a while and she tells me she has had a tragedy in her life and she comes back here and with all that trouble, she has lost a pound. Raise your hand, Josephine so we all can see you.'

Josephine laughs and blushes and says that she has been trying.

'You know that when there is something bad we eat and Josephine is down 37 pounds.'

Many look at Josephine and say 'Wow' and 'That is wonderful' and most clap.

'Lena has two beautiful pounds gone, and she is down 11 1/2 in four weeks, and that is very nice.'

Many clap and agree that the loss is good and Lena smiles and says 'thank you.'

'We haven't seen Rose since April, and Rose didn't stay with us long enough so she is back up there again, but we are glad to have her back. She said that she needed me again and I am glad she came back to Mama.'

Rose says that she is glad that she came back.

The lecturer says that she will not embarrass Rose by saying how much Rose gained—the important thing is that Rose is back.

There is silence and some look at Rose and whisper that she does look fatter than the last time they saw her.

'Now Mary even with her daughter getting married made it four pounds this week in the face of much temptation. A big clap.'

Many clap and smile at Mary.

'Now, Margaret, you have lost two and one-half pounds in three weeks but that is not good enough for you and you weren't here last week so I will have to get my fish hook after you.'

Margaret says that she is determined to try harder.

The lecturer adds that Margaret is not doing so bad since she has lost 20 1/2 pounds in three months.

All clap.

'Now the new grandma over there, and she looks so young I can't believe she is a grandma—only lost one-half pound but a total of 30 so let's give her a hand.'

Many look at this woman and clap but she says she won't clap for herself until she loses more and it must be the canned fruit that is not letting her lose more.

'Now Rose, you have lost two and so it is two pounds in four weeks. Any questions or problems on the diet?'

Rose replies that she is enjoying the diet and it is unbelievable that there is so much to eat on it.

'Georgia, you can kiss that handsome husband of yours for me and tell him that you lost two pounds and he will be very happy. A total of 34 pounds gone now.'

Georgia replies that she is happy and her husband has been nagging her to lose.

All clap.

'Now Ruth you have been a little naughty and had a little gain but you can make up for it next week and get with it—I know you tend to retain fluid.'

Ruth says that she has been holding water but she has been eating chocolate candy too and she will work hard now for sure.

'Now Joan has lost three pounds and all together, 41 pounds.'

Joan says that she was just plain determined and she had two weddings to go to and rehearsal dinners, but she managed to go right back on the diet after cheating a little.

The lecturers stressed that cheating sins were over and done with—they were errors of the past; they tended to accentuate the positive and pep up members to do better on the diet rather than to scold and condemn members for poor weight progress. Holy dieting was the order of the day, something all could do if they just put their minds to it.

In some meetings, Trim-Downers seemed to "worship" the Ideal of Thinness in a direct physical way when they exercised as part of their group dieting *careers*. The exercises seemed to show parallels with religious genuflections and more vigorous bodily movements, as well as with the recitation of Hail Marys with rosary beads. In this period, Trim-Downers revered thinness with their bodies as well as with their words.

The Trim-Down method did not include strenuous exercising as the primary mode of weight reduction—some said that such exercising only made one ravenously hungry. Yet, one minor aspect of the Trim-Down cure was mild, isotonic exercising for the chest, stomach, rear end, thighs, arms, legs, and chin. The idea was to firm up and tone the muscles as well as to lose weight. If nothing else, these exercises made some Trim-Downers quite body-conscious of their excess flab. Many, huffing and puffing, talked about how they were out of shape. The exercises convinced some members that they required more healing—they had not yet achieved the Ideal of Thinness in their persons. To quote from my field notes:

Exercise 9 reads: 'Curl fingers backward. Scoop down and pull arms back until elbows are level with your shoulders. In this position pull back three times.' Lecturers stress that this exercise will strengthen and firm up the breast muscles; it will not increase or decrease the size of the bust. Members laugh as they talk about the size of their breasts; some say that their breasts are too large now and do not need to be increased. Others say that they do not have any breasts to begin with, and even wish they could gain some weight there. Members laugh as they talk about this exercise making their bosoms 'firm and fully packed.'

This exercise has many sexual implications. Some members make short comments, as 'My husband likes something to grab on to up there,' or 'My husband wishes there was more to hold on to.' Some say that they have to be careful when they do this exercise so they will not pop buttons or tear blouses and sweaters. Some talked about how the Marilyn Monroe look was not 'in' anymore; the flat-chested look is now in vogue. Others say that they would not mind having bosoms like some of the big-breasted movie stars. This exercise seems to stress body-consciousness, sex-consciousness, and fashion-consciousness.

During this exercise period, many *laughed* loudly—some from nervous tension, others in a release of multiple pent-up feelings about their bodies. Some laughed so hard that they got tears in their eyes. It was not certain whether some were laughing or crying, or, in fact, doing both.

Some "laughed at" their own and others' bodies, with remarks of ridicule and mocking. Others attempted to "laugh away" their bodies, trying to minimize the "badness" of the size and shape of their bodies. They rid themselves of "bad" pounds by "laughing them off." Some thinnish Trim-Downers seemed to be "laughing up their sleeves" at other members. In their laughter, they expressed in a rather cruel way their superiority over fatter Trim-Downers. Some were "having the last laugh"—they were losing weight in spite of their cheating binges or in spite of their skepticism about the diet. Some of these members described themselves as "having their cake and eating it too." As they exercised, many Trim-Downers seemed to laugh *with* and *at* themselves and others. (Allon, 1975, pp. 61–62)[11]

The meeting was finished. Trim-Downers then partook of their *last processional march* of their group dieting *careers* from inside to outside the door in their *rite of exit* lasting between three and 15 minutes. Their exit also might be viewed as a *rite of initiation into* the "outside" world of the non-dieting as well as the dieting population. (van Gennep, 1961, p. 20) Lecturer-healers appeared to be coaches who offered short pep-up farewell phrases, as "Bye, I'll see you back here next week with a good weight loss," or "You can do it—take it meal by meal." One lecturer stated:

> We've got to remind them to stick with it when they go out the door and how we say good-by is important, we have to say it with a tone of 'I'll see you again real soon' in our voices so they will come back to us. When I say good-bye, I say good luck and watch out for the holidays and some bad foods. You have to give them a kind of warning of what not to eat so they will have it last on their minds as they leave here and go into the world of temptation.

"Exit-partner" healees wished each other good luck and happy eating. They did not look over each other's bodies in bidding each other farewell as much as they did at earlier times in the meeting. Verbal good-byes seemed to symbolize the end of "body-readings" of others. Jackets or coats "defended" or "protected" many from further body perusals. Trim-Downers put on their wraps and closed off their bodies from their own as well as others' glances. These actions signified the end of the meeting, just as their verbal farewells did. Many said that they just "hated" to leave their friends and acquaintances in the meeting, but they were looking forward to seeing each other soon again.

Many looked each other straight in the eye when they said good-bye. They seemed to have arrived at a certain quality of honesty in tackling a common problem by the end of the evening. A sense of group unity and solidarity of sisterhood seemed to be implied in these straightforward eye-to-eye contacts. "I know how much Sue and I are helping each other when we look at each other eye-to-eye, uneasy about separating, but knowing that we will expose our inner selves to each other again next week." This woman added that one knows that one is being really straightforward and honest with another if one can look another right in the eye. (Goffman, 1967, p. 41; Simmel, 1969, pp. 356–61)

Some remained before their final march out the door. Lecturers asked newcomers to stay so that they could explain the diet in detail to them. Some lingered to seek out more verbal and visual encouragement from lecturer-healers and sister-healees—"I need something extra at the end, to go over the details of my eating to convince myself I can do it." Some stayed to challenge the Trim-Down healing method, or to question whether the cure from fatness was necessary or even legitimate. Some thought that the ultimate cure was the realization that overweight need not be cured but be endured. "I stay here to get her to break down and admit you'd have a horrible life if you never cheated, and to get her to agree with studies that dieting does cause depression."

Glaser and Strauss have defined the *awareness context* as the ". . . total combination of what each interactant in a situation knows about the identity of the other and his own identity in the eyes of the other." (Glaser and Strauss, 1964, p. 670) Some lingerers tried to make lecturers admit that everybody cheated a little when they dieted. These lingerers wanted to bring cheating into the *open awareness contexts* of lecturers and members alike; they wanted lecturers to admit candidly that cheating was an understandable part of dieting. Sometimes members insisted that they did not cheat on the diet as they spoke with lecturers. Such members did admit such cheating to some friends or at least to themselves. In these instances, lecturers or members, or both, often operated within a *pretense awareness context*. That is, they were fully aware of cheating as an integral part of dieting, but they pretended not to be so aware. (Glaser and Strauss, 1964, pp. 669–79) Most Trim-Downers showed *conflicting and contradictory commitments* to dieting and cheating in various instances; many hoped to minimize but never to obliterate cheating on the diet.

For some, the end of the Trim-Down meeting meant that the time had come to practice the preachings of Trim-Down leaders; the real work of dieting had to go on outside Trim-Down meetings. Others chose to more or less reject the idea of striving for thinness ideals outside the context of Trim-Down meetings; they were purely "Sunday worshippers" at group meetings who were often prone to dieting sins after they left meetings.

TRIM-DOWN MEMBERS AS HEALEES

Certain types of Trim-Downers emerged in the dieting groups who had varying perspectives toward the *Fat-Thin Morality,* and the Cure for Fatness. Such types appeared to crosscut age, class, ethnic, and religious lines. Such a *Fat-Thin Morality* could be conceptualized as the interrelationship between actual weight progress and the attitude toward the Ideal of Thinness. Four basic orientations toward confronting the stigma management of overweight existed within this *Fat-Thin Morality,* and therefore led to four types of Trim-Down group dieting *careers.* Each *career* developed its own rationales and strategies for *self-validation.* Each *career* showed much *self-absorption* in one's own body and weight. Women self-consciously perused their own bodies and other—consciously examined the bodies of others. *Conflicting commitments* to group dieting were shown by believers and doubters.

FAT-THIN MORALITY

		Weight **Lose pounds**		**Progress** **Gain pounds** **or no weight** **change**
Moral code: Attitude to Ideal of Thinness	Positive	1. Saint-in-the-Making	2.	Theoretical saint- Practical sinner
	Negative	3. Theoretical sinner- Practical saint	4.	Proud sinner: Devil's advocate

1. Belief in the Ideal of Thinness with the behavior of losing weight. The Saint-in-the-making type indicated a congruence between attitudes and behavior.

2. Belief in the Ideal of Thinness but with the behavior of gaining weight or no weight change. The Theoretical saint-Practical sinner showed a belief in the value system of thinness, although actual behavior in terms of weight change appeared to belie this belief.

3. A negative attitude toward the Ideal of Thinness, but with the behavior of losing weight, almost in spite of one's professed ideology. This theoretical sinner-Practical saint viewpoint suggested the possibility that one might protest too much only in theory. Behavior seemed to demonstrate an allegiance to the value system of thinness.

4. A negative attitude toward the Ideal of Thinness with the behavior of gaining weight or no weight change. With this orientation, the most manifest Devil's advocate or Proud sinner stance emerged, with the double negative emphasis. Such challengers often became Fat Power advocates, believing that they would and should stay overweight to some degree—

whether due to a sour grapes attitude or to a realistic assessment of themselves and their bodies.[12]

Some Believers in the Trim-Down "sect" of group dieting had strong faith in the Ideal of Thinness, and were working very hard to achieve the Ideal in their own bodies. They put their trust in the Trim-Down healing system as the most effective way to reach their goal of thinness. Some of these members were "true believers," who had been converted to the Trim-Down healing system, and who were out to proselytize to as many others as possible. (Hoffer, 1951) Some affirmed that they never need search for another cure for fatness—they would stick with the Trim-Down cure for life.

Some would never be cured of their temptation to eat the forbidden fruit, and their Trim-Down affiliation would remind them to stick with the straight and narrow. Continual Trim-Down healing was a way of life for them—they would stick with the Trim-Down diet in general even after they had lost all their excess pounds. One was never completely healed from the mental affliction of overweight. That is, one would always have desires and thoughts about delicious fattening foods in one's head, even if such fantasies were not acted out in practice. Indeed one could make peace with herself about being a Trim-Down healee for life, as a basic means of *self-validation*. One said:

> I really go all the way with the Trim-Down diet, and I will until the day I die—it is comfortable to know that I can come here for the rest of my life. They had to work at me to win me over; I didn't convert overnight. But in three weeks time being pretty good, I lost 10 pounds, and was loving every bit of the food I ate. I was never hungry. It was wonderful to begin to feel my ribs, and my cheeks were starting to sink in. You don't know how happy and healthy you feel getting thinner until you are on your way down. Everybody laughs and cries with you here about the struggle. Now I feel that the world is mine and I can do anything. I am a whole new person, out to conquer as a new mental outlook. I have guts and ambition and I have more patience and don't holler at my family any more. The group really gives me a fix for the week—I want to do well for all the girls to show them that they can do it too.

Such *Believers* often walked around to different healees in the meeting to win them over to the Trim-Down healing system. Some members joked with these proselytizers, and told them that they should be on the Trim-Down payroll. Sometimes these *Believers* seemed to push themselves upon others so as to *authenticate* themselves. They interrupted others' conversations to declare the goodness of the Ideal of Thinness and the Trim-Down healing system. One woman interrupted another's conversation:

> Excuse me, but what you are gossiping about can't be as important as what I must say. This diet has changed me into a different person—I don't hide in my mu-muus and I have come out of my shell. I have energy to do everything, and my husband is proud to show me off to his friends. The Trim-Down desserts are delicious. All I can do is rant and rave. Just stick with it, and you will be 100 feet above the ground like I am.

Other devout *Believers* had a quiet but radiant glow about them, and they waited to be called upon by others for their proselytization efforts. Once asked to speak, such *Believers* could not say enough good about Trim-Down healing toward thinness. Self-congratulating, the *Believers* were eager to spread their joyous tidings to others.

> Joan: Come on, Alice, pep me up—you are doing so good and I can't seem to stick with it.
> Alice: Well, I am so glad you have asked me to help, and now you will never be able to turn me off. You are full on this marvelous diet all the time. The free foods are great, and the fruit and diet gelatin satisfy your sweet tooth. I love to eat 12 or 15 cans of the Unlimited Vegetables a day. The frappes are even better than the high-calorie kind. I feel great now that I can stick my hand down the waistline of my skirt.
> Joan: I have trouble going to parties.
> Alice: The best thing is to fill yourself up on the right foods before you go out. Then you won't be tempted to gorge on the wrong ones. And think about that smaller dress size. I already bought it to stare at it, so I have something to look forward to. There is no greater accomplishment in the world than to lose weight.
> Joan: Thanks, I need your push. I hope I can get back into a size 14. Maybe you can spread some of your angelic powers over me.

Thus, some Trim-Downers seemed to believe heart and soul in the Ideal of Thinness and the Trim-Down healing system. Some *Believers* appeared to worship this Ideal and were eager for a cure from their fatness. Yet, they had some reservations about the Trim-Down healing system as the way to get there. They believed in the ultimate cure of thinness, but questioned the particular Trim-Down curing process. One commented:

> Look, I am a vain woman, and I know that to be beautiful in this society you have to be thin. You do look so much better in your clothes when you are thin and you can wear the big plaids. And you are a lot healthier because you don't have all that flab crushing your internal organs. But I am not sure about the Trim-Down diet plan. I hate to eat breakfast. It is a pain in the ass to weigh in all my foods on a postal scale. I get cramps and constipation on the diet, and it makes me bloated. There is too much food on it for me to lose—I need to starve myself to lose. The group is just a big lonely hearts club and a social gossip session—you really don't get down to your eating problems. My husband will kill me if I don't lose, but I have to find a diet where I don't get nauseated. I need quicker results than a one and one-half or two pound loss a week to prove to myself that I can do it.

Another important category of *Believers* included those who seemed to revere the Ideal of Thinness in the abstract, although their bodies in the concrete belied their devotion. Many of these Trim-Downers had wanted to get cured from their fatness for many years. They had tried a variety of diets to heal them, but only stayed the same or gained weight.

> With all my belief in getting thin, You'd think I'd weigh 90 pounds. I just can't get my body to look like my ideal self-image. It is important for me to lose and

keep off these extra 35 pounds. I dream about how sexy I would look in a bikini and how I would make my husband jealous. Sometimes when I look in the mirror, I squint my eyes and see a slim hour glass figure. I kid myself that I am thin when I stand up tall and hold in my stomach. When I squish in the fat all over, I end up with very fat feet and a fat face. I know that I would feel freer to do other things if I would get over my weight hang-up—I am trapped by it. I can't seem to stick to a diet, though I am gung-ho when I start for the first ten days. This time, I want my good intentions to pay off.

The healers of the organization attempted to perpetuate a self-fulfilling prophecy—that the Trim-Down healee who lost weight was a better and happier and healthier person. Many *Believers* seemed to "buy" this party line. The major themes of the *confessional,* the *testimonial,* and *redemption* for one's "sins of cheating" were integral parts of *Believers'* group dieting *careers.* In confessing to others throughout the meeting, these *Believers* made known to others the past and present errors of their ways in terms of eating patterns—"after you confess all your cheats here, then you are motivated to be good and eat right." Some proclaimed their holiness on the diet, often in the expression, "I was as good as gold." In the *Believers'* testimonials, they solemnly declared their belief in the goodness of thinness; they offered personal evidence (thinner bodies or lower weights or smaller-sized clothing) in support of the Ideal of Thinness and the Trim-Down diet plan.

In their redemption, the *Believers* sought out salvation from their eating sins through the atonement of the earthly representatives of the Ideal of Thinness—the group leader and the scale. "We ask the scale to forgive us and we apologize to the leader and promise we will only think thin for the next time." In redeeming themselves, they sought to gain possession of thinness by paying money, and to set themselves free from fatness. Some seemed to compensate for their fatness by paying money which acknowledged their state of sin. For the *Believers,* therefore, the group stressed the rhetoric and practice of *guilt-atonement* cycles in relation to eating behavior, based upon the Protestant ethic value of ascetic impulse control over the self-indulgent immorality of overweight.

Some *Believers* did state that Trim-Down leaders allowed some degree of "sinning" on the diet—such healers would grant absolution for the small weight gains of *Believers.* Legitimate excuses for sinning, such as water retention or a menstrual period, were dispensations for the otherwise godly. Cheating due to the lack of correct foods in the house or to yielding to the enticement of friends was less easily excused. "Sometimes I tell my devilish friends that I am allergic to their baking—I am, because I will break out in fat." Indeed, one could prepare herself so as to resist such temptations to evil.

Believer-healees seemed to partake of a *morality play* in the groups as they competed and "antagonistically cooperated" with each other to lose their excess pounds. (Sumner, 1940, pp. 30–32, 58, 297) They told on each other's "sinfulness" and "saintliness." "Our friends can't get away with lying to the lecturer, because we tattletale on them." *Believers* developed a guilty conscience about their fatness as they learned how to change their eating habits by Trim-Down strategies and tactics. (Smith, ed., 1971) The group made the *Believer* feel bad about her overweight—then she was prepared to lose her excess pounds. Some talked about how they wanted to achieve "high grades," which in this case were low weights, in the Trim-Down "school." Indeed, written records of weight progress were called "report cards" in Trim-Down lingo. Many *Believers* were eager to "graduate" from the Trim-Down groups—that is, reach their ideal weight goals. For *Believers,* the Trim-Down group might be viewed as an educational process with a spiritual side to reinforce the classroom situation. For the *Believers,* the Trim-Down healing sessions involved the acceptance and processing of the stigma of their overweight.

Group dieting with particular reference to the *Believers* did encounter a contradiction:

> If they attempt to convince the critical sector of society to be sympathetic to overweight persons, to discard the (negative) stereotypes . . . they may well impair the motivation of the individual to overcome his problem. As a result, more so than AA, these obesity groups tend to be entirely oriented toward the condition, not the social condemnation of it. Here, in the American tradition of activism, of every man a master of his own fate (and fat), people are told first that they have a problem, and second, that they, and they alone, can solve it. All it takes is will power which . . . is obtained through mutual reinforcement—not, however, of the need for self-acceptance, but of the desire, willingness, and feeling of ability to change. (Sagarin, 1969, p. 73)

Believing Trim-Downers seemed to *externalize* their stigma of fatness in the groups, and, hence, got rid of it. Friendships which developed in the groups often protected the fat self and offered an incentive to reduce— "Sally and I defend each other and lean on each other here—we spur each other on to lose." Many *Believers* nevertheless knew that they would be stigmatized even in their nurturant Trim-Down subgroups if they gained weight. Some *Believer* gainers left groups early to avoid this public stigmatization during the period of the reading off of the weight losses and gains. *Believers* often admitted that they were tempted to cheat, whether or not they did. Some gainers had elaborate excuses for their "poor" weight progress—for example, their sons were being sent to Vietnam, and they were eating out of nervous tension. In contrast, the losers often rationalized away their cheating binges, and considered themselves "good girls with some minor relapses—the main thing is that the scale has gone down."

Other Trim-Downers were more reluctant to "swallow" the Trim-Down "pill" than were the *Believers.* They were *Doubting Thomases* or *Agnostics* in their dieting *careers* with reference to the Final Cure of Thinness and the Trim-Down healing system. Sometimes their belief in being healed the Trim-Down way was overshadowed by their skepticism about Trim-Down healing. Some of these members were gripers who complained about dieting in general and about some specifics of the Trim-Down plan. One said:

> It really isn't worth the two bucks a week—they don't give you that much, and they must be laughing their way to the bank. They make such a fetish about stepping on the scale in fear and trembling, as if the scale is God. She is a disorganized speaker and says the same old things every week. The recipes are sickening—most turn out too sweet. The exercises are nothing. I am starving. If people pretend to care about you, it is in a nosy way.

Some gripers were malingerers who stayed after meetings to attempt to break down lecturers and make them condone cheating. They seemed to seek private dispensations from the moral pressure to lose weight, in a time and space where they were not visible to most Trim-Downers. One said to a lecturer:

> Now, come on and tell me the truth—now that we are alone. You really don't expect all of us to be perfect angels like you say, do you? My son and daughter-in-law are preparing a big feast for me this weekend. What kind of parent would I be if I didn't go all out and enjoy myself, if I only had a few nibbles? I want to be happy while I am losing and not feel cranky and deprived like a martyr. Admit it, a little mayonnaise on my tuna won't be so harmful.

In such instances, Trim-Down healers held firm to their party line, saying, "I can't stop you but don't get me to say it's all right with me if you cheat." Other *Agnostics* did not so much question or attack Trim-Down healing, but were "in waiting," holding the Trim-Down diet plan "in abeyance." One said:

> I don't want to say too much one way or the other yet. I have lost nine pounds in a month, but I am not sure. I am giving myself some time to get used to the diet—I do get headaches. It is too early to make a judgment. Time will tell. I am not sure if I can hold out on it to lose all my 29 extra pounds.

Some of these low-keyed *Skeptics* not only were unsure about the Trim-Down healing system, but also questioned the Ideal of Thinness as the be-all and end-all Cure as well.

> I don't know why we have this thinness mania—I am beginning to question why we should all look like Vogue models. Cooking and baking are part of the way I live, and that will be hard to change. I can't resist tasting my own cooking and I am not sure if the sacrifice of not eating my own goodies is worth it. If I lose, I will probably put it back on anyway. People like me this way—it's just that I am being brainwashed by advertising.

Some more vociferous *Doubting Thomases* showed even stronger disbeliefs in the Final Cure of Thinness.

> Maybe it will be the strong and sturdy types like us who will survive, not the weak and feeble ones. Why should we all be one basic size and have the dress

manufacturers dictate to us? To fit into any slacks these days, you need to chop off your hips. I think it may be propaganda—that I will die young if I don't lose. Yet I am getting to be for fat power—eat and be happy—are all fat people really sick? Why live long and be miserable by not eating?

An interesting group of *Doubting Thomases* included the rather small percentage of those who proclaimed their disbelief in thinness as the Final Cure, who had little faith in the Trim-Down healing system, but who were losing weight anyway. Some seemed to be losing their pounds in spite of their protestations, while others seemed to lose almost because of their "fighting spirit." Some seemed to think it was rather fashionable to talk up some rebellion against losing weight, but they still were committed to the behavior of losing weight.

> I don't know how or why I am doing it. I am amazed that the scale keeps going down. I tell her how lousy this diet is and I say I do need my chocolate ice cream every day. Some friends brainwashed me to come here to lose 22 pounds. I came out of curiosity, not because I believe in this madness. I am very active and athletic, a little overweight. There is some magic in my losing—it has nothing to do with the way I am eating.

This woman was saying that she was an ordinary, "regular, normal" kind of dieter and cheated like everybody else—"I'm no goody-goody, just because I happen to be losing." With her skeptical facade, this woman perhaps did protest too much!

The *Agnostics* and *Doubting Thomases* seemed to be quite ambivalent about the Ideal of Thinness and the Trim-Down healing system—they waxed "hot" and "cold" on curing their Fat Affliction. Sometimes they called the Trim-Down cure "enjoyable medicine" and "painless." At other times, they questioned "whether it is worth my time and effort." Some admitted sadly and angrily that for many years they had been indoctrinated into believing that fat should be lost—through their families, friends, and the mass media. Some said that it was probably too late for them to change their basic attitudes, and most likely, "I'll be stuck believing in this Thinness Ideal for the rest of my life." Yet, some began to question whether the cure for fatness was "worthwhile" or "necessary." Perhaps some would function more effectively if they "started living and quit worrying about dieting and losing so much."

The *Devil's Advocates,* or *Atheists,* were a small but loud minority of Trim-Downers. They rejected all healing approaches to fatness and the notion that fatness need be healed at all. These *Devil's Advocates* objected to one main tenet of the Trim-Down healing system—that of giving up self-determination of one's weight and one's eating. They were critical toward the totalitarian connotations of Big Sister healers and healees' control over Trim-Downers, not to mention that of the inanimate scale. They often seemed to utter a sigh of relief that the groups were not so "successful," in terms of pounds shed. "Otherwise, I would be worried about the destiny of this society full of people of blind conformity."

Thinness is a religion in this country and I am proud to say that I have joined the ranks of the nonbelievers. Everyone wants the fastest and easiest cure to lose. Why not eat and have fun instead of dieting and feeling anxious? Why should anyone tell me how to look? I have got the right to eat and weigh what I want to—as it is, our lives are too programmed. This is like *1984* here, like the scale and people here are supposed to have power over you. At least, and I've checked it out, 80 percent of the people here are healthy enough to resist the pressures—they don't lose or they gain it back fast if they do lose. I love Italian and Jewish foods too much to follow this crazy diet for the rest of my life. I want to find one of those new types of doctors who realizes the hoax of this dieting mania. I am proud to say that I love food, and it is a sign of health, not weakness to love to eat. Why hide myself in a thinness costume?

Some *Devil's Advocates* blamed the medical profession for being one of the first groups to consider fatness a sickness, and they blamed Trim-Down healers for following suit.

The doctors are behind this fascist plot, but the blind led the blind. Medical schools brainwash doctors how it is ugly and un-American to be fat. And then they show that fat rats die fast. The doctors brainwash the patients to lose weight and there is a big business in brainwashing masses to be thin. Then Trim-Down jumps on the bandwagon. Nobody really has all the answers about fat, but there is money in getting people to be thin.

Some *Devil's Advocates* in group dieting *careers* were proud to reject any and all cures for their fatness—they were Happy Fats. They resisted changing themselves and their lives by losing weight. Eating a certain way was an integral part of their life styles, which they had no desire to alter. These people felt that they were what they ate, and they resented changing who they were. They asked rhetorically: what is the meaning or the goodness in the Ideal of Thinness?[13] One commented:

The reason why this group has done me so much good is that it has made me proud to say that I am happy and I am fat—I can shout it to the rooftops. I am not about to change me—I have been this way for over 25 years. Coming here has made me realize the absurdity of this whole weight-losing bit. I am thankful to this group for relieving me of my reducing obsession. Now I can start to live, and appreciate myself for who I really am.

Predictably, most of these strong protesters were about to quit their Trim-Down healing *careers*. Some needed to convince themselves of their genuine Atheism for one or two more weeks, and were Ending-Timers. Other disbelieving Final-Timers had "had it for the last time, and we have realized that we are through with dieting for good." In contrast, many Believers gave the strong impression of being perpetual Middle-Timers on the diet—they were constantly in the midst of the Trim-Down healing process, never at the beginning and never at the end of it.

In contrast with these clear-cut cases of *Believers* and *Disbelievers,* some Trim-Downers were purely *Socializers*. These members never talked about their overweight, and it was difficult to determine what they thought about being healed from their fatness purely by observing them. These *Socializers* insisted that they came to the group to "have a good time" and to engage in "juicy gossip." They "loved gathering the dirt" about many people at the meetings. Weight-reduction appeared to be almost a side issue for them—they seemed to attend meetings to renew old acquaintances and form new ones. They gossiped about their families, friends, and social activities. The group dieting rituals seemed almost incidental to their primary interest in conversational rituals of chatting about their own lives and the lives of others.

These *Socializers, Atheists, Agnostics,* and *Believers* lost varying amounts of pounds which were not correlated systematically with their attitudes toward the *Fat-Thin Morality*. The common denominator for all seemed to be the regularity of their attendance at Trim-Down sessions. If they came week after week, they did lose pounds. If they skipped one or a few meetings, they tended to lose little, or even gain. The steady appearance of their bodies at healing sessions, more than their words and feelings, seemed to be the most meaningful indicator of weight reduction.

These different types of healees "tuned into" the group process in various ways. The healees, regardless of their weight reduction "progress" or their beliefs, called into question what "group" meant in reference to Trim-Down healing. For some, the group appeared to be similar to an extended family or a close-knit neighborhood gathering. These healees exchanged feelings and information about dieting as well as about many other parts of their lives. For such members, the publicity of weight "progress" to all other healees was the climax of the entire meeting.

In contrast, other Trim-Downers seemed to view the healing sessions as a heterogeneous audience in a theater, or a rather loose-knit collectivity. These members had rather personal and private motivations and interests in their own weight-losing *careers*. They resented the "publicness" of announcements of losses and gains. They appeared to "perk up" when their own weight records were announced. They seemed primarily concerned with their individual healing process. Such an individualistic stress upon one's own weight record rather than upon the healing "progress" of all made the term "group" in reference to the Trim-Down meetings questionable. Some believed that the "schooling" and "grades" which they achieved through Trim-Down healing were their "private affairs;" they need not share their "grades" with others. Some even just came to the meetings to weigh in, and then left.

Many Trim-Downers, however, did seem to find much meaning in their group healing experience. They talked about needing other healees to watch out for them and to encourage them. They wanted to "perform well" before the eyes of others; they would be ashamed to "do poorly" in front of sister healees. Also, the group healing session helped some take gains in their stride—there was comfort in numbers in the "fatty cliques" of gainers. Many stressed that all faced the same problem together when they announced their weight progress to each other. Coming to the healing sessions kept the Trim-Downer "in line," even though she might not lose much weight. She got into the spirit of dieting, even if she did not follow the diet to the letter.

Some emphasized that they made good friends in the group, and they bolstered each other's ego when they complimented each other for becoming thinner. Trim-Downers felt "at home" with their friends in the group, and they got together with them outside the group for lunch and parties. Some admitted that they were lonely, and the group gave them a sense of belonging. Some said that people in the Trim-Down "lonely hearts club" understood each other better than did those "on the outside." The groups were "fun" for chatting and for entertainment by the lecturers. The meetings meant "a night out with the girls," and were the "reunion of one big happy family." Group experiences led to *self-validation* for many.

Thus, there did seem to be some differences among Trim-Downers in regard to how "public" or how "private" they viewed their Trim-Down weight-losing *careers*. Those who stressed the functions of sociability in the healing sessions seemed to regard their weight-losing as quite public; those who emphasized weight reduction as their primary motive for group participation seemed to view their weight-losing as a private, or an individual, affair.

TRIM-DOWN LEADERS AS HEALERS

The Trim-Down leaders exalted the Ideal of Thinness and the Trim-Down diet plan. At the meetings, group lecturers publicly stated their names and the number of pounds which they themselves had lost through the Trim-Down healing method. Thus, they affirmed their personal relationship to the dieting cure in general, and the Trim-Down diet method in particular.

As Trim-Down "healer-pastors" preached, *Believers* nodded their heads in agreement, laughed, and uttered, "Yes, we know what you mean." Some *Disbelievers* frowned, wrinkled their noses, and stuck out their tongues. Often the lecturer-healer appeared to be the Solo-Testifier; then member "lay-healees" "sang" the choral refrains of her message. Healers led in repeating and underscoring the Final Cure of Thinness and the Trim-Down healing system; members followed in agreement or dissension. Healers spread the Gospel of Thinness among the Trim-Down laity, and encouraged the laity to carry the Word to those outside the Trim-Down meeting.

In a rather serious tone, most healers stressed the goodness of thinness.

To be thin is to be happy, healthy, beautiful, and young—the main goals in anybody's life. Everything in this country shows that it is *in* to be thin. Even the ads for specialty clothing for overweight women never picture fat women.

Seats and aisles in theaters are geared for the thin. You really get it in the rear in subway turnstiles if you are fat. You can't sleep comfortably in the same bed with your husband with those extra pounds. You can have that new look in mod clothing if you are thin. People won't be able to tell you apart from your teenage daughter. You will be walking on air when you are thin, in your bright reds and yellows.

Most healers stressed that the Trim-Down diet meant a total reeducation of one's eating habits. They said that Trim-Downers always must be prepared like good Girl Scouts—they must always have the filling and tasty Trim-Down foods in the house. Trim-Downers must be selfish; they should not offer their special foods to nondieting family members. Their own dieting welfare must be uppermost in their minds. The more you ate of the correct Trim-Down foods, the faster you would lose weight, and you need not count calories—the diet would have a "magical" effect because of its chemical balance. To make the diet work the best, you should stick to it seven days and nights a week, and not go on weekend binges. "Beware of evil temptresses who urge, 'Come on, just one little bite won't hurt.'" The Trim-down method was preached as the most effective plan of all—it was better than exercising, doctors' diets, and diet pills.

Some lecturers were detailed *Autobiographers* of their own dieting-healing efforts.

I got fatter with each pregnancy. And then there were sicknesses and deaths in the family, and I ate and ate all through the night. I was too ashamed to eat in front of my family, so I would sneak out of bed at four in the morning. Then I got hooked on the diet pills. I became a nervous wreck, and was unfit to live with. They make you feel hopped up. My daughter couldn't take it, and she moved out of the house. Really, I was worried that I was on the brink of a divorce. I had trouble with my legs when I decided to go off the pills, because then I gained back all the weight. My legs became paralyzed, and I could not walk. The doctor said it was because my legs were carrying too much weight, and he didn't know what to do with me. I couldn't lose on his medications. Well, then the gods in heaven blessed me. I was ready for surgery on my legs and a mental institution. I was active in the sisterhood of my temple, and a Trim-Down group started there. I decided to go to make a good showing for my temple, although I knew of course that they could never help me. But I stuck to the diet and it worked. I have been born again, and my whole way of life has changed. I feel proud to shop in the stores for size tens. I am acting 20 years younger, and my husband and I go to the drive-in movies and neck like kids. I am full of energy, and my legs are in perfect shape. And my daughter loves me again. With me, it was a question of life and death. The Trim-Down diet gave me the gift of life.

Such *Autobiographical* healers often pointed out how they and other dieters tried to evade the Ideal of Thinness. They used phony excuses for cheating on the diet. What was there to do but eat that small piece of cake which broke off from the larger cake? Who could resist the morsel of chocolate or that nut which fell off the cake when you leveled it? It is a "sin" to waste food, so why not scrape the pan for the last spoonful of the creamy casserole? How could you see if you were eating the right food in a dark restaurant? Why should you deprive yourself of the tasty food that you are serving to the rest of your family? Think of all the poor starving children in Europe—you have the obligation to lick all unfinished plates clean! Who else but you could eat the leftovers in the refrigerator? After all, the others were out most of the time. You were the only one who was near the refrigerator quite often, and had the time to finish the unconsumed goodies.

Other lecturers were *Entertaining Story-Tellers,* talking about the assets of thinness and the liabilities of fatness. The humorous anecdotes of these healers were often quite personal in nature, as:

> My husband is in the automobile business and he buys me this Valiant which is cheap and easy to run. I get in, and my stomach touches the wheel, and there is no button to push the seat back. I tell him that I need a bigger car, but I'm ashamed to say the real reason why. So I say that I need more room to pile up lots of kids in the back, and that I don't like the shade of blue of the car. Really, the seat belt would not go half the way around me. But there is a happy end to this story. Now that I am skinny, my husband rewards me with a big car. He brings me a huge Ford that I can fit 47 people into. And, I feel like Twiggy.

Some *Story-Tellers'* tales were full of humor and pathos. Tears of laughter and weeping seemed to trickle down the faces of some members, as one lecturer spoke:

> The most terrible time was when I had to loosen my girdle after a big party. I tell my husband that I must do this when we are driving home—I was stuffed to over-capacity, and was about to burst. We stop and park, and he unbuttons me. I am undressed in the car, and I breathe a heavy sigh of relief now that I am not trapped in that thing. Oh, the glorious mounds that are just hanging out and don't need to be stuffed into a girdle any more! Then a policeman comes up and sees me in the nude. He is about to arrest us for indecent exposure and necking. I swear that we are married, and I tell him the facts. He laughs and says that he'll let us go, because his wife has the same problem.

One lecturer told a story about a fat lady who was trapped in an elevator which was caught between two floors. The mechanic bored a hole for the passengers to get through, but the lady got stuck in the hole—she could not get her fat rear end through the hole. She was caught, and nobody could pull either end of her out. Finally, five men pushed her through. This woman was so embarrassed that she went on the Trim-Down diet, and lost 40 pounds.

Some lecturer-healers seemed to be "vicarious" *Entertainers.* They served as catalysts for the member-healees to amuse each other. Such healers provided the tactics and strategies for their healees to become entertainers. For example, some lecturers used role-playing techniques in their groups, with the result of much laughter. In these "plays," lecturers sat back as part of the "audience," while entertainer-members made other members laugh. In such instances, members became active healers in meetings—they were not merely healees.

One lecturer asked for three volunteers to act out a "play"—a waitress in a restaurant, a good dieter, and a bad dieter, who tempted her "good" friend to go off the diet.

Waitress: Have some nice, gooey, chocolate dessert—it is delicious.
Bad dieter: Come on, it is only one night.
Good dieter: No, I am going to be an angel tonight—I will have a fruit cocktail if it is fresh fruit.
Bad dieter: Why not have the beans and franks?
Good dieter: No, the shrimp salad will be fine, with no mayonnaise.
Waitress: We specialize in greasy hamburgers and frappes.
Good dieter: Do you have a diet menu?
Bad Dieter: Who needs that? We are here to have fun. If this is the way you eat, I am never going out with you again. I will have a strawberry milkshake—I am on a vacation from my diet.
Waitress: Fine—no, we don't have a diet menu.
Good dieter: Well, I don't know what you put in your food, so I better have a cheese sandwich on white bread. Really, you are going all out with chopped liver too—I hope you gain five pounds. I am going to tell the lecturer on you.
Bad dieter: Oh, big tattletale! It is fun to live it up.
Waitress: You dieters drive me nuts.
Good dieter: Please watch out for her—she is not supposed to eat all that fattening stuff.
Waitress: I am not my brother's keeper.
Bad dieter: I am having a ball—I will have a hot fudge sundae.

The three role players laughed and blushed. The lecturer and members clapped and congratulated the three for an "outstanding performance.' Most healees agreed "it really hits home when you see it this way—sometimes our own members are funnier than our leader."

Lecturers who encouraged their members to perform with and for each other also used the buzz-group technique. In this method, lecturers divided the entire group into subgroups of three to six members. They posed a general problem, as what the Trim-Downers liked most and what they liked least about the diet. Lecturers asked each subgroup to discuss the question for about ten or 15 minutes. The members of each subgroup chose one of their members to write down their impressions and report the responses of her subgroup to the group meeting as a whole.

Some lecturer-healers and member-healees considered the tasting party variation of the group meeting to be the "biggest barrel of laughs and the most fun of all." The lecturer and the members in a group would decide collectively to have a tasting party—all brought in food prepared according to Trim-Down specifications. One lecturer considered this group strategy to be very entertaining:

I don't have a natural plus personality and I'm not a comedian. The group enjoys having a ball more with each other in the tasting party than listening to me try to make jokes. I give the signal to dig into the food, and they are off and running like a pack of horses. They laugh and yell in their bacchanalia.

Indeed, some of the mouth-watering and exotic names of the Trim-Down recipes made the "diet medicine" smell and taste delicious!

A minority of lecturers did not appear to work so hard at being *Amusing Entertainers,* or at providing the stimulus to make their members respond as *Amusing Entertainers* for each other. Rather, they were *Solemn Preachers* on behalf of the Trim-Down cure for fatness. The Trim-Down "denomination" was the best of all its competitors in "worshipping" thinness. These sober healers made Trim-Downers feel guilty about their "sinful fat." One stated:

> Shame on you if you're overweight! It is a sin to be fat when you don't have to be, and you feel that you are the lowest of the low. When you start to lose weight, you are on the road to salvation. You are unattractive and clumsy when you are fat, and look much older than your years. You get a rash when your blubbery thighs rub together. Your fat is killing your internal organs. Oh how glorious thinness is—it is the pot of gold at the end of the rainbow, or should I say gem of gold: Thinness preserves your physical and mental well-being. Let the guilt you feel serve as an incentive for you to reduce. We sinners have the power to save ourselves.

Another *Solemn Preacher* type of healer praised the merits of the Trim-Down diet cure. This lecturer herself actually was an evangelical minister. She believed that faith in God and devotion to the Trim-Down cure worked hand-in-hand. "If people would trust God, He would help them stick to this diet and lose their weight."

> How wonderful this group therapy is—we each become a little more saintly by helping each other. We confess our cheats to each other and help each other be born again. We help our fellow dieters get on the path to righteousness. We scold each other for our sins, but we are kind to our backsliders as we teach them the way. It is not just your penance you are doing when you come to this group. The diet is a real joy and you get a true sense of accomplishment from being on it. This diet is happiness for you, and you can praise and thank God for finding us. Don't be a martyr on the diet—tell your loved ones that you are on it. You don't need to be a bottom of the barrel sinner to come here. We accept you even if you want to lose only a few pounds. You are reborn here, and we help everybody fight those cheating temptations. If you stick with us, you will feel like an angel on your way to heaven when you know that you are eating the right way.

In all cases, the Trim-Down healers exposed much about themselves; healers had an intimate association with the content of their messages. The powerful and dynamic personalities of many of these lecturer-healers seemed to hold a "charismatic sway" over the members—"you do feel the spirit move you and like a magnet you attract others to you to follow you in getting thin." It appears that many Trim-Down healers had been "called" to their missionary vocation; they had not merely "rationally" chosen a "job" for themselves. "I was called by a higher spirit to preach about thinness—this was special and not just any old job for me to make a buck." Although many said that they were not "in it for the money," some admitted that their income as healers meant that they could indulge in "extras" for themselves and their families.

It is important to stress that almost all lecturers served as *authority* figures upon whom some Trim-Downer members depended. Some healers called themselves "mothers," "big sisters," and "housewife diet doctors." Some lecturers discussed how particular members indeed were losing weight for their healers—they "pledged their allegiance" to these healers. "They want to prove to us that they can do a good job and make us proud of them."

One healer stated, "I will get the fat off my patients if it's the last thing I do. I like them to cry and to run back to Mama's arms to help them." Many lecturers felt that they were personally responsible to help their members lose weight—they were more important as helpers than the diet or the group. "I am the most important force here and I get depressed when my ladies do badly—I blame myself for their poor progress losing."

However, other lecturers felt more squeamish and uneasy about members who insisted that they were losing weight for their lecturer-healers. One stated:

> I keep telling them that they are not doing it for me. They are doing it for themselves, and maybe for some members of their families. I don't hold their fate in my hands—I am just here to help them a little and give them inspiration to stick with the diet. It is a real problem for me to get some not to cling on to me as if I knew all the answers. If I am absent for a week, they go to pieces and gain. They insist that they need me to make them lose, but I tell them that they would lose just as well with another leader. I really don't know how to handle their strong reliance on me. Frankly, it scares me."

SELF AND BODY IMAGES OF GROUP DIETERS[14]

As Trim-Downers chatted with each other throughout the various rituals of group dieting, they encouraged each other to express various negative and positive self and body images. Many stated that as they confessed their cheating on the diet, they had the incentive to let go of many of their bottled-up tensions. They felt relieved in their general catharses of self-hatred, anger, depression, and loneliness which surrounded their eating and weight problems. "I really clear the air for myself when I talk about hating myself for my fat and I am getting rid of my ulcer by getting stuff out of my system."

Many Trim-Downers stated that once they felt free to express negative feelings about themselves in the supportive social networks of the groups, they were more open to see the positive assets in themselves and others. "I start realizing that I should stop being so hard on myself and realize how good a mother I am." A few said that they did come to the dieting groups to "get a shot in the arm to build up our self-confidence." Trim-Downers encouraged each other to develop positive self images, and reciprocally accepted such encouragement from others. "We do unto others and are done unto with compliments on clothes and hairstyles and our good traits as wives and mothers and our talents in our creative artistic hobbies."

Trim-Downers stressed that by leveling with each other in words as well as eye-to-eye and body-to-body, they really confronted their strengths and weaknesses as people. "Honesty hurts but we get self-knowledge here to give us some direction of where to go as people, as to stop using our fat as an excuse not to go out in the world and find an exciting job." Many said that they arrived at such honesty by vacillating between crying and laughing about parts of their lives and their bodily problems "in an atmosphere of most sympathetic understanding with people we feel like we've known all our lives." One said that she cried when she thought about how desperate she was in hiding food under the bed and in the bathroom, "but then I giggle a lot realizing that we all do these crazy things." Some smiled and chuckled as they felt that they were triumphing in self-control and increasing their self-esteem as they began to say "no" to others who were always trying to entice the women with temptations of fattening foods.

Trim-Downers increased their positive self images as they were able to share many of life's ups and downs with others in the groups, whom they labeled as "pals," "buddies," "good friends," and "even closer than a friend, really like a sister whom I have known forever." Many felt a very shared reciprocal liking and caring with and for each other, beyond the limited scope of dieting and weight foci. "Having the security of steady predictable friends here who you can call at four in the morning makes you realize you must have some good traits for others to fuss over you so much." Trim-Downers often repeated that they could accept their burdens of weight and dieting problems and take pleasures in the joys of their family lives "as we unload our pluses and minuses on our Trim-Down family."

Group dieters said that they were beginning to feel more comfortable and at ease with themselves as they deeply probed their psychological motivations for eating as well as engaged in rather superficial, cheerful, and lighthearted gossip with each other in Trim-Down groups. "I have learned to be more at peace with myself since coming here because a lot of us have irritable husbands and I can paint to calm my nerves and not eat a chocolate bar." Some added that they felt quite secure as well as curious about investigating the whys and hows of their eating binges "with friends who really know what you mean so you can start to control the binges." Many said that the groups were "recreation fun nights out with the girls" which encouraged the women to forget about some of their troubles and see their lives "in a more balanced perspective of goods and bads."

Group dieting encouraged Trim-Downers to dwell on their self-destructive daily routines as well as on their pride of small accomplishments—such as small weekly weight losses, or showing anger to husbands and not retreating out of guilt. In openly discussing various aspects of their self images, Trim-Downers underscored their fears of and wishes for success. Many agreed that they were afraid to really lose all their excess pounds, because then the only way to go on the scale would be up— "if I really succeed big, then I will fail and gain, but this way, even one-half pound a week is a success." Some stated that they had grown somewhat accustomed to their complacent overweight selves, and had even begun to enjoy joking with others about being "pigs" or "hippopotamuses." Some were nervous about how to manage themselves as "really attractive as thin—I am scared because it will go to my head and I will go wild on buying clothes and I'll get totally wrapped up in my beauty and not care about anybody beside me." For some Trim-Downers, there was the security of predictability in routines of scolding themselves for their overweight.

In their ambivalence about success, Trim-Downers said that they had mixed feelings about achieving in life—"I use my overweight as an excuse for being lazy and sloppy and lying in bed all day and hardly leaving the house." Some said that they did not want to push themselves so hard; some stated that as they were losing weight, they were making plans to go back to college or graduate school. Trim-Downers were ambivalent about competition. "If I get thin, I will have to compete hard or wear the latest in fashion, and being fat means that I don't have to be in the competition." Some did add that they could "beat" many thin women in cooking and cleaning contests, and in giving "lay" psychological counseling. Trim-Downers had mixed feelings about how to deal with pressures which they felt to please others. Some said that they were beginning to resent and fight off pressures from family members to pay attention to everybody's eating preferences, except their own. Some said that they were too generous and masochistic in catering to family members' passions for rich desserts, "and it's hard to be a martyr and just watch them eat and pretend you don't want any." A few said that they were trying to become "nastier" and "more stubborn" in sticking to their correct diet foods.

While group dieting firmed up women's self images as it was an outlet for specific fears and worries, it was also an arena for the giving and receiving of concrete, practical knowledge. Group dieting prescribed aids for daily living which helped participants feel and behave more happily and productively as they took more pride in themselves. Information exchanged included pragmatic tips on diet recipes, as well as on food stores and restaurants which catered to dieters. Suggestions about grooming, cosmetics, and clothing, including stores which offered attractive clothing in large sizes, and about the pros and cons of exercising to lose weight were made.

Particular bodily and temperament problems on the diet were discussed, and some solutions were offered, including: gas and constipation (to be cured by an iced drink followed by very hot coffee or tea); fluid retention (to be helped by cutting down on salt intake, particularly the hard cheeses); excessive urination (a good sign not to worry about because it meant that the fat of the body was turning to liquid and leaving the body); headaches; neck wrinkles; chills; hyperactivity; irritability; and fatigue. Trim-Downers discussed the relationship of overweight to multiple ills, as viruses, colds, skin conditions, muscle aches, diabetes, heart, and gastro-intestinal conditions. Some practical tips offered had little to do with dieting, as: where to get the best buys, interior decorating, party and gift ideas, recreation, vacation and hobby ideas, and educational and occupational opportunities. As some group dieters became better informed as consumers of everyday goods and services, they increased their self-esteem.

The most positive encouragement given by Trim-Downers to each other so as to increase their feelings of self-worth was based in the dieters' helpful solutions to emotional problems. Trim-Downers discussed how to increase their self-respect beyond their self-doubts. For the group dieters, self-respect meant a more open-minded and effortless self-acceptance, in which "I can take it easy, roll with the punches and not work so hard to keep proving myself to myself and others." Self-respect involved "being relaxed and loose, with an easy-come, easy-go feeling." "Not being so hard on myself" and "just letting go and relaxing" were basic to self-respect. "Sue here taught me to lie down, close my eyes and listen to my heart beat instead of shoving cake down my throat when I'm tense." Self-respect also included flexibility, and "not thinking so rigidly in black or white or feast and famine terms." One woman said that her pattern had been to eat non-stop for 24 hours or to eat no more that one-half grapefruit a day. In the group she learned how to "moderate and tame my eating habits and to know if I cheat a little on the diet, my day isn't ruined." This woman added that as she was losing weight, she was becoming more open in hearing what others had to say and really learning from them.

Some Trim-Downers stressed that self-respect meant "being nicer to yourself and being honestly selfish." Some said that they were becoming number one to themselves in terms of eating and their social activities—"I am sick of obeying my husbands commands to eat exactly what he eats and to go to boring baseball games with him." For some Trim-Downers, self-respect meant "taking off my rose-colored glasses and seeing my life and the world for what they really are." Some described this idea when they said that they were becoming more "reality-oriented." One woman said that she gave up her delusion of grandeur that she would look smashing in a bikini and short-shorts once she lost all her excess pounds, because she would always tend to have a "rounded rump." She realized that she must stop pressuring her three daughters to become super-thin, "so that I can get vicarious kicks through them." She was beginning to admit that her daughters as well as herself simply did not look their best in hip-hugging clothing.

And for some Trim-Downers, self-respect meant the acknowledgement that there were no magic panaceas in life. They said that fast fad diets did not work. What was harder for some to admit was that their husbands and children might not idolize them or even like them any better and shower the women with attention and gifts, even if the Trim-Downers lost weight. "My husband loves my cooking and he won't hire a maid for me even if I get thin; he is a home body and won't take me out on the town a lot if I'm thin, so I see the real limitations in my life, thin or fat." This woman added that the group was encouraging her to stop selling herself short or defensively degrading herself, "in measuring myself up to ideals that I probably don't even want."

For some Trim-Downers, self-respect entailed courage in "sticking to my guns" and perserverance, "so you keep trying and never give up." Some said that as they developed the courage to eat what and when they wanted to, which often meant alone and not with family members, they became more determined to stick to certain decisions which would lead them out of the home. Such choices included getting or changing jobs, or getting higher degrees in education. Some stressed that their steady and reliable work at their weight-losing on a day-to-day basis made them more patient and hard-working in coping with uncertainties about physical illnesses, marriage and family problems, and economic pressures.

Group dieting helped quite a few women develop and implement this goal of self-respect. With their increased self-respect, Trim-Downers began to have the courage to stand up for their convictions in many areas of life, including sticking to their diets. They were working hard to keep on top of their dieting and in various tests of self-control. Increased self-esteem and self-respect meant a clear-sighted view of the actualities of one's life, with a minimum of illusions and rationalizations. Self-respect entailed a rather relaxed self-acceptance with a moderate amount of self-centeredness and open-minded flexibility, whereby one would reexamine and perhaps change attitudes and behavior toward many parts of one's life.

The services of group dieting latently and ambivalently reinforced as well as mitigated against negative self feelings. Orientations in the dieting groups permitted and prescribed revelations of self-hatred and personal anguish. Group dieters did dwell on their unhappy lot in life. Still, one latent function of group dieting sociability was the opening up of philosophical and practical possibilities for the dieters to make their lives more meaningful as they improved their self-esteem. Group dieters expressed despair and hope about their bodies and their lives. Group dieting legitimated the venting of many feelings about oneself. In their catharses of sorrows and joys with each other, group dieters cleared the air of their tensions. Expressing themselves with others who shared a weight problem, group dieters mustered up emotional strength and courage to continue to fight life's battles, including the battle of the bulge. Group dieting was a supportive social service which offered aid and comfort for coping with multiple tensions. (Allon, 1975, p. 68)

CONCLUSIONS

There is much cultural and historical variability with regard to the aesthetic, health, and moral dimensions of overweight. In economies of scarcity, when food is not so taken-for-granted, overweight is valued as a sign of prestige and success. In economies of greater abundance, with the opportunity for the overconsumption of abundances, one can afford to worry about overweight. Much money, time and energy is spent to wipe out fatness in contemporary America. Still, the paradox of a mouth-watering dessert with few calories shows the urges for repression and gratification of eating desires in contemporary America. To complicate the picture even more, there are no clear-cut, objective standards for the overweight phenomenon, and people have many different subjective ideas about how fat or thin they are.

Trim-Down group dieting was a profit-making voluntary association which was run and led by lay women who had lost and were losing weight. Trim-Down groups displayed a missionary fervor of commitment and conversion to group dieting as well as a business-profit-prestige orientation of recruiting more members. Trim-Down offered a basic diet plan for members, which was made up by a medical consultant along with some Trim-Down executives.

I have analyzed much of my data about Trim-Down group dieting in the frameworks of a spiritual movement and a secular religion. Through the rituals of group dieting, Trim-Downers themselves used much religious terminology, such as "confessing one's cheating sins" and following the "diet Bible." Trim-Down group dieting established and reinforced the stigmatization of overweight people as bad sinners, while at the same time mitigated the stigmatization of the overweight. Some began to increase their self-esteem as they saw that others shared their condition. To become a thin saint, one must start off as a fat sinner—one does not become such a saint if one has been thin all along. The groups emphasized the processes of becoming thinner, not the final state of being thin. As Trim-Downers weighed in, chatted with each other, and heard group leaders' advice, Believers stressed the merits of thinness and dieting, Doubting Thomases questioned aspects of dieting, and Devil's Advocates rejected the notion that fatness need be healed. Group leaders offered autobiographies of their own dieting efforts, entertaining stories about the struggles of dieting, and sermons about the guilt of overweight and the atonement of dieting.

Trim-Downers expressed negative and positive body and self images. Some were full of self-hatred, anger and sadness because of their overweight which they viewed as basic to some of their problems. In the supportive social networks in the groups, Trim-Downers began to increase their self-esteem as they let out gripes, expressed specific fears, exchanged practical knowledge and helped each other construct helpful solutions to emotional and interpersonal dilemmas. Through both deep searching into their feelings and motivations and through lighthearted sociability for its own sake, quite a few Trim-Downers began to develop or increase their self-respect.

How many of us struggle with negative and positive self and body images based upon our sizes and shapes? How many of us are free from the multiple social pressures which push us to cultivate a certain appearance, often based upon our body weights? How many of us are fighting the pressures to conform to certain body images? Whether we go to dieting groups or not, many of us are not so different from Trim-Downers in our preoccupation with eating and dieting. By focusing on aspects of the body in group rituals, group dieters as Trim-Downers merely underlined in a bold-faced manner some of our deep wishes and fears, joys and sorrows about our bodies. Whereas some of us feel that we want to care for our bodies by ourselves or with the help of some formally established professionals, others among us prefer managing our bodies in group atmospheres of mutual support.

SUGGESTED TOPICS FOR THOUGHT AND PROJECTS

Group Dieting

1. Investigate further historical and/or cross-cultural variations with regard to ideal and actual body size and shape for females or males. How are orientations toward obesity related to specific aspects of social structures, as sex, age, race, ethnicity, social class, occupational, and educational perspectives? Can we arrive at what an "objective" standard of overweight is?

2. How are moral views about body styles, as thinness/fatness, related to health/illness or attractiveness perspectives? Why do you agree or not agree with the secular religious analogy of worshipping an Ideal of Thinness used in this chapter?

3. Probe in depth one aspect of the stigma of overweight and investigate one or two aspects of the discrimination of fat people in contemporary America. How can one gather evidence about such discrimination?

4. Discuss some pressures in American society which encourage repression/suppression as well as gratification of eating urges.

5. Are dieting groups degrading or uplifting ceremonies for participants? Compare dieting groups to one other type of self-help groups, as groups for alcoholics or drug addicts.

6. Compare group dieting as described in this chapter with another form of weight-losing. Comment on the presence or absence of professionally trained experts in dieting attempts.

7. Compare the qualitative research methods used in studying group dieting in this chapter with quantitative methods which could be used—as a survey analysis which could focus on pounds lost and

gained, or an experiment which might try to differentiate a fat from a nonfat personality.

8. Investigate one aspect of the body and/or self images of overweight persons.

NOTES

[1]This idea of responsibility is often a basic characteristic used in distinguishing crime from illness—so perhaps overweight is often considered more "criminal" than "sick" in contemporary America. "Crimes" are deviant acts or attributes for which people are held responsible, and "illnesses" are those for which they are not held accountable. The reactive consequence of imputing a "crime" is punishment, whether by fine or imprisonment; the consequence of the label of "illness" is permissiveness conditional on treatment. For such a distinction, see: Eliot Freidson, *Profession of Medicine: A Study of the Sociology of Applied Knowledge* (New York: Dodd, Mead & Company, 1972), esp. pp. 224–43. See also: Vilhelm Aubert and Sheldon L. Messinger, "The Criminal and the Sick," in *Medical Men and Their Work: A Sociological Reader,* ed. Eliot Freidson and Judith Lorber (Chicago: Aldine-Atherton, Inc., 1972), pp. 288–308.

[2]For a basic overview of research on overweight, see:

Brent Q. Hafen, ed., *Overweight and Obesity: Causes, Fallacies, Treatment* (Provo, Utah: Brigham Young University Press, 1975).

Norman Kiell, ed., *The Psychology of Obesity: Dynamics and Treatment* (Springfield, Ill.: Charles C. Thomas, Publisher, 1973).

Albert J. Stunkard, *The Pain of Obesity* (Palo Alto, Calif.: Bull Publishing Co., 1976).

[3]The rest of this section has been informed by my reading of: Marie Killilea, "Mutual Help Organizations: Interpretations in the Literature," in *Support Systems and Mutual Help: Multidisciplinary Explorations,* ed. Gerald Caplan and Marie Killilea (New York: Grune and Stratton, Inc., 1976), pp. 37–93.

[4]For some discussions of contemporary group dieting processes and efforts, see:

Natalie Allon, "Group Dieting Interaction." Ph.D. dissertation, Brandeis University, 1972.

———, "Group Dieting Rituals," *Transaction/Society* 10, no. 2 (January/February 1973): 36–42.

———, "Latent Social Services in Group Dieting," *Social Problems* 23, no. 1 (October 1975): 59–69.

Benjamin J. Becker, "The Obese Patient in Group Psychoanalysis," *American Journal of Psychotherapy* 14, no. 2 (April 1960): 322–37.

Joseph R. Buchanan, "Five Year Psychoanalytic Study of Obesity," *American Journal of Psychoanalysis* 33, no. 1 (1973): 30–41.

Eileen N. Goldwyn, "Weight Watchers" A Case Study in the Negotiation of Reality." Ph.D. dissertation, University of California, Berkeley, 1970.

Herbert Holt and Charles Winick, "Group Psychotherapy with Obese Women," *Archives of General Psychiatry* 5, no. 2 (August 1961): 156–68.

Henry A. Jordan and Leonard S. Levitz, "Behavior Modification in a Self-Help Group," *Journal of the American Dietetic Association* 62, no. 1 (January 1973): 27–29.

S. William Kalb, "A Review of Group Therapy in Weight Reduction," *American Journal of Gastroenterology* 26, no. 1 (July 1956): 75–80.

Benjamin Kotkov, "Experiences in Group Psychotherapy with the Obese," *International Record of Medicine* 164, no. 10 (October 1951): 566–76.

Barbara Laslett and Carol A. B. Warren, "Losing Weight: The Organizational Promotion of Behavior Change," *Social Problems* 23, no. 1 (October 1975): 69–80.

Albert J. Stunkard, "The Success of TOPS, A Self-Help Group," *Postgraduate Medicine* 51, no. 5 (May 1972): 143–47.

Marvin B. Sussman, " 'The Calorie Collectors': A Study of Spontaneous Group Forma-tion, Collapse, and Reconstruction," *Social Forces* 34, no. 4 (May 1956): 351–56.

Hans Toch, *The Social Psychology of Social Movements* (Indianapolis, Ind.: The Bobbs-Merrill Company, Inc., 1965), pp. 72–75.

Samuel Wagonfeld and Howard M. Wolowitz, "Obesity and the Self-Help Group: A Look at TOPS," *American Journal of Psychiatry* 125, no. 2 (August 1968): 249–52.

Sarah Wernick, "Obesity and Weight Loss in Weight Watchers; a Study of Deviance and Resocialization." Ph.D. dissertation, Columbia University, 1973.

Janet P. Wollersheim, "Effectiveness of Group Therapy Based upon Learning Principles in the Treatment of Overweight Women," *Journal of Abnormal Psychology* 76, no. 3, pt. 1 (December 1970): 462–74.

[5]This diet was based upon an obesity clinic diet worked out by medical doctors. "Musts" and "Shall Do's" on the diet included:

1. You must not skip a meal.
2. You must not substitute foods. (The diet was considered chemically balanced for the most effective weight loss, rather than being a calorie-counting diet.)
3. You must weigh all proteins and Limited Vegetables with a postal or food scale.
4. You will have three fruits a day (at any time), excluding cherries, watermelon, dried fruits, and grapes.
5. You will have two glasses of skim milk or buttermilk a day at any time.
6. You must have no more than four eggs a week.
7. You will have five fish meals a week.

Unlimited Vegetables which were a "must" for lunch and dinner, and allowable at any time of the day in any quantity included: asparagus, broccoli, cabbage, cauliflower, celery, cucumber, lettuce, mushrooms, peppers, radishes, rhubarb, spinach, French-styled string beans, and zucchini. Four ounces of Limited Vegetables were prescribed for daily consump-tion. They included: artichokes, beets, carrots, eggplant, peas, tomatoes, and turnips.

First Choice meats, fish, and poultry which were the lowest in calories and most preferred included: chicken breast, clams, crab, flounder, haddock, halibut, lobster, scallops, shrimp, sweetbreads, and trout. Second Choice meats, fish and poultry were: dark meat chicken, liver, swordfish, tuna, light meat turkey, and veal. Third Choice meats which were to be eaten only three times a week included: beef, dark meat turkey, lamb, frankfurters, and tongue.

Free Foods which could be eaten in any quantity and at any time of the day or night were: low-calorie carbonated beverages, low-calorie gelatin, bouillon, salt, pepper, herbs, spices, lemon, lime, tea, coffee, vinegar, mustard, soy sauce, and water.

The recommended breakfast included: four ounces of orange, grapefruit, or tomato juice, or any fruit; one egg or two ounces of cottage cheese or two ounces of fish or one ounce of hard cheese; one slice equaling one ounce of enriched white or whole grain bread; and a beverage.

The suggested lunch was: three ounces of cooked fish or poultry or two eggs or six ounces of cottage cheese or two ounces of hard cheese; any amount of the Unlimited Vegetables; four ounces of Limited Vegetables; a fruit; and a beverage.

The recommended dinner included: six ounces of cooked meat, fish or poultry; four ounces of the Limited Vegetables; a fruit; and a beverage. Two cups of skim milk or buttermilk were allowed in between meals.

This basic diet was given to all Trim-Downers. All Trim-Downers were urged to check with their doctors to make sure that the diet was compatible with their health requirements. Trim-Down leaders adjusted the diet to fit individuals' health needs.

[6]For relevant discussions about religious process in groups, see:

James H. S. Bossard and Eleanor S. Boll, "Ritual in Family Living," *American Sociological Review* 14, no. 4 (August 1949): 463–69.

Emile Durkheim, *The Elementary Forms of Religious Life,* trans. Joseph Ward Swain (New York: Collier Books, 1961).

Sigmund Freud, *Totem and Taboo,* trans. James Strachey (New York: W W. Norton & Company, 1960a.)

Paul W. Pruyser, *A Dynamic Psychology of Religion* (New York.. Harper & Row, Publishers, 1968).

Philip E. Slater, *Microcosm: Structural, Psychological and Religious Evolution in Groups* (New York.. John Wiley & Sons, Inc., 1966).

W. Lloyd Warner, *The Living and the Dead,* Yankee City Series, 5 (New Haven, Conn.: Yale University Press, 1959).

[7]For the idea of monetary exchange meaning an objective valuation as well as reciprocity between giver and receiver, see the summary of some of Georg Simmel's views in Nicholas J. Spykman, *The Social Theory of Georg Simmel* (New York: Atherton Press, Atheling Edition, 1965), pp. 217-51, esp. p. 220.

[8]For a discussion of the ambivalent fusion of everlasting reliability and ungiving indifference in the stone deity, which is similar to the scale, see: Slater, *Microcosm*, pp. 9-10. For discussions of totem, see: Freud, *Totem and Taboo*; and Claude Lévi-Strauss, *Totemism,* trans. Rodney Needham (Boston: Beacon Press, 1963).

[9]Trim-Downers did not seem to have global and inarticulate responses as some researchers have discovered in overweight people. Rather, they seemed to be very psychologically differentiated in reference to their perceptual spheres, having a piercing eye for detail with regard to their own and others' body parts. See: Stephen A, Karp and Herbert Pardes. "Psychological Differentiation (Field Dependence) in Obese Women," *Psychosomatic Medicine* 27, no. 3 (May-June 1965):238-44.

Also see: H. A. Witkin, R. B. Dyk, H. F. Faterson, D. R. Goodenough and S. A. Karp, *Psychological Differentiation; Studies of Development* (New York: John Wiley & Sons, Inc., 1962).

[10]For a discussion of the use of sacred texts in religious services, see: Myron B. Bloy Jr., ed., *Multi-Media-Worship* (New York: The Seabury Press, 1969); and Paul F. Johnson, *Psychology of Religion,* rev. ed. (New York: Abingdon Press, 1959), pp. 130-230.

[11]For some insightful discussions of laughter and humor, see:

Rose Laub Coser, "Laughter among Colleagues," *Psychiatry* 23, no. 1 (February 1960): 81-95.

Sigmund Freud, *Jokes and Their Relation to the Unconscious,* trans. James Strachey (New York: W. W. Norton & Company Inc., 1960).

Martin Grotjahn, *Beyond Laughter* (New York: McGraw-Hill Book Company, 1957).

Jacob Levine, ed., *Motivation in Humor* (New York: Atherton Press, 1969).

[12]I am very grateful to Samuel E. Wallace for helping me work out this typology.

[13]For the idea of "unbelief," see: Martin E. Marty, *Varieties of Unbelief* (Garden City, New York: Doubleday & Company, Inc., Anchor Books, 1966). For some literature about the growing movement of fat and thin people who are questioning and protesting thinness norms as well as gathering evidence about discrimination against overweight people, contact: Fat Liberation Front, Box 342, New Haven, Connecticut, 06513; The Fat Underground, Box 5621, Santa Monica, California, 90405; National Association to Aid Fat Americans, Inc., Box 745, Westbury, New York, 11590. This latter association is the largest national organization of its type. Also see:

Abraham I. Friedman, *Fat Can Be Beautiful: Stop Dieting, Start Living* (New York, Berkley Publishing Corporation, 1974).

Marvin Grosswirth, *Fat Pride: A Survival Handbook* (New York: Jarrow Press, Inc., 1971).

Llewellyn Louderback, *Fat Power: Whatever You Weigh Is Right* (New York: Hawthorn Books, Inc., Publishers, 1970).

Stella Jolles Reichman, *Great Big Beautiful Doll: Everything for the Body and Soul of the Larger Woman* (New York: E. P. Dutton, 1977).

Eugene Scheimann with Paul G. Neimark, *Sex and the Overweight Woman* (New York: New American Library, Signet Book, 1970).

[14]Ideas in this section are developed in: Allon, "Latent Social Services in Group Dieting," pp. 59-69.

Health Spas

3

with Hannah Wartenberg

INTRODUCTION

Throughout history in many cultural settings in the world, the idea of a spa has often connoted a fashionable place for the upper classes which combines health treatment, luxury, and a mingling of various societal leaders and members of "high society." People have mixed in a healthy and beautiful natural and human-made environment in the spa, with natural springs, fresh crisp air, beautiful vistas of mountains and valleys, and elaborate architecture. A spa often has implied the idea of a health resort which has grown up around the location of natural mineral spring waters which are considered to have therapeutic value for people bathing in them as well as drinking them. Some spas have been recommended by doctors for the treatment of different ailments, depending upon the chemical composition of the waters. Some springs at spas were believed to have deities or sacred guardians who cared for people who came to the spas. Spas throughout history have shown a combination of myth, mysticism, faith healing, formal religion, ordinary hygiene, hydrotherapy and nature cures. (Duguid, 1968; Graves and Graves, 1970; Turner, 1967; Wilkens, 1976) The term "spa" stems from the town of Spa in Belgium, where the mineral springs and baths made its name so popular that the word "spa" designates similar health resorts.

Some famous European spas which were the playgrounds of high society reached their zenith in the nineteenth century. Royalty, nobility, heads of government, and high level diplomats converged at the spas. Sometimes there was an aura of international intrigue as such people walked, exercised, and rested in the spas. In addition to the high nobility and society, hangers-on, confidence men, jewel thieves, gamblers, charlatans, and courtesans came to the world famous resorts. The casino and the promenade represented the two sides of spa life. The promenade, where guests walked while taking the mineral waters, represented the health aspect of the spa, which treated diseases as gout, liver trouble, and diabetes. The casino, with its elegant dining, glamorous balls, and games of chance highlighted the amusement aspect. Some spas have included places for sleeping, structures for bathing, physical therapy, entertainment, and relaxation as well as religious edifices. Commercialism clearly moved into the picture as merchants did good business in the towns that sprang up around the spas.

The democratization of European spas has accelerated in the twentieth century throughout the world. Greater ease and speed of transportation, the findings of medical science leading to a decline in the appeal of the spas, and the increasing visits of the middle classes at spas meant that many spas were no longer just the haunts of glamorous and elegant high society. (Turner, 1967, p. 14) Today the spas throughout the world offer: treatments and services for physical fitness, including weight reduction, restoring energy, alleviating the pains of some chronic diseases of old age, such as arthritis and rheumatism, and promoting longevity. (Graves and Graves, 1970)

Medical treatments, such as antibiotics, are used for curing many of the illnesses formerly treated by mineral waters. With increasing technology and medical knowledge, spa treatments have changed significantly. For example, electrotherapy, physiotherapy, and the use of complex machines for shaping up the body have been added to spa treatment. Spas have become part of preventative medical efforts in relieving people of their various tensions and so warding off or at least alleviating various diseases. (Chelminski, 1974, pp. 58–65; Graves and Graves, 1970, pp. 19–21; Sarton, 1971, pp. 30–31, 56, 68)

In fact, one major reason for the large numbers of French spas and their continuing prosperity has been the Social Security system which was introduced by General de Gaulle after World War II. All people belong to this system, and the system has enabled anyone with a chit signed by a doctor to have three weeks of spa treatment. The use of the spas is practically classless and some spas have been taken over entirely by the state for patients. (Graves and Graves, 1970, pp. 42, 52) This process of democratization has been extended even further in Eastern Europe, where socialist policies encourage the workers to use spas so as to maintain the workers' ability to work or to restore the workers to health so that they can resume work. Thus, spas are viewed as being in the interests of the national economy. (Jordan, 1967)

For many years before the arrival of white settlers, various tribes of Indians used many mineral springs in the United States for religious and health reasons. With the arrival of white people, health resorts grew up around mineral springs for therapeutic reasons. American spas appeared to imitate European spas in regard to the fashionable as well as the therapeutic aspects. America, lacking royalty and a hereditary upper class, never developed the types of luxury spas which were social playgrounds that flourished in Europe in the eighteenth and nineteenth centuries. The exclusiveness of many spas in the United States has been based primarily on money, not on social standing. Sociability, including husband-hunting, became a basic reason for frequenting the spas. Attractions at the spas included entertainment, gambling, and race courses. (Duguid, 1968; Flythe, 1972, pp. 88–89, 129; Kelley, 1975, p. 23)[1]

The demise of some of the fashionable spas in America occurred in the early twentieth century with the rise of railroads and the automobile, leading to a faster style of life, so spas were bypassed. New techniques in American medicine discouraged people from coming to the spas for specific cures. Also, many different kinds of people in America were showing a passion for physical fitness, and not just the rich. America had to modify the spa concept so that many parts of the population could partake of the health benefits of the spa. (de Tocqueville, 1956, p. 209; Duguid, 1968, p. 23; Wamsley, 1975, p. 18)

Since the early and mid-twentieth century in the United States, there has been an extensive growth of many different types of so-called health spas. Many of these spas have not been promoted by doctors, they have not claimed to cure diseases, and they have not centered around watering places with mineral springs. These spas have not encompassed entire towns whose whole existence has depended upon the spa activities, as was the case for some fashionable European spas. Many of these spas have not had casinos, balls, or fashionable amusements.

Super Spas as exclusive beauty farms have catered to upper-class or wealthy women in particular. They continue to offer a multiplicity of services, machines, exercise and diet programs to shape-up, lose weight, and maintain one's figure, sometimes charging a few hundred dollars a day. These spas' strategies have protected and pampered participants in women's and sometimes men's exhausting pursuit of attractiveness. These Super Spas often consist of large luxury hotel complexes which contain many facilities of a modern spa: exercise rooms and apparatus, physical therapy equipment, massage rooms, whirlpools, steam baths, saunas, and swimming pools. (Kelley, 1975; Wilkens, 1976)

Many women who come to these spas do not aim to display their fashion or wealth, nor relax at leisure, as was the case in some European spas. Indeed, a woman's mere presence at a particular Super Spa indicates her place in the socioeconomic status hierarchy. Most women come to these spas to engage in a rigorous regime of physical exercise, body care, diet, and beauty attention so that they can achieve the body beautiful that enables them to look like conforming members of white upper—and upper-middle class contemporary America. Super Spas offer plans for physical restoration and rejuvenation, youthful beauty, buoyant good health—and the opportunity to rub thighs with the Beautiful People, including social and political leaders, as well as entertainment and sports stars. These spas reflect the increasing specialization and differentiation of contemporary America by not being total resorts like the nineteenth century spas where people took vacations. Often limiting time requirements for customers to several days, these spas as specialized institutions are devoted exclusively to one aspect of body care: physical fitness, which includes beauty culture. (Berland and eds. Consumer Guide, 1977, pp. 214–25; Kelley, 1975; Wilkens, 1976; Wyden, 1966, pp. 101–17)

Some modest and relatively inexpensive versions of such Super Spas which have shown quite a democratization of the spa concept have been made available to broad sections of middle-class and even some working-class women, in particular. The main focus of these spas is often upon weight reduction. Reducing the time and space needed for spa activities, these spas are in no way resorts, and participants are not so pampered by staff members as those in Super Spas. Many emphasize active exercise and weight loss much more than enjoyment and luxury which is still part of much Super Spa life. The egalitarian ideologies in these spas state that all can attain attractive bodies.

The spas which people come to for one or a few hours during the day or evening are different than the live-in spas in some important respects. Most people come to the day spas for mild or vigorous exercise workouts, in the midst of their other daily activities. They often pay less than a few hundred dollars a year for the unlimited use of the spas. The day spas no longer stress the rather all-encompassing goals of revitalizing the body and restoring energy, but they encourage constant body maintenance through exercise every day or at least a few times a week. The intense and detailed care of one's body, once the privilege and part of the life styles of the nobility and upper-middle classes indulged in during prolonged periods of spa sojourns, has become a way of life accessible to many people in contemporary America. These spas are part of mass culture and are not merely fashionable retreats for the elite leisure class. (McCannell, 1976, pp. 5–7)

Stripped of their faith healing aspects, these spas show the secularization, democratization, and commercialization of the body culture in contemporary America. Various kinds of health, reducing and exercise spas, diet spas, and gyms are part of a big business which have become available at sometimes fairly low cost to many Americans. The growth of these various kinds of spas has been aided by medical authorities who have been promoting the benefits of exercise as a preventative measure to avoid diseases and prolong life. These spas often have circumscribed exercise programs for working people who need only spend limited periods of time at the spas. Many of the spas are located in one or two floors or merely a few rooms of hotels, high rise office buildings, or in stores in shopping centers. Many spa participants are not in touch with the idea of spas as fashionable retreats for the elite. Indeed, the definition of "spa" in contemporary America as become rather loose and all-encompassing. One of the latest developments in the democratization of the spa concept is that people are building and bringing some equipment to their residences so that they can have spas at home. One can perform the routines of the fashionable Super Spas in one's own home, at little or no cost. (Becker, 1975, pp. 88–89, 118, 128; Flythe, 1972, p. 89; "On Gym Nests and Spa Spots," 1974, p. 86; Oursler, 1929; "Spa at Home," 1973, pp. 60–61; Wyden, 1966, pp. 84–100)

In the contexts of *leisure* and *work, play* and *seriousness,* contemporary American health spas frequented by a broad range of middle-class people exhibited certain manifest *leisure* functions.[2] In the tradition of Greek ideals, leisure was an *end in itself* for some health spa participants. The functions of leisure were in the doing or in the experiencing—people came to the spa because they liked the spa. Secondly, some spa members stressed the *instrumental* character of the spa. They used leisure as an instrument to attain certain goals—in particular, that of physical well-being. Thirdly, some participants viewed the spa as important in the *development of themselves*—" . . . a willing cultivation of the physical and mental self over and above utilitarian considerations of job or practical advancement." (Kaplan, 1975, p. 144) Some experienced the spa as a relaxing and refreshing escape into a total concentration upon themselves—away from the necessities of the outside world. (Kaplan, 1975, pp. 142–46)

Health spas also showed some latent *leisure* functions, conceptualized in a series of dichotomies. Health spa patrons viewed leisure as both *movement* and *rest. Movement* was a form of mastering space, a means toward bodily change and improvement, and also a value *sui generis. Movement* in the spa was mainly task-oriented—done by one's body for the benefit of one's body; sometimes, *movement* was applied to one's body by exercise machines. Some spa members said that they wanted to actively use their bodies to counter their passive spectator roles in front of the television set. Push-button technology discouraged them from moving around too much. Special recreation rooms in the spa provided space for movement in planned ways. (Kaplan, 1975, pp. 146–48)

Spa members channelized their restlessness into movement in the spa. In moving physically, they felt refreshed, recuperated, and restored from physical and mental anxieties. At peace and at ease, spa patrons *rested*—they sat or lay in the sauna or steam bath, in the whirlpool and on lounge chairs around the swimming pool. Such relaxing rest was just short of sleep or sometimes turned into sleep. Spa patrons viewed their quiet resting periods as mental and emotional therapy. (Kaplan, 1975, pp. 148–50)

Spa members found *freedom* and *discipline* in their activities. *Freedom* meant: ". . . freedom from the toil of obtaining the necessities for life; freedom from familiar tasks, faces, and places; freedom from the clock; freedom from responsibility; freedom from family." (Kaplan, 1975, p. 150) "*Freedom for*" is distinct from "*freedom from,*" and can derive through restraint and is also built on strong, positive attractions. Of their own volition, spa patrons partook of the *disciplined* regulations and procedures of the spa, including certain weighing, measuring, and exercise routines. (Kaplan, 1975, pp. 150–51)

In stressing Huizinga's play elements, spa members viewed their experiences as *play* and *entertainment. Play* in the spa meant voluntary activity, an interlude in ordinary life, secluded and limited with its own course and meaning. *Play* meant that an in-group of people shared common experiences in the spa with their own sense of order and rules. *Play* connoted active participation for spa members. Some spa members who felt *entertained* by exercises or by others in the spa believed that they were acted upon, rather than acting. In a rather passive way, they received, observed, listened, and watched. (Kaplan, 1975, pp. 151-53)

Spa members showed various orientations to *sociability* and *isolation*. Some wanted to remain private in the spa and separate themselves from others. They wanted to be alone to observe themselves and to grow stronger in the knowledge of themselves, even if they became bored. *Sociable* participants wanted to be bound up with others in the group; they said that they could find themselves and also be less lonely if they were involved with others. (Kaplan, 1975, pp. 153-54)

Spa participants were motivated by *construction* and *distraction*. They wanted to *construct* themselves in the sense of transforming, building, affecting, or changing themselves, especially their bodies. The spa was a most basic "do it yourself" movement, catering repeatedly to one's own body. Some members did want to *distract* themselves from the harsh realities of everday life—the spa was a kind of "escapist opiate" for some. In *distracting* themselves at the spa, participants tried to separate themselves from, negate, or reverse other parts of their lives. Some came to the spa to *distract* themselves from loneliness, boredom, anxiety, anger, or hectic demands of work. Such *distraction* gave the participants mental relaxation or freedom from worry and grief. (Kaplan, 1975, pp. 155-58)

Quite a few spa members were oriented to *self-growth* and *recreation*. *Self-growth* meant development, expansion, enlargement, creation, achievement, and evolvement. It was an active, moving concept which encompassed bodily changes, increased self-awareness and increased sensitivity to one's environment. *Recreation* meant the refreshing of one's mind or body through some diverting activity after hard work. For some, going to the spa was a distinctive, separate activity apart from the rest of one's life—it was a kind of respite, jocularity, and interruption from regular life. (Kaplan, 1975, pp. 158-59)

Spa participants showed feelings of *self-worth* and *self-defeat*. Some began to appreciate themselves and became more content as they lost weight or inches or firmed up flabby muscles. They felt that their time and money were paying off in bodily accomplishments. In accepting themselves, those experiencing *self-worth* recognized their strengths and limitations. Such patrons felt that they were calling upon their own inner resources. Others who were not so successful in changing their bodies according to norms in the spa often experienced *self-defeat*. Some found no meaning in exercising and dieting and regarded themselves as "hopeless cases" in terms of bodily changes. They stated that their useless spa activities were a waste of time, giving them aches and pains, getting them nowhere fast and only increasing their appetites to eat more. Those experiencing *self-defeat* in the spa stressed that they were being untrue to themselves, imitating others, heeding false standards beyond their means, skills or real desires. (Kaplan, 1975, pp. 159–60)

Kenyon has provided a useful summary of the basic characteristics of physical activity which clearly apply to the spa: (1) physical activity as a *social experience* where people can share something important, meet new people, and perpetuate existing relationships; (2) physical activity as possible and desirable for *improving one's health and fitness;* (3) physical activity for the pursuit of *vertigo,* providing at some risk to the participants, an element of thrill through the medium of speed, acceleration, sudden change of direction, with the participant usually remaining in control; (4) physical activity as an *aesthetic experience,* as pleasing to the eye, possessing beauty or artistic qualities; (5) physical activity as *catharsis,* which provides a release of tension precipitated by frustration through some vicarious means—the venting of one's hostilities, aggression, and pent-up emotions through physical activities; and (6) physical activity as an *ascetic experience* with long, strenuous and often painful training with some punishment of the body, and stiff competition with oneself or others demanding a deferment of many gratifications. (Kenyon, 1969, pp. 73–77)

HEALTH SPAS: MAIN THEMES

In the health spa, *self-absorbed* participants focused inwardly on themselves as they expressed many feelings and thoughts about their bodies in particular. They stressed taking care of the beauty and health of their bodies, graceful bodily movements and shaping up/keeping up their fitness as basic goals in their lives. Sometimes sharing bodily concerns with each other, many maximized their sensory experiences in the spa as they pampered and moved themselves in an atmosphere of warm and cool air and water. Particular interests in others' bodies were often grounded in self-conscious concerns about one's own body as a main and dominating involvement.

Some health spa patrons did view their bodies as geographical territories or marketplace commodities which were worth more or less depending upon shape and size, and sometimes gracefulness and strength. Generally, small numbers in terms of pounds and inches were held in higher esteem than larger numbers. Health spa patrons took time out from part of their lives so as to put time into catering to their bodily selves. They sought to strengthen and control their bodies so as to fight potential and actual kinds of body-weakening, including sedentary life styles, illness, and aging. Some viewed their bodies as machines, which they tried to master and perfect through exercise routines. Most spa patrons could achieve some limited goals in the spa. At least many could prove to themselves that they could discipline themselves to exercise for a small period of time. Standards for proving oneself to be a success or failure were quite concrete and clearcut in the spa. People's worth could be measured in the quantitative terms of pounds and inches.

Showing *conflicting and contradictory commitments,* spa patrons vacillated between concealing parts of themselves and revealing parts of themselves. Sometimes spa patrons guarded the private territories of their bodies; at other times, they exposed themselves most publicly to scrutiny by others. Some spa patrons chose to be independent and alienated from others as they minimized communications with others as they exercised. Others wanted to be interdependent and merge with others as they shared attitudes and feelings while exercising. Some showed rigorous self-control in skillful exercising, and they also gratified themselves in pleasurable and sensual ways in long sauna, steam, and whirlpool baths. Spa patrons talked about feeling guilty about yielding to all the fattening foods which they loved. Then they showed that they were purging themselves for their self-indulgence by doing vigorous exercises in the spa and by trying to diet. After one was an ascetic martyr for a while on a strict diet and exercise regimen, one could then allow oneself to cheat on one's diet.

Spa patrons viewed the spa as serious work and as playful leisure. Those stressing that the spa activities were hard work were quite self-disciplined, diligent, and sober in their exercise routines. The serious spa patrons had a steady and enduring commitment to improving their bodies, because they felt that the state of their bodies had important consequences for their lives. Often these members viewed the spa as a place where there were compulsory and obligatory rules to follow, as exact kinds and amounts of exercises. Serious spa members stressed that body-management and body-improvement were part of their everyday routines of life, not anything so special. They were concerned about past, present, and future states of their bodies as a basic part of their lives.

Those stressing the goal of playful leisure stated that they came to the spa to enjoy themselves, let out a few tensions, have some laughs, and gossip with friends. They found a temporary time-out play period in the spa as a voluntary setting of recreation. These patrons, wanting to leave the cares and troubles of their serious lives, found their spa sojourn to be a diverting interlude in their everyday lives, an activity quite limited in time and space. Some playful spa patrons stressed the enjoyment of the immediate sensual pleasure of the here-and-now in the spa. Playful spa participants often viewed their spa activities as "special" and "different" and "exotic" in their own special costumes of leotards and tights. Their spa experiences were quite set apart from their prosaic everyday lives.

Although feeling degraded by their bodily imperfections, spa patrons could *validate* and uplift themselves by actively changing their bodies. *Authenticating* oneself involved self-examination as the basis for self-improvement, and much sensitivity to the responses of others. Spa patrons sought reassurance and compliments from others for coping with or changing their bodies which were stigmatized as somewhat inferior or inadequate. Some wanted to prove that they were reliable and responsible people who could be respected for showing self-control and willpower in their dedication to exercising and dieting.[3]

Spa patrons sought to *validate* themselves as they shared a common base of problems with each other, especially the stigma of bodily imperfections. The atmosphere in the spa, encouraging *self-validation,* stressed that all could be somewhat successful in a bodily endeavor, whether firming and toning parts of one's body, losing a few pounds or inches, or performing an exercise more skillfully or quickly. With this positive approach stressing willpower, perseverance, and concentration, participants corrected and aided each other, especially when someone was wavering in resolve, to stick to parts of the spa's bodily improvement plan. Many showed others by themselves as living examples that the spa's program worked.

Self-validation in the spa was also aided by the sharing of much information about technical details concerning bodily problems and guidance for difficulties in abiding by the spa's program. Participants offered each other concrete suggestions of what and how to eat, and of the best exercises for losing weight in particular body areas. Quite a few members taught specific exercises to each other and critically evaluated each other's performances. Participants themselves became exercise leaders for others, beside the spa's regular staff of employed exercise leaders. Such action beyond mere words which could clearly lead to bodily changes enhanced one's *authenticity* about oneself. There were concrete indicators of achievement for the active pursuit of working out in the spa, as the scale and the tape measure.

Routines and rituals of bodily exercises according to one's own exercise program and in a class setting enabled spa patrons to clarify and improve parts of themselves. Many members spent much time and energy on the *careers* of their bodies as they developed ideologies, vocabularies, and skills in regard to their bodily *careers.* Many held high aspirations for achievement in their bodily *careers.*

As part of the health-weight social movement in contemporary America, through a community of membership, the spa aimed to produce changes in individual's attitudes and behavior with regard to their bodies. One's own problem became identified as a common collective problem— such as the lack of physical fitness. The spa socialized people into revering ideals of thinness and physical fitness. Physical fitness as an ideal to strive for meant working hard on many aspects of one's body in the here-and-now. In terms of offering behavioral monitoring and psychological support, health spas have been adjuncts to formal and professional caregiving systems, especially medical doctors, psychologists, and social workers.

As part-time and supplementary communities to other communities in which people lived and moved, spas have offered supportive solidarity, catharsis, control, and hope for participants, providing plans for maintaining and changing one's body. Spa patrons, coming with or making new friends in the spa, sometimes formed close-knit primary groups where people shared many feelings and interests, beyond aspects of physical fitness. Health spas have been part of a subculture of body preoccupation, with norms about exercising and eating certain ways for the sake of one's health, attractiveness, and moral integrity. As an agency of social control which resocialized people into believing and practicing physical fitness as a desirable way of life, the health spa was a microcosm of a more general public concern over excess pounds and flab. The spa showed aspects of a therapeutic method as patrons worked through and resolved dilemmas.

Many of us, sometimes unthinkingly, perform various bodily rituals with regard to exercising and eating on a daily basis. Many of us hold the same values about the goodness, attractiveness, and health of the body as did health spa members; we agree with such norms of white upper-middle class America. The health spa was an intensive concentration in a restricted time and place setting for a show of attitudes and behavior about the body which many of us take for granted. Many of us contemporary American women, in particular, are quite preoccupied with our bodies and seek to change our bodies through diet or exercise, whether we go to a health spa or not.

THE HEALTH SPA SETTING

The spa which Dr. Hannah Wartenberg and I attended was located amidst stores in the middle of a shopping area. It was open between 10:00 A.M. and 10:00 P.M. Mondays through Fridays; on Saturdays and Sundays, it was open between 10:00 A.M. and 6:00 P.M. The spa was completely closed only on two or three major holidays during the year.

When we attended the spa at one particular time, there were between five and 60 members present. Many were self-identified as wives and mothers between 21 and 65 years old, most of whom did not have full-time jobs. We also observed and talked with quite a few single women (never married, or separated or divorced) who were 35 years old or younger, and who did have full-time jobs or careers. Many of these younger women held secretarial, clerical, sales, and public relations jobs. Some of the younger women were trying to break into show business and modeling. Some women were former models and dancers, trying to keep in shape.

Most of the women we focused on in this study were white middle-class women of various ethnic and religious backgrounds. We did observe some women who were lower-middle or upper-working class, judging by their conversations about their lives. A few women with whom we spoke were black, Latin or Oriental. About 70 percent of the women we observed wanted to lose weight or inches; about 20 percent wanted to firm up and maintain their present body build. Many women wanted to lose between five and 15 pounds; quite a few wanted to lose between 25 and 50 pounds. These women often talked about losing pounds or inches in particular body areas, especially on rear ends, hips, thighs, and stomachs. The remaining 10 percent contained a few women who wanted to gain weight or add inches,

FLOOR PLAN OF A COED RECEPTION AREA IN A HEALTH SPA

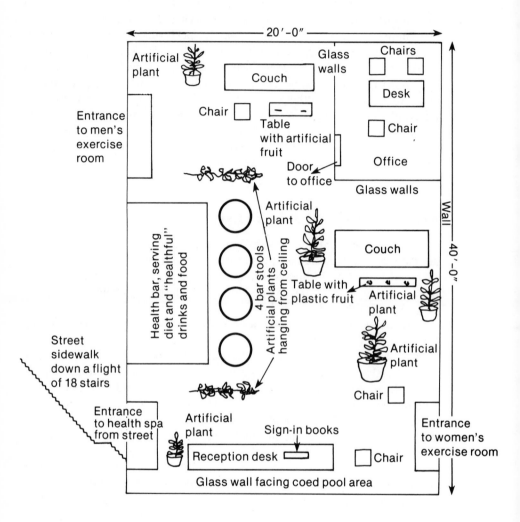

FLOOR PLAN OF A WOMEN'S LOCKER ROOM IN A HEALTH SPA

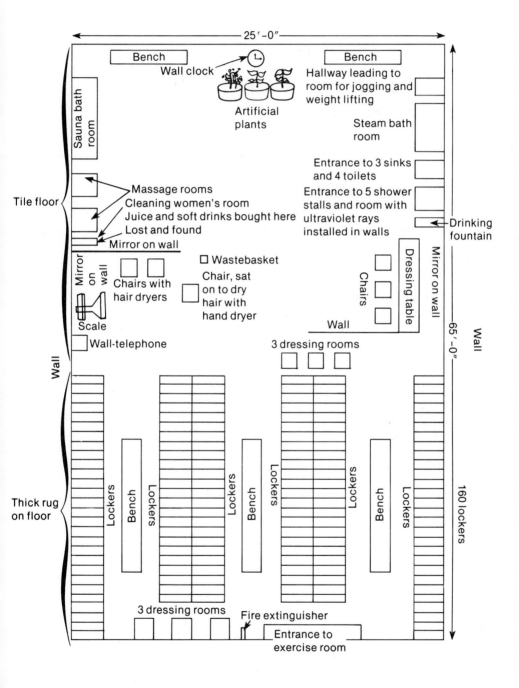

FLOOR PLAN OF AN EXERCISE ROOM IN A HEALTH SPA

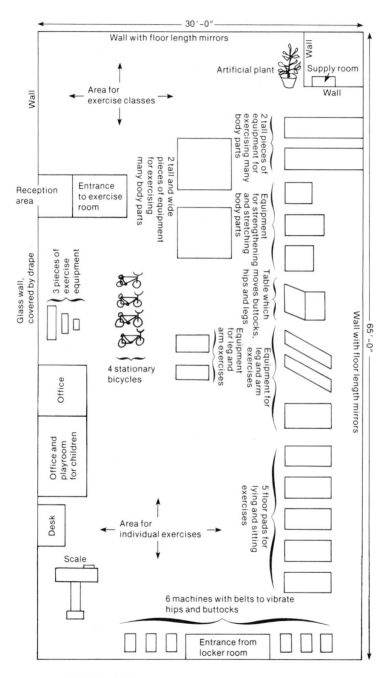

30'–0"

Wall with floor length mirrors

Artificial plant

Wall

Supply room

Wall

Wall

Area for exercise classes

Reception area

Entrance to exercise room

2 tall pieces of equipment for exercising many body parts

2 tall and wide pieces of equipment for exercising many body parts

Equipment for strengthening moves buttocks, and stretching hips and legs body parts

Table which exercises buttocks, leg and arm

Equipment for leg and arm exercises

Glass wall, covered by drape

3 pieces of exercise equipment

4 stationary bicycles

Office

Office and playroom for children

Desk

Area for individual exercises

5 floor pads for lying and sitting exercises

Wall with floor length mirrors

65'–0"

Scale

6 machines with belts to vibrate hips and buttocks

Entrance from locker room

FLOOR PLAN OF THE COED POOL AREA IN A HEALTH SPA

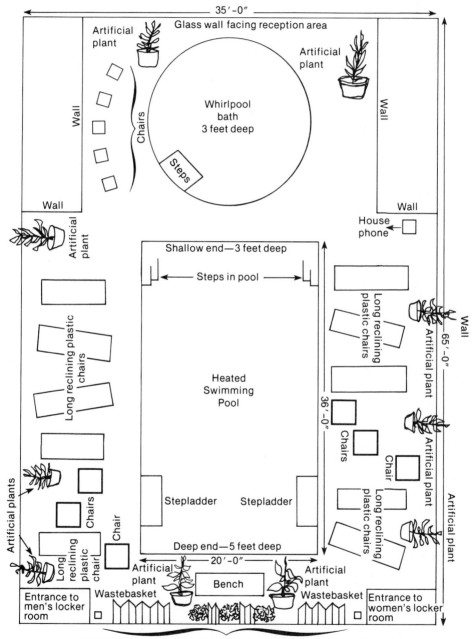

35'-0"

Glass wall facing reception area

Artificial plant

Artificial plant

Wall

Chairs

Whirlpool bath 3 feet deep

Steps

Wall

Wall

Artificial plant

House phone

Wall

65'-0"

Shallow end—3 feet deep

Steps in pool

Long reclining plastic chairs

Artificial plant

Long reclining plastic chairs

Wall

Heated Swimming Pool

36'-0"

Chairs

Chair

Artificial plant

Artificial plants

Chairs

Stepladder

Stepladder

Long reclining plastic chairs

Artificial plant

Long reclining plastic chair

Chair

Deep end—5 feet deep

20'-0"

Artificial plant

Bench

Artificial plant

Artificial plant

Entrance to men's locker room

Wastebasket

Wastebasket

Entrance to women's locker room

Plastic canopy suspended from wall—plastic flowers in wall

especially to bustlines, and more women who stressed that they came to the spa for relaxing recreation, than to change or improve their bodies.

The newcomer signed a contract to join the spa, which stated that for a set fee, the member could use the spa as many times and as often as she liked for the designated period of time, usually six months, one or two years. A member could stay as long as she liked each time that she came to the spa, and she could use any of the spa's facilities. The regular membership fee was about $300.00 a year. Special membership rates enabled people to join the spa sometimes for less than $100.00 a year. Members who got other people to join the spa had their own memberships extended for various periods of time with no additional fees required.

Young female employees who were exercise leaders introduced themselves by first name to newcomers who were told to put on leotards and tights. This employee gave the newcomer a certain number which would identify her record in the files. The employee measured the woman's height, weighed the newcomer on the scale, and took various measurements of her body parts with a tape measure, as bust, waist, hip, and thigh. The worker wrote down the newcomer's weight and measurements on a card, along with any particular health problems which the newcomer was asked to state. Then the worker set ideal weight and inch goals for the member, both paying attention to the desires of the member and referring to height-weight-body build-age charts. Workers then demonstrated about ten to 12 exercises for the newcomer to do, watching and correcting the newcomer perform the exercises.

Many female spa members used the spa environment in similar ways. First, the spa member entered the thickly carpeted reception area of the spa after descending 18 thickly carpeted stairs from the entrance on the street. She signed her name and the date of the expiration of her membership in a book on the reception desk, often saying a brief "hello" to a young female exercise leader who was standing behind the desk. Sometimes this leader asked to see a patron's membership card. New and continuing members sometimes negotiated their financial transactions in regard to membership in the glass-walled business office in the reception area.

People waited in chairs and couches for others of the same and opposite sex in the reception area. Sometimes they rested alone or chatted with others in these seats. Sometimes members partook of special health spa foods and drinks, prepared by an employee behind the health bar. The spa staff promoted its own ideas of what was "healthful" food, often stressing high protein diets. A few times a week for a few hours each time, a nutritionist was available on the premises for consultation about individuals' diet plans, at no additional fee to members. There were many artificial plants and a few pieces of artificial fruit in this area, which were rather effective imitations of live plants and fruits. Such decorations indicated that the spa was striving for a "natural," perhaps even fertile and "outdoors" look.

After signing in the reception area, the female member then walked through part of the large exercise room so as to enter the thickly carpeted locker room. She often put on her leotard and tights, unless she was going straight to the swimming pool, in which case she put on her bathing suit. Some members wore their leotards and tights to the spa with some additional clothing. Most members brought their own locks to fasten on their lockers. Sometimes members weighed themselves in on the scale in the locker room as they were changing their clothes. Most did not use the six dressing rooms to change their clothes, although a few did. Quite a few used toilets and sinks at this time. Again, there were a few plant decorations in the locker room to convey a fertile, "natural" look.

Next the member went out into the thickly carpeted exercise room, carrying out her individual exercise routine which she had learned in previous visits to the spa. Different exercises and equipment were available for beginning, intermediate, and advanced exercise programs. The member gave her record number to an exercise leader in the room who often asked the member if the woman needed help in carrying out her exercise program. Leaders helped new members learn their programs for the first few visits. As a leader pulled the card of a member with her number, the leader checked to see whether it was time for the member to get weighed on the scale in the exercise room or measured by the leader. Such measurements and weights of patrons were taken every fifth or sixth time that a woman came to the spa.

There were only a few machines in the exercise room which operated so as to move members around as they passively lay down or stood. One example of such a machine which moved sedentary members around was a flat table on which a member would lie, turn on a switch, and the table would move that portion of her body from her buttocks through her legs. A machine called the "conveyor belt machine" was operated by turning on a switch after putting a thick cloth belt around one's buttocks and hips. The machine then jiggled one's rear end, hips, and thighs. Members were advised to use such machines which moved them around if they so chose at the beginning of their exercise routines to loosen them up—they would then firm themselves up by more active exercises in which they moved their own bodies.

Individuals' active exercise routines were done in lying, seated, and standing positions, involving bending, raising, lowering, twisting, and turning many body parts. Some exercises were done with the aid of exercise equipment and machinery, which focused on particular body areas. Other exercises were performed solely by moving one's body parts. Most members cycled from two to at least five miles on one of the four stationary bicycles as part of their exercise routines. Most members spent between ten and 45 minutes in their individual exercise routines.

After performing their individual exercise routines, sometimes members put on their street clothes and went home. Quite a few stayed for exercise classes which were held about once an hour and lasted for about one-half hour. Various exercise leaders conducted these classes, occasionally in the swimming pool. Leaders led participants in a variety of mild and vigorous calisthenic exercises in which people moved all parts of their bodies. The leaders often announced that certain exercises were "good" for firming and toning certain body parts and as aids to lose inches in certain body parts. Often leaders demonstrated the exercises and then walked around the room, correcting the members who were exercising. A few yoga routines as well as jogging were sometimes done in exercise classes. In a group or individually, some women went to a room connected to their locker room where they could jog around a small track and lift weights.

After their group and individual exercises, members often took a sauna bath (dry heat) or a steam bath (wet heat). Women covered themselves with towels, wore bathing suits and robes, or were completely nude in these all-female baths. A few women took a massage from a masseuse who was on the premises a few hours a week, paying an extra fee for this service. Many women then showered, washed, set and dried their hair, and went home. Anywhere from one-tenth to one-half of the members we observed got into a bathing suit so as to swim or dunk in the swimming pool or to sit or recline in the whirlpool. The swimming pool temperature was usually between 75 and 80 degrees. The whirlpool temperature was usually between 90 and 110 degrees.

Often women alone or in small same-sex or cross-sex groups relaxed and lounged in reclining or sit-up chairs around the swimming pool and whirlpool bath. These people either appeared to be involved in their own thoughts or in sociable chatter, as they passed some time in rest. In this pool area, there were many artificial plants, some even inserted in the walls under a plastic canopy. The canopy and plants conveyed a leisurely and somewhat affected "natural outdoors" environment. There were many small lights in this area all over the ceiling and on some walls; some lights were in the form of candle decorations.

After women lounged around the pool or sat in the whirlpool or sauna or steam baths, they usually took showers in one of the five shower stalls with curtains. A few women took a form of sunlamp and heat treatment in a room connected to the shower area, in which ultraviolet rays were installed in the walls. As mentioned before, quite a few women went into the sauna to sit or lie down, covered with a towel, dressed in a robe or bathing suits, or in the nude. Some dried off their wetness or dampness from showers or pools in the sauna. Some took showers after sauna baths, saying that they perspired in the sauna. A few women took steam baths, and usually showered afterward, stating they really perspired a lot in steam baths and needed to shower to clean themselves.

Quite a few women washed and set their hair in the spa, spending a long time in front of mirrors for such purposes. Some dried their hair under the two standing hair dryers which the spa provided. Others brought their own blow dryers to dry their hair. As women set and arranged their hair, put on creams and makeup, and got dressed to leave the spa, they often focused on particular body parts—either with their eyes on themselves alone or in conversation with others. Often talk centered around how to improve one's bodily appearance, including discussions of particular clothing styles. Women then left the spa alone, with others with whom they came, or with others they happened to meet at the spa.

A woman (often a black woman) dressed up in a white uniform who was referred to as a "cleaning" or "maintenance" woman by others was based in a room which contained cleaning equipment as well as beverages, as juice and soft drinks, which were sold to members. Lost articles could be claimed in this room. These cleaning women were usually quiet, occasionally chatting with members. They vacuumed the locker room rug quite often, usually at least once or twice every hour. They also cleaned the shower, sink, and toilet areas quite often.

Rather soft music from various radio stations permeated the locker room and exercise room areas, and sometimes the pool area, through a public address system. Popular songs of present and past years which were fairly slow and quiet in tempo and mood (as distinct from loud hard rock or jazz or classical music) were the main kinds of piped-in music. This music seemed to have a relaxing, calming, soothing effect on some members who hummed or softly sang along with the tunes. The music provided a mild secondary focus for members as a calm background as they were mainly concentrating on other activities. Some members exercised according to the rhythm of the music.

Sometimes the radio was turned off for spa employees to make announcements to members, as when exercise classes were starting and when spa hours were ending for the day. Employees announced special membership offers to entice members to renew their memberships at fairly low costs and to get even lower membership rates or time added on to their memberships if they got their friends to join the spa. Articles of clothing, jewelry, and other accessories were offered as bonuses to members who got others to join the spa. Exercise leaders paged each other for business reasons through this internal public address system.

ORIENTATIONS TO THE HEALTH SPA SUBCULTURE

The complicated and ambivalent intermingling of *seriousness* and *play* as part of leisure and work norms was a basic part of health spa life styles, as it is in many parts of our lives. Another basic dimension of health spa life which we focused on was that of being *alone* or being *with* someone as one partook of spa activities. In the spa, being *alone* referred to attitudes and behaviors of participants which stressed that women wanted to keep to themselves, to undertake their routines of spa activities with minimal interactions with others. Being *with* someone meant that spa participants were open and active in initiating "with" relationships with others; verbally and nonverbally, such women sought to be with and talk with others. These latter women wanted to share publicly part of themselves, while many *loners* kept to themselves—they valued their privacy even in the public territory of the spas and wanted to be left alone. The women who valued *withness* might come with one, two, or three others to the spa setting; others might come alone but sought to join with others soon after arriving at the spa. Those seeking togetherness stated that they did not desire to remain isolated, alone, and self-contained in the spas—they wanted company as they engaged in spa activities. So, *lonelys* often longed for companionship and they wanted to be with others in the spa as or soon after they entered the door; in contrast, *loners* desired to remain somewhat isolated, remote, and aloof in the spas—some stated that they did not want to be bothered by others.

The single *loner* is by himself or herself. A *with* ". . . is a party of more than one whose members are perceived to be 'together,' " according to Goffman. (Goffman, 1972, p. 19) Single *loners* in the spa did not approach others to obtain or offer help as did the *withs*.

With these distinctions in mind, there emerged four basic types of spa participants, and these types also apply to many of our daily activities.

ORIENTATIONS TO THE HEALTH SPA SUBCULTURE

		Loners	Withs
Attitudes to	Serious	A	B
Spa Activities	Playful	C	D

A. First, there were the *serious loners,* often concerned with the quality and quantity of their own efforts and achievements in the spa. Coming to the spa for these loners meant putting time in to concentrate on oneself alone, with a minimum of distraction from others. Some stated that they faced up to themselves as they perused their bodies. Some stressed that people could always make their bodies better and more successful in terms of health and beauty standards. Some of these loners worked hard on improving their body potency and body control, shown in their intense efforts in exercising and their involvement with their weights on scales and the inches of their body parts measured by tape measures. These loners said that coming to the spa was a productive and constructive use of their time. They stated that they might need to suffer and be masochistic to achieve their goals of better bodies, but the final goal was worth the painful means to get there. These women looked to the future consequences and payoffs of their hard work in the immediate present—to be happier, healthier, or more attractive. Some exclaimed that they were serious professionals in learning about the body through reading and live experimentation; some added that it was a full-time job or career to be so intensely involved in their bodies. A few laughed and said that it was too bad that they did not get paid for their energetic efforts.

B. Second, there were the *serious withs,* who in verbal and nonverbal communication with others showed much concern over the successes and failures of their bodily shapes and sizes. These withs engaged in much reciprocal give and take, of speaking and listening, in sharing with others multiple feelings and thoughts about bodily changes and bodily improvements. Some said that they liked to be together as sufferers in the same boat working toward the goal of some bodily change; they could be very empathetic with others with similar bodily problems. Some stressed that others around them in the spa spurred them on to work hard on their bodies; others acted as an incentive to motivate the women to keep at it in exerting much effort in the spa. These withs showed a constant involvement with others in their talking and eye interaction. Some of these withs seemed to engage in a team sport by coming to the spa and competing as well as cooperating with others. In comparing and contrasting themselves with each other, self-defined *body-superiors* and self-defined *body-inferiors* emerged in the spa.

Drawing on Watson's discussion, the *serious withs* and *loners* often showed work-oriented interactions. They stressed the usefulness and productivity of their efforts aimed to reach specific goals at the spa. They wanted to show and prove their individual competence and achievement. They only presented parts of themselves in the spa; they often restricted their focus to putting forth much effort and succeeding in a particular bodily accomplishment. These serious types talked of making progress, getting something done, completing a task. These participants had to accomplish a job on their bodies. (Watson, 1958, pp. 269–72)

C. Third, there were the *playful loners,* who delighted in the sensuality of their bodies, openly enjoying their narcissistic self-caressing, as they showed skin and muscle eroticism. With their self-mothering and self-pampering, these women enjoyed their self-indulgence when they could be carefree and engage in free-associative thinking in a leisurely way. These loners talked about how they liked to be lazy and have the luxury of idle time with no pressure so they could come to the spa. They stated that they enjoyed being selfish in the spa and catering to themselves—they could kill time or shoot the breeze in the spa with no definite purpose or goal. The spa was a soothing diversion for these women, who stressed that they could relax and take it easy in the spa, sometimes to counter feelings of restlessness and boredom. The spa had a soporific effect on some, who stressed that they were very peaceful when they gave in to their sensuality as they felt pacified and tamed by their spa routines. Some stated that they got pleasure in increasing their bodily strength by exercising. Women mentioned that they were glad that they did not need to use their heads in the spa, and they could really unwind in the spa; the spa worked against their self-destructive tendencies, and gave them a hopeful and an optimistic view toward life. Some stated that the spa was a good vacation or escape from their everyday work routines as wives, mothers, and office employees. Some *playful loners* who often smiled as they were being good to themselves seemed to have much time and patience to pamper their bodies, as in long sauna baths, and by elaborate hairdressing and makeup rituals.

D. Fourth, there were the *playful withs,* who talked about taking time out from their regular lives to have fun in the spa; they wanted to get away from the negative pressures in their lives. Some of these withs touched each other and bumped into each other as they talked and so appeared to be body-horseplayers. Most of these withs seemed to enjoy sociability for its own sake, and in their laughing and gossiping, they talked about many common interests beside the body. They stated that they really enjoyed being with each other in the spa, which was a diverting recreation, and added a bit of novelty and excitement to their lives. Many of these withs made new friends and kept up old friendships in the spa, with whom they spent time outside the spa context. Yet beside passing the time in idle chatter, some of these withs shared some problems rather superficially in a lighthearted spirit. They talked about how they could forget their troubles and be happy at the spa, where they could let off much steam and have a cathartic tension release. Generally, these withs were quite relaxed and low-keyed as they chatted about families and friends.

Drawing on Watson's discussion, the *playful withs* often showed sociable interaction in that they supported and reinforced each other's feeling and attitudes about bodily changes and bodily improvement. The *sociable withs* joined together to create and maintain a world of special meanings for themselves as insiders in the spa subculture. Shared values and shared definitions of reality emerged in cliques of *sociable withs*. The *sociable withs* emphasized nonhierarchical qualitative distinctions between people—much importance was given to the unique personal qualities of each person. In stressing the unique, some *sociable withs* sought out and created novelty, festivity, and entertainment for themselves in the spa; they enjoyed frivolity. Many were looking for new people and/or for new bodily experiences, as they were eager for dramatic and unfamiliar "happenings." (Watson, 1958, pp. 269–72)

Sociable withs did get together to reduce anxiety, to enhance self-esteem, and to offer supportive protection to others. Sometimes there was a kind of unconditional acceptance of all people joining in conversation—there was an implicit guarantee that all "sisters" in the spa were harmless and well-intentioned; everybody in the group would be liked and would like others. Such automatic liking responses often are taken-for-granted assumptions in familial-types of interaction. Sociability also provided a clear picture of reality for some of the *playful withs*. It provided acceptable explanations for aspects of the external world which were puzzling or threatening; problems with others would be alleviated by spa members' shaping up of their bodies. *Sociable withs* gained reassurance from others about their own worth and importance. (Watson, 1958, pp. 272–76)

Watson most perceptively and subtly distinguished familial interaction as a style as separate from such sociable interaction, but which could be incorporated into sociable interaction. In terms of Watson's scheme, *playful withs* showed the familial style when they presented problematic and routine aspects of themselves with the listener's personal interest in the speaker being taken for granted. Some *sociable withs* showed the familial style in being repetitive, dealing again and again with the same routine concerns, often focusing on the details of daily life. And quite significantly for the *playful withs* and *loners,* the familial or pseudo-familial aspects of the spa led to an opportunity for privacy and for retreat from society. For some *playful* types, the spa did serve as a sanctuary for the individual away from the outside world which was viewed in some sense as alien. Some of the orientations of the *playful withs* and *loners* were quite antithetical to those of the *serious* spa attenders—the playful stance was antisegmental, antiachievement and antiproductive. (Watson, 1958, pp. 277–80) Are we *playful* and *serious* in these ways in our everyday lives?

It is important to remember that these four types were united by one common theme—the *body* was the *main* and *dominating* focus. Taking off from some of Goffman's ideas, the body absorbed the major part of the spa members' attention and interest, visibly becoming the principal determinant of their actions. (Goffman, 1966, pp. 43–44) Spa norms and ideologies contrasted with many of Goffman's examples, which held various preoccupations with the body to be side and subordinate involvements ". . . sustained in a muted, modulated, and intermittent fashion . . . ." (Goffman, 1966, p. 44) Not only did the spa legitimate such bodily concentrations which we attempt to minimize or hide in everyday life. The spa also elevated such bodily foci to a position of central and major importance. In many spheres of life, concentration on one's own body is viewed as a kind of alienation, a withdrawal, an "awayness" from interaction with others; in contrast, in the spa, concentration on one's body was an involvement obligation. (Goffman, 1966, pp. 64–74; Goffman, 1967, pp. 113–36)

Serious Loners

Many *serious loners* were quite self-consciously body-absorbed. They were of all ages and all shapes and sizes, but quite a few were between 21 and 35 years old, and relatively slim—some almost looking like magazine "cover-girls." Many of these loners smiled and frowned, clicking their teeth, sighing and chuckling as they perused their body parts while dressing in leotards and tights for exercising or putting on bathing suits for swimming or the whirlpool. These *serious loners* viewed some version of the Protestant ethic as being basic to their motivations and activities at the spa. Exercising in the spa, and often dieting at home as well, were viewed as hard work—they were instrumental and productive activities to lead to the improvement of one's body. Such improvement meant: a morally better body—"Your conscience is clean when you put your body in good shape;"

a healthier body—"It's less strain on your heart and your blood pressure to be in good shape;" and a more attractive body—"You can look great in the slinky mod clothes when you lose." Ascetic self-denial, impulse control, rigorous self-discipline, thinking of the future goal of greater body perfection to be planned for in the present—such aspects of the Protestant ethic applied to hard work as a means toward success were prevalent in the spa as they are in many parts of our lives. One reflected:

> I frown at my chubby parts as I stare in the mirror here; I chuckle at how wide my hips are as they stick out in my leotard. Ten pounds is my obsession which I have got to get off by the lifting leg exercises. It is tough and hard work and you have to concentrate on lifting your leg higher and increasing the speed of the leg lifts for it to work. And it's a killer to deny yourself the yummy carbohydrates which put weight on the hips. But I am being tough on myself and pushing so I can be one of the beautiful people—no giving into sweets. Knowing how good you'll look in the future pushes you to sweat and strain a lot in the present. I want to get rid of all my flab, and my greatest achievement will be to have no fat to pinch on my waistline or upper arms.

These loners stressed that coming to the spa was a constructive way to work on a specific bodily problem—the spa made one confront one's body in a most essential way, which was a basis for *self-validation*. One woman commented:

> You can't escape from looking at yourself from all angles in the mirror here, when you are in the nude or when you are dressed. You gotta work hard here to get the pounds off and it's best to come three or four times a week and stick to a strict diet. You huff and puff here, but you can't reward yourself by a big feast or by pretending you'll get rid of your dieting cheats by sweating in the steam bath. You work hard on the diet at home and hard on exercising here. If you don't diet and exercise, the flab turns to muscle and you gain weight. If you diet and don't exercise your skin gets loose and flabby. So you slave over the exercising and dieting; you can't afford to let your body relax. Twenty of my extra pounds are on my waist which I see in my leotard, so I have to push myself to keep bending and not eat.

In relation to the hard work, diligence, and sobriety of these *serious loners,* Wax has made some insightful comments:

> Interestingly, plastic control of grooming involves not only creativity but the application of the capitalistic ethic: beauty becomes the product of diligence rather than an inexplicable gift from the supernatural. Thus, those with an interest in the elaboration of the grooming ritual (e.g., charm schools, cosmetic manufacturers, cosmeticians, beauty shops) issue advice that has a hortatory, even a moral character. The woman is informed of the many steps she must take to maintain a 'beautiful,' that is, socially proper, appearance. She is praised when she fulfils every requirement and condemned for backsliding. (Wax, 1957, p. 592)

These loners stressed that they did not want to have much to do with others in the spa. If a woman tried to initiate a conversation with one of these *serious loners,* the loner often shook or nodded her head, smiled, said a quick "yes" or "no"—but quickly turned her face and/or body in another direction or actually walked away, silently stating, "I acknowledge your existence and I don't want to be mean, but I really want to be alone, with feelings and thoughts about working hard on my body."

Some loners said that they wanted minimal sociability with others— they did not want to meet openly others' eyes, they did not want to exchange even brief greetings and chats with others. They would socially or personally place others in general social categories through *cognitive* recognition, but they wanted to minimize *social* recognition—". . . the process of openly welcoming or at least accepting the initiation of an engagement, as when a greeting or smile is returned." (Goffman, 1966, p. 113) Do we sometimes merely want to acknowledge the existence of someone without wanting any reciprocal interaction?

Some loners told us that they did not like to be rude to others, but they were in the spa to work hard on their bodies, and they did not have the time or patience to be bothered with small talk—"it's not a casual social hour here, but it is the time for me to look at myself under the microscope." Some added that they had to keep drilling themselves and could never let up. Once they lost any extra weight, they concentrated on the exercises to firm them up—focusing on the appearance and movements of their bodies meant that they hardly noticed anyone else. One woman stressed:

> Coming here is time in to achieve losing a half-inch more around my thighs. I am dead serious about concentrating on myself here and I don't want anyone to distract me and I try to come here during off hours. It is a serious scientific study to figure out how to remodel my body like clay and how to correct the bulges. If I am not working on this remodeling by exercising, I am thinking about strategies in my head. I close my eyes and think about this in the sauna and so I'm abrupt if somebody talks to me, but I am not here to go to a party, but to change myself for the better. It takes a lot of drive and perserverance— it's not fun and games.

Many loners stressed that it was a never-ending process to perfect their bodies and that no one ever arrived at any final goal of perfection. In principle, the level of skills which they could attain was inexhaustible. (Csikszentmihalyi, 1975, p. 39) One could always work at different kinds and increasing degrees of body control as shown by being able to stand on one's head for a long period of time, or by firming and toning muscles so that there was a minimal amount of fat anywhere on one's body. "Everybody's body can be improved in some way—at the very least by increasing the strength of your muscles." One stated:

> The more I do to shape up my body here, the more I realize that I can and should be working even harder to shape up. My goal is to constantly perfect my body through hard work, and I don't ever want to think I will have a final perfect body, because then I will relax and get sloppy. My body is in pretty good shape now and at the age of 40 I have been asked to model in some local clothing stores. But it doesn't mean that I can let up, or I'll go to pot, literally.

I am not the kind who can stop with a small piece of cake—I have to eat the whole cake so I have to keep resisting the first small piece. I have to work hard at keeping my body in good shape, now that I've gotten it this far. I can keep making my body be a success—it is all in my power and it is up to nobody except me. This gives me a great feeling of power and responsibility.

These loners stressed that the means of suffering were well worth the final rewards of a happier, healthier, or more attractive body. Painful means were necessary to reach the pleasures of a better body. These women often looked to the very positive future consequences of having better bodies. Such future fantasies about and achieved realities with bodily satisfactions seemed to make all the hard work in the present worthwhile, perhaps true for some of us. One woman commented:

It is hard work to resist temptation and not give into the gooey food. And it is not very pleasant to stare at your body and see all its imperfections. You have to work hard on your mind to convince yourself not to be lazy and too self-satisfied with how your body is. You can't give up and throw in the towel; you have to be a harsh taskmaster on yourself and really get angry at yourself for putting on the extra flab. You have to mentally beat yourself to goad yourself real hard to lose and firm up. You have to make yourself feel anxious and nervous so you will feel guilty with every cheat on your diet. You work like a dog here—you get aches and pains and pulled muscles and back strain and you limp around. You get smelly and sweat and pant and grit your teeth. You get out of breath. It is no picnic here—you get exhausted. But then what's it all for comes out in the final payoffs. You realize how much you can do with your body and it is like a symbol—if you can control your body, you can control other parts of your life—it is like a key to success. In my case, with my greater body control, I am more in control of my moods with my family. Now I am a glamor queen wearing bright plaids and my blood pressure is down so my hard work here is paying off. My success with my body makes me want to go back and finish college. You put in your time and you get the payoff of a lower dress size and fewer medical bills. I am even an amateur athlete now, running long distances with my kids. You are winning a contest with yourself if you can be a martyr and stick to the diet and exercises. It is dreary drudgery but you get a sense of accomplishment and get prettier on the outside. Nothing really good comes naturally—it takes hard work.

This sense of hard work with potential of actual future rewards for one's labor led some *serious loners* to consider their involvement in the spa to be a full-time job or *career*. (Hughes, 1958, pp. 62–67) Some stressed that they were serious professionals about improving their bodies in the spa; they were not lighthearted amateurs or merely "Sunday spa-worshippers."

It is a full time occupation to come here four times a week and to stick to the diet they suggest—you have to keep pushing. If you really concentrate on this stuff, you don't have time to think about anything else. It is a real career to fit in the exercising everyday and to think about every bit that goes into your mouth. It is real hard work for me not to lie around and eat chocolates. It is like I have three jobs—one as wife and mother, a second as an executive secretary, and the third—my body career which is part of the other two. I am on a schedule, whether doing my housework or coming here and working on my body—a woman's work is never done. I am a real pro now—I am getting more and more knowledge about the details of foods and exercises. You can never turn off the job with your body—it goes on 24 hours a day; it is not like an eight hour a day job. I have enough mental knowledge to deserve a Ph.D. in dieting and exercising—I could teach the stuff. But to apply all this mental knowledge on yourself is harder and that is really where the hard work begins—making yourself pay attention in your heart to what's in your head. It is a real big job to feel in your gut that you want to keep off extra weight and stay in shape—it is not just a rational thing.

The systematization and regimentation of the spa routine with many calculations made with regard to bodily achievements, with a minimal amount of spontaneity and carelessness, meant hard work for the *serious loners.* (Huizinga, 1955, p. 197)

Serious Withs

The *serious withs* were quite body-absorbed in their own as well as in others' bodies. These women were of all ages and all shapes and sizes, but quite a few were between 35 and 55 years old, and wanted to lose 15 to 35 pounds. These withs were constantly going back and forth between looking at others' body parts and then scrutinizing their own body parts. Some withs stared at others for as long as five or seven minutes, and then gave a critical evaluation of their own bodies to somebody nearby. Most pointed out how they were failing in some ways, yet succeeding in other ways, in improving their bodies, as they were self- and other-conscious. (Goffman, 1967, pp. 118–25) Two women conversed:

Sally: At least coming here gives me a conscience and makes me watch what I eat, and I feel like a success if I don't give into a binge. And I can prove that I am some kind of a success by swimming 25 laps here. But I am not doing so hot because I am not coming here often enough to do the exercises. I like to look hard at the others here because it gives me a sense of where I am not too bad and where I can stand improvement.

Jane: Me too. I think you are doing good because you stick to your swimming and jogging. Now I was doing good on the diet until the wedding last week and now I feel miserable but I can't stop eating and I am a failure. But at least I am succeeding in pushing myself to come here and sweat off the calories.

Sally: Yeh, when I exercise here, I feel that I am succeeding in doing something good for myself, and it will spur me on to diet.

Jane: They balance each other out, so you succeed in the exercises but fail on the diet or succeed on the diet but fail in the exercises. But the real sign of success is reaching close to your ideal weight or ideal inch measurements, and I'll feel like a failure until I get closer to them.

Sally: I agree, but you have to think of little successes along the way, so you don't feel completely miserable, like feeling proud of your accomplishment of losing even two pounds and being proud of resisting the temptation to give into the delicious desserts.

Many of the *serious withs* did mention their fears about getting old as a basis for their energetic efforts in the spa, a fear shared by many Americans. "You have got to keep fighting that creeping old age from getting the better of you and you need your own kind to help you." "Since I have been coming here I have recaptured the fountain of youth, and people keep telling me that I look 25 though I'm almost double that." "We have to fight evil Father Time together." As Wax has suggested, such women were examples of self-discipline through diet and exercise, and were:

. . . engaged in the valiant battle against being classed as old. Our culture classifies old age as retirement from sexual, vocational, and even sociable activity, and the woman who is battling age is trying to prevent too early a retirement. She employs the techniques of grooming to conceal the signs of aging and to accentuate (and expose) the body areas where her appearance is still youthful. (Wax, 1957, p. 592)

In such dialogues, people spoke *with* and *to* each other. Sometimes the women picked up on what others said, and commented on such remarks in relationship to the other women or themselves. At other times, women just sounded off to each other. They seemed to need an ear, but they did not care about getting a response back from another. Indeed, some women virtually ignored responses given back, as they were quite involved in their own heads in concentrating on their multiple feelings and thoughts about the progress and lack of progress of their own bodily achievements. *Self-absorbed,* the *serious withs* were eager to *validate* themselves.

Some emphasized that misery needed and loved company—they wanted to feel that others were suffering with them in the same boat working toward some common goals. "We can really understand each other and empathize here—a lot of us are on the same wave length about changing our bodies through dieting and physical activity." One stated:

We know it's no fun and games, no picnic. We are not enjoying ourselves here, but we have to push each other. Being with the others sweating and panting and gritting their teeth makes you put up with it. Together we put in the time and pat each other on the back. We need to hold each other's hands, because we know that we could not endure this austerity and these rigid routines all alone. We suffer together and we will celebrate together and throw a party when we turn out to be beauty queens. Another person's success or failure here becomes our success or failure. I can feel for and I can be that very person who goes on a wild eating binge or the person who is in to a hard push and loses eight or so pounds in one week. Everyone is a lot like each other here.

Many of the *serious withs* stated that others kept them on their toes and kept them working hard in the spa. "Everybody charges each other up here, so it is mutual motivation; you can't just charge up your own battery alone." One commented:

The others here make you work harder because they push you and they are always watching you and don't let you get away with being lazy in the exercises or gain weight. Some even tell you that you look a little heavy or they frown at you and you know that you have disappointed them and not lived up to their expectations. It is like you have a silent and unwritten contract here to work hard and show some change for the better for others are watching over you sort of like police. It is an incentive to others to push you—you need these external controls, because sometimes your own conscience is a little weak. It makes you want to improve when you see how good others are at some exercises. It is like friendly competition when you see the beautiful bodies working out so hard here; you want to be one of those beautiful bodies, so you will work harder and harder and harder at the exercises. You wouldn't work so hard if you were alone just staring at the mirror. You would get lazy. Here there is like group pressure to get into the spirit of it with others. You get pushed from both directions. You see you are doing better as losing more weight than some here, but you aren't doing as good as others. This comparing business spurs you on.

In their pushes to achieve, some of the *serious withs* seemed to compete with others around them; they tried to move their bodies faster, more vigorously, or more gracefully than women in close geographical proximity to them. For example, some *serious withs* tried to peddle stationary bicycles faster and longer than did other women on the bicycles at the same time. Some panted, huffed, and puffed, said "Whew" a lot, hung their heads down as they took deep breaths, but smiled as they won their self-defined contest of bicycling more quickly or vigorously than somebody else. Some withs strained and trembled and groaned as they stretched their legs wider apart than others, or as they raised their legs higher than others when exercising.

Such withs were also competing with themselves to do bigger and better exercises than they had done in the past. Trying to get quick positive results, these withs often accompanied each other as they weighed and measured themselves three or four times within a one and one-half to three hour period when they were at the spa—they smiled or frowned, depending on whether they had or had not lost weight or inches. These *serious withs* showed their involvement in spa exercises by their obvious perspiration. In the spa, such perspiration was a sign of correct or appropriate involvement in the scene, not evidence of overinvolvement which it would be in other contexts. (Goffman 1966, p. 62)

While concentrating on their own measurements, these *serious withs'* eyes glanced up and down the bodies of others, often seeking out strangers across crowded rooms. In particular, these glancing onlookers perused from head to toe particularly overweight women (with more than 40 pounds to lose) or particularly thin women (even underweight by some standards) who were located in different sections of the room than they were. Some said that they liked to feel that they were "in the middle" and not the fattest or the thinnest women in the room. Indeed, some *serious withs* did focus on the intricate details of others' bodies. Some undertook a very detailed analysis of a friends' body, telling her her strong and weak points, and what exercises to do to lose weight in certain body parts. Such women elaborated on what styles of clothes did and would look the best on their friends, "accentuating their good points and playing down their weaknesses—sometimes a friendly outsider can be more objective about the best clothes for you better than you can."

Many stated that it was easier and less threatening to do an analysis and even try to help somebody else with regard to their bodily aspects than to do a rundown on oneself. Some added that in judging others' bodies, they have begun to change their views about the most appropriate body styles for themselves. Some had started to consider that some stocky body styles were firm and strong looking and quite attractive; "maybe I don't have to look like a string of spaghetti after all."

Two types of *serious withs* were quite conscious of others as well as themselves as they showed the spirit of *competition,* or at the least of *antagonistic cooperation,* in relationships with others. (Sumner, 1940, pp. 30-32, 58, 297) The self-defined *body-superiors* were often between 21 and 40 years old, and were either as thin as fashion models in contemporary women's magazines or solid and muscular with little flabby fat. These *superiors* knew that they were close to the goal of almost-perfection in terms of their bodily shape, and, full of much self-confidence, they seemed to want to show and tell others how others could follow the *superiors'* righteous path to perfection. These *superiors* talked about how it was a real "ego trip" for them to come to the spa, "because you get a lot of flattery and it makes your head feel good and you can teach others how to do it with your own diet and your own exercise routines." Some of these *superiors* were rather self-righteous and holier-than-thou ex-fatties, who seemed to have little pity and compassion for women who insisted that they were trying but they could not help giving into the wrong foods. "Look, it was hard for me too, but if I could do it, so can you," was the common answer.

Some of these *superiors* stated that they liked to "flaunt my body—it makes me feel I am a real success in something." Some said that they were proud to show off and exhibit themselves. They felt that they deserved the reward of others' applause, because they worked hard for a long time to get that applause, and they would have to keep working hard to deserve the applause. Some *superiors* admitted that they needed to keep coming to the spa to watch themselves—"it's sort of like you need the watchdog control here, the big sister looking over your shoulder to keep your body O.K. so you won't backslide." Are we ever *body-superiors?* One said:

> I have won the contest here and I want to show others they can win too. Maybe I am a little too pompous and even sadistic in parading myself around and showing that I am better than many others here, but I feel it's deserved, because I worked hard to get this way. I have a bloated head now but I fought so many inferior feelings in the battle of the bulge for years. The exercises are the key thing here because they firm you up and you see the inches go which show up more than losing pounds on the diet. I deserve praise here, but I want to help others. I have to be tough and not feel sorry for the fatties—they just

have to pull themselves up by the bootstraps and get a hold of themselves like I did and not eat at every whim or problem. But it's not just because I love to be appreciated that I come here. Deep down, I need to come to stay this way and not let myself slip. Even if I stay thin, my muscles will get flabby if I don't keep working out. I hold my tummy in, stand up tall, and strut around the room so all can see me here. I prance around tall like a show horse and people do see that I am proud as a peacock of my shape, gotten through much work—others can follow me.

These *superiors* often displayed their bodies by taking strolls in the nude in the locker room, or by lying or sitting in the sauna for long periods of time. Others stood tall and walked slowly around the swimming pool in their bikinis, smiling as they caught the eyes of others. They smiled at themselves, stroked their hair, touched and rubbed their arms, necks and legs, silently saying that they were quite content with their bodies. Some of the *superiors* stood out all the more when they wore brightly colored leotards and bathing suits. Some stated that they were "proud to prance around in my shoestring bikini—it is quite an accomplishment at the age of 37."

In contrast to the pride shown by the self-defined *body-superiors,* the self-defined *body-inferiors* were often between 35 and 50 years old, with at least 25 pounds to lose. They often looked down at the floor, slouched, slumped over, frowned at themselves, or stuck their tongues out at their bulges in the nude or in clothes. These women often expressed a negative body image to friends and acquaintances, often calling themselves "ugly" and "sexually unattractive." These women often called themselves derogatory names, as "butterball," "hippo," "piggy," and "fat ass." They talked about ways to hide their bodies in large nightgowns, muu-muus, and dark colors. Some discussed how they were embarrassed to wear bathing suits and appear in the nude. They discussed how it was hard for them to find clothes which were flattering. The negative body images expressed by some health spa patrons were often quite similar to those expressed by group dieters.

These women were careful never to appear in the nude in the dressing room. They quickly covered themselves with towels after showers, and mostly did all their dressing and undressing in the privacy of small dressing booths. They blushed and sighed as they finished the details of their dressing and makeup in front of mirrors in the company of others. They frequently mentioned that a piece of clothing did not fit correctly or that their hair was impossible to fix, and their hair always looked terrible. In contrast, the *superiors* often talked about how glad they were to find the perfect makeup or hairdos for themselves as well as clothing to do the most for their figures.

Many self-defined *body-inferiors* sighed and talked about how they would never get there—down to that desirable figure—"I really don't think there is any hope for me—I've tried everything." Some said that at least coming to the spa helped them to maintain their weight and not gain. These *inferiors* exercised slowly, not performing the full quantities of exercises suggested by the group leaders. They stated that they had bodily pains or that they were exhausted. Some *inferiors* cried a little when they saw women whom they thought had better bodies than they did; they felt somewhat disheartened and defeated—"I could never possibly look like that." Some said that the spas should have different classes or sessions "for the skinnies and the fats so that these thin beauties don't make us feel so bad and set up an impossible standard for us." Some *inferiors* put on baggy bathing suits with skirts and quickly went into the pool or whirlpool and dunked, so that only their heads were out of the water. Such a hiding of the body stance was in sharp contrast with the *superiors* in bikinis who strutted around the pool and whirlpool several times, holding their heads high, smiling, smacking their lips, and winking at others. One woman bemoaned:

> I need to talk about how bad I feel about my body and how ugly it is for me to be hepped up enough to do something about it. I can't blame my husband. Who wants to go to bed with an elephant? I have got mountains of flab to take off before I can even feel my bones. The people here understand how horrible you feel. But when I get into one of these exercise classes with the thin beauties, I wish there were a hole in the floor for me to drop into, because I am so ashamed to stand next to them. I change my clothes in the bathrooms here—I don't dare let anybody see me in the nude. I wear baggy housedresses here so nobody knows how fat I really am. I get discouraged fast and I don't think I can make it—I go on an eating binge and I run five or six miles to work these 30 pounds off, but it doesn't work. I kill myself in exercising for nothing, and really I don't eat that much. I wish they wouldn't allow the skinnies to come here and make me feel bad. I feel too fat to put on a bathing suit here. People will frown or laugh.

Playful Loners

Many *playful loners* were quite self-consciously body-absorbed in a leisurely and low-keyed way, enjoying their bodies, in contrast to the mode of restless or even frantic anxiety of some of the *serious loners*. These *playful loners* enjoyed touching their skin and feeling their muscles; some smiled and said that the spa was a legitimate place for them to let themselves go and love themselves or caress themselves and even masturbate. "I really can feel the delight of my body here and I have spontaneous orgasms." Some stressed that they really could take care of themselves with various wet and dry heat treatments. Some said that it was a delight to let their minds wander to all kinds of topics as they were being good to themselves. "I like to pamper myself here and feel hot and cold and it is like taking a long massage treatment here—you actively massage your muscles and you are passive and soak in the heat and water." *Playful loners* were of all ages and body types. When are we such *playful loners*? One woman said:

> To do something nice for your body you can really use it a lot in exercises here and pamper it in the sauna and whirlpool. It is like you are taking care of yourself here like your mother used to take care of you when you were a

baby—you mother yourself here. I love to feel and touch myself here. The self-massaging is a real joy here and it turns on all my senses. I love to look in the mirror here and take a long time to comb and brush my hair; I love to experiment with my makeup here. I guess they call it narcissistic to keep looking at yourself and touching yourself like this but it is a great soothing relaxation. Here it is legit to pamper yourself and not just lose yourself in doing things for other people. I smile at myself here and am self-satisfied even if I could lose ten pounds, no big deal. I enjoy myself alone here and I don't want to be nasty but I am having so much fun with myself that I don't want to bother with anybody. Usually when people start talking to me, I say I'd love to talk, but I have a bad headache. I like the luxury and leisure of total self-indulgence here, and I don't want to be distracted from my carefree thoughts and the absorption in myself. I turn my body on in the steam and the sauna and I feel very sensuous. I love to touch my soft skin and feel my muscles getting hard. It is like hugging myself all over.

Some of these *playful loners* stressed that they liked to leave their pressure-cooker lives and just hang around or lie around the spa—they enjoyed the feeling of idle time when they had nothing much else to do but come to the spa.[4] "It's like the clock stops when I am here and I just do what I feel like here; I love to be so selfish." Some said that they enjoyed lying around the pool or in the sauna bath, and almost falling asleep—"just collapsing in the heat and the nice feeling that you don't have to push yourself to achieve anything." Many used the word "relaxing" to describe their spa experiences, "which means that you let it all hang out and go at your own pace—you do real things here so you are not anxious wondering what to do with your time."

Some women did say that they were upper-middle-class wives and mothers who did not want to work at full-time jobs and had a few hours to kill in afternoons; the spa was viewed as a "good time-killer." One stated:

The spa does two big things for me—it stops me from being bored and it really is like a pacifier. I move around a lot here so I am not just sitting around the TV set bored or resting in a boring afternoon half-nap. I get sleepy here and I wash my hair and fall asleep under the dryer. It is a wonderful feeling to just be here and do what you want to do because you feel like it—with no specific purpose or meaning or goal—you just are who you want to be here and you don't have to worry about living up to anybody else's expectations. It is an ego trip to develop muscles and control the graceful movements of my body here. It is a high to feel the power of your own body and you feel good about yourself and then nobody can really get to you. I feel really at peace and free when I float on my back in the water. So I move a little, so I rest a little. It is an easy life here, not a care in the world when you plop in the pool. I guess it is a mark of the idle rich to be able to come here and not work for money, but I feel fine about it, no guilt.

Many stated that while they were feeling good about the increasing power and strength of their bodies, they could "turn off my mind and all my worries and just be body-involved."

Playful loners said that their time at the spa was a "scheduled time of relaxation when I turn off my worries and my frantic thinking of 100 miles an hour." One women defined playing in the spa as "not thinking too much and just letting my body do what it wants to and getting real pleasure from the movement of my body—moving my body faster and more energetically each time I come here." Do we ever play in these terms? Some of these *playful loners,* therefore, seemed to define a rather low-keyed and relaxed competition with themselves in their own improving bodily efforts as a *playful* and not a *serious* orientation. Rarely did any *playful loner* mention the goal of weight or inches' loss as a central or even peripheral reason for attending the spa; it was the *serious loners* and *serious withs* who stressed such purposeful achievement intentions.

When the *playful loners* emphasized that they could "let it all hang out in the spa," they spoke about releasing many tensions through exercising, working out angers and fears by "sweating all this anxiety out of our bodies," and "unwinding, so I don't just stay tied up in knots." They stated that they were very content and happy to let go of tensions by and for themselves at the spas. These women were quite self-possessed and self-contained—"I don't need anybody to help me let it all hang out, I just do it myself—I don't want to dump my load on anyone and I don't want anyone dumping their stuff on me." Some pointed out that the spa encouraged them to be good to themselves, to accentuate the positive parts of themselves and not be so self-critical, and so *validate* themselves. One woman reflected:

> Coming here really makes me less of a masochist. I feel that I really allow myself to feel pleasure here and I get off the kick of thinking about everything that is wrong with me. I am easy on myself here and tolerant of my weaknesses of a few extra pounds. It makes me realize how hard I beat myself and condemn myself when I am not here—I blame myself for everything. Here I take it easy and turn off the self-destructive push to be a perfectionist in everything. I get a sense of courage and hope here—things will get better in my life and my life won't fall apart. My body feels good in the warmth and water here and it makes me feel that other things in my life will be good too.

So the spa made some *playful loners* feel and think good and happy views about themselves, and often tended to make some women question or lessen some of their masochism, at least for a limited time and space. Some said that at the spa they began to realize that everything that went wrong at home was not their problem or their fault and they were getting sick of blaming themselves for all problems. Some said that their quiet reflection in the spa made them feel that they were responsible for a lot of things that went well or right at home. Some said that they were happy to feel good about themselves at the spa, and that they were going to tell their family members to start appreciating them more. A few mentioned that as they felt better about themselves and gained more self-confidence in the spa, they were beginning to feel resentful and angry at others, "instead of just getting mad at myself all the time." For some, the spa was "a catalyst to let me feel real legitimate anger at my husband for the first time and I really explode all my anger in fast exercising here." One woman commented:

Maybe when you are good to yourself and pamper your body here, you realize you are a fine and O.K. person and people better start seeing the good points in you that you are discovering about yourself. You are proud to feel that you are doing good things for your body. Others better start being good to you because you deserve it and you are not going to take their shit any more—you are going to announce to them that you are a good person and they better stop giving you a hard time. You want pleasure in all of your life, just like you feel the pleasure in the spa.

Most *playful loners* stressed that the spa experience was a most important time-out period for them; in particular, coming to the spa meant time out from these women's hard-working responsibilities as wives and mothers. Coming to the spa was "a respite, a necessary escape from all the responsibilities you are up to your ears with—the cooking, cleaning, husbands, and kids." Some said that the spa was a necessary vacation from everyday routines—they felt that they needed such a time-out vacation to freshen them up, to renew and reinvigorate them—"to slow down to give me time to charge up my battery more to go back into the battle lines to fight the real tough serious battles of life." Some women mentioned that they did run away to the spa for a few hours so as to escape harsh reality— "you need to come here to get away from the harsh realities of illnesses and problems which are pounding on your head like thunder." The spa was a place of recuperation and restoration for some. (Gross, 1963, pp. 44–46) One woman said:

> I am so good and responsible and so conscientious all the time that I need to turn off my worrying so much about other people. You need time out from catering to everybody else when you practically forget about yourself. My husband says he needs time out from his work pressures so he plays handball and drinks with the boys and I need time out from being such a dutiful wife so I come here. I really can breathe slow and deep here as I sigh and take a long coffee break from my 48 hour a day work at home with keeping a big house clean, doing the laundering, and chauffeuring my three kids around. I need this country club to get away from the kids' screaming. I pay a babysitter so I can come here sometimes. I'd go crazy if I didn't come here to escape pleasing everybody so hard. I muster up strength here to go back home and face all the little details of running a home. I have to come here to stop myself from my compulsive thing about doing more and more for other people.

A few *playful loners* who had full-time jobs or careers said that they needed to come to the spa to divert their minds from the pressures of "hard pressure cooker work, which you can never forget thinking about, even in your sleep." Some stated that they came to the spa so that they would be in a very different world than their world of work, "and being in this really separate world of the spa, you clear your head, and get a calmer and better perspective on your work."

Some *playful loners* appeared to go away and enter their own little worlds—they inwardly emigrated from the gathering while outwardly participating in spa activities. In going away, these loners relived past experiences or rehearsed future ones—in reverie, daydreaming, or autistic thinking. As Goffman has suggested, such individuals demonstrated their absence from the current situation by preoccupied, faraway looks in their eyes, by a sleeplike stillness of their limbs, or by certain kinds of side involvements that could be sustained in an abstracted, almost unconscious manner, as humming, drumming the fingers on a surface, hair twisting, nose picking, and scratching. Some *playful loners* appeared "away" when they talked to themselves, muttered, or laughed to themselves—they were carrying on dialogues with themselves, not unlike other spa members were doing with each other. (Goffman, 1966, pp. 69–73) Perhaps many of us go "away" in this sense in various activities in our everyday lives.

Playful Withs

The *playful withs* stressed that they wanted to have "fun" or "a good time" in the spa, whether they did or did not focus on aspects of their own or others' bodies. Some said that it was "fun and games" or a "real recreation to come to the spa which is like an amusement park, except the rides don't move you around—you have to move yourself around." The *playful withs* were of all ages and all shapes and sizes—quite a few were between 25 and 50 years old. Many said that they wouldn't mind losing anywhere between five and 30 pounds, but they stressed that they really were not coming to the spa to lose weight, because the main way to lose weight was to stick to a diet. Many said that exercising really would not help them lose weight, "because after you move around a lot you are really starving and you deserve to eat because you have been so good and knocked yourself out exercising." Many of the *playful withs* did not want to achieve precise goals of body changes in the spa, but, similar to the *playful loners,* did come to the spa "to get away from the buzzing tensions of everyday life so the pressure won't make your ears pop."

> You forget about all the pressure cooker problems when you can come here and just be silly. You are all pent up inside, and here you can have some good jokes with the girls. Sometimes you are the entertainer for others and sometimes you are just part of the audience, but it is like being in your own comedy here and you laugh about your problems and even your body bulges—and your real tensions are far out there and not so real to you when you are here. But you got to get a rise out of others so you don't stay wound up in your own head and it is like being a child again and playing with others on the playground here. We scream and laugh and even play tag with each other here. It is pure fun to forget all hardships of being a grown-up.

Some of the *playful withs* seemed to define "fun" in terms of much *bodily horseplay.* In contrast with some of the *serious withs* who glimpsed and stared at others often, these *body-horseplayers* laughed a lot as they joked and bumped into each other, calling each other "clumsy" and "klutz." These women kicked each other, pushed each other, hugged each other, kissed each other, pinched each other's cheeks, and slapped each other on the back. Some stated that they really hated and loved each other, and the spa gave them the opportunity to show such feelings in a direct physical way. A few added, "I am taking out how I feel about other people like my husband and kids on my friends here in the spa." Some stated that they really felt that they were together with each other and communicating with each other when they touched each other—"it is really a more basic and genuine way of being with somebody than just talking with words." One woman mentioned, "I feel more alive and aware of my own feelings when I touch somebody else."

Thus touching was a way for some women to get to know themselves better as well as to get to know others; touching symbolized a reciprocal sharing of the self. Besides this mutual give-and-take aspect of touching, some women stated that they learned about their physical strengths and weaknessss through exploring each other's body. "I never realized how strong I was until I picked Mary up." "You really find out how strong your arms are when you hand-wrestle here." "It is fun to bump into each other because then you know the difference between the soft and hard fat." For a few members, these direct physical contacts in the spa served as an outlet for aggressive and sexual urges. "I do let out a lot of anger when I punch Sue in fun and then when we hug it does sort of arouse me."

Many *playful withs* stressed that coming to the spa was a "cheap way to have a lot of fun—it takes less time and energy than going skiing." In underlining the idea of *fun,* these women pointed out that they were enjoying *sociability for its own sake* in all their laughing and gossiping.[5] They said that it was a pleasure to realize that they had many interests in common besides the body. Coming to the spa added something "new and different and exciting to my life." One woman said:

> We all jiggle our bodies around and it really is a kick—it sure is something different than we do in our everyday lives. It is a big social party here—everybody is all over you and asking you how you're doing, even when they don't know you very well. It is like a friendly country club—everybody wants to be your friend. You do the activities here really as a way to meet people. You talk to people all the time everywhere, in the suanas, showers, pools, and in the dressing room. It is very relaxing to talk about light subjects and to let yourself go and laugh together. Sometimes I forget what I am supposed to do here—I meet people from my neighborhood and we catch up on all the dirt. There is always somebody new and different to talk to here and there are a million things to do so you never get bored trying out an activity with a friend. You keep meeting nice new people and as an afternoon out with the girls, it is more of a novel and unique experience than just going out to lunch. It is a ball to gab and let yourself go and shoot the breeze and just play with each other. It is amusing and diverting to do something different like this with each other.

Some of these women added that it was exciting to come to the spa because they talked about everything under the sun and they never knew for sure what they might talk about next. Some said that coming to the spa was a really good way to keep up old friendships, "because it is a scheduled way to see old friends and to really have something fun to do together." Others mentioned that they were always eager and open to make new friends, and "you can always add to your friendships here because we all have lots in common in the way we live." One woman stated, "The spa is a big social mixer with a different twist—it is mainly just for us girls." These women often made plans in the spa to see their old and new friends at social occasions outside the context of the spa.

Some of the *playful withs* did point out that they felt relaxed to share some of their problems in a lighthearted way—"you can get things off your chest and unbosom yourself and then laugh about your problems and realize you don't have it so tough." One said, "We all let out our troubles here so we can forget them and be happy together." Many women seemed to view their collective catharsis of tension releases as a means to the very important end of having fun together—"sharing juicy gossip is a great way to have fun." One commented:

> You let your hair down and empty your mind here. All you have to do is tell jokes and count your exercises and your mind is emptied of all burdens. You laugh about the woes of middle age and you realize you don't have all the troubles of the world on your shoulders. You laugh at the little problems of your body and your eating and you can calm each other down about specific things. Like Mary calmed me down about my daughter going out with the wrong kind of guy and I tried to soothe her about her fears of taking her first airplane ride. So then we felt better and we laughed and splashed around in the pool. We enjoyed the sauna together. It's like we go on a little vacation with each other once or twice a week. You get too heavy and serious and dramatic about making a big deal of your troubles alone in your head at home. Here, you treat your troubles in a lighter vein and more casually and you realize you are not so bad off. The spa makes me realize that I should try and be more superficial—I take things too much to heart.

Some of the *playful withs* said that they were "leisurely, lighthearted amateurs" in the spa, who liked to chat and do a few exercises, "but I am not out to win any athletic contests or any medals; this is the one part of my life where I don't have to push." In contrast, many of the *serious withs* and *loners* labeled themselves as "hard-working professionals," who were out to try to succeed in achieving certain goals. The *playful withs* stated that the main thing was to have a good time "with the girls" and not to worry too much about making definite progress in losing weight or gaining weight. Some said that they were gaining more self-confidence in handling their lives by coming to the spa, "which is more important for me than following their literal rules here of losing 17 pounds." These women stressed that it was fun to share their experiences at the spa, and talk about how good the activities at the spa made them feel. Women gave each other tips about different routines of using the showers, sauna, whirlpool, and steam bath so as to make one's body feel even better.

You empty your mind and have a great escape from your work and your problems when all you do is concentrate on how your body feels wet or dry, hot or cold, exhausted or full of energy. It is gratifying to talk about these simple body things with others who really understand. You realize that such simple feelings really may be basic to what life is all about.

One woman clearly summarized the main foci of the *playful withs*:

It is fun to come here and horse around and be frivolous about your body with others. You can be lighthearted here in contrast with your involvements with your family and work. We snort and laugh and push each other around and pinch each other's fat. We laugh and tease each other and are not so serious about it as most of us six have lost zero or even gained in the last few months. It is a happy afternoon out with the girls and you put your body through the machines that make you wiggle like in an amusement park. It is real recreation here—not like pushing a mop at home. You flop around here and laugh with others and it is a big break from real life. No purpose or goal here as I scream and kick—I realize here that if I took every little bulge so seriously, I would go crazy. I have to try and act serious around some of the fanatic sweating types here—put on a show of trying hard and sincerity. But boy do we laugh about it all in the locker room! I feel like I am walking on air after I leave, after putting down everybody in the neighborhood with the girls here—I think they call it insult humor. I love to come here for four or five hours one day a week and laugh and act crazy and do nothing with the girls, like guys do when they go out and drink together. I tell my husband it is my one afternoon for a merry escape and just playing like a kid—after all, I am working hard for him the rest of the time.

Riesman, Potter, and Watson have described the three values of *sociability* as artfulness, solidarity, and intimacy, clearly exemplified by some *playful withs*. The artfulness of the ephemeral product of sociability means that attention is focused on the conversation and not on the individuals themselves. Intimacy implies the kind of conversation, often dyadic, which permits participants to gain some experience of each other as individuals, to participate vicariously in the experience of another person, and so get a sense of what kind of person the other one is. By the same token, one gets renewed impressions of the kind of person one is oneself. Collective solidarity is a third value in sociability, often found among groups of persons already linked together by institutional ties. In these groups, there is less than the usual amount of freedom to pick and choose one's close associations. Too much differentiation inside the group would threaten the group's ability to achieve collective institutional goals. In such groups, sociability allows for some individuation, some recognition of unique individual qualities and achievements. The predominant theme, however, is the assertion of continuity and solidarity. The same people gather together time after time and discuss the same topics and the same grievances. (Riesman, Potter, and Watson, 1960, p. 27)

In their sociability, the *playful withs* were spectators and performers who watched themselves and watched each other. These *playful withs* often defined the spa as an *open region,* where staring was a permitted and even a preferred activity, and was quite legitimate. Such staring was not at all viewed as an invasion of territoriality or as an impertinence or as a hostile act. (Goffman, 1974, p. 373)

Spa members were often open to each other, as actresses and audiences. *Playful withs* were mutually accessible to each other in their informality and solidarity which led them to recognize each other as being of the same special group. Their positions were exposed and opening. (Goffman, 1966, pp. 131–32) The spa as an open region was a physically bounded place ". . . where 'any' two persons, acquainted or not, have a right to initiate face engagement with each other for the purpose of extending salutations." (Goffman, 1966, p. 132) Some of these spa members contradicted the general rule suggested by Goffman, when bodies are naked, glances are clothed, as in nudist camps. (Goffman, 1972, p. 46) Often glances were vividly and unabashedly naked in the spa where bodies were almost if not completely naked.

SEPARATENESS AND INTERMINGLING OF SERIOUSNESS AND PLAYFULNESS

The sense of coming to the spa as a time for *serious hard work* as distinct from *playful leisure* has been captured in the following dialogue:

Nancy: It is hard work to come here, and it is not a game or a joke or a kick. You have to take it seriously to beat the weight off. You do the exercises as hard and fast as you can in the exercise class and you do them at least 15 minutes a day at home. You want it to pay off so you go home and work hard on your diet and don't give into temptation.

Betty: Maybe, but you are too intense about it. You should come here like me and horse around and have fun and laugh and let yourself go. You get rid of your tensions. So if you feel like it, exercise, but you kill yourself exercising—you are going to collapse. I find out all the dirt from the girls here and we talk about where we will go for lunch. Why are you such an angel?

Nancy: You are trying to tempt me and you are teasing me for being a goody-good. I don't like to see you or anybody I know here. I prefer to come here alone so I can concentrate on the exercises and not get distracted. You have to work at making over your body—it doesn't come naturally. I push myself and it makes me feel good to lose even a pound or one-fourth of an inch. I don't like it when you tell me to stop pushing—if I want to joke around, I will do it on the outside, at a social party.

Betty: But you are so hard on yourself. Who are you competing with anyway? Look, you are not going to become a movie star or a fashion model or professional athlete. So come here, forget your troubles, do things that make you feel good, like the whirlpool and the sauna—forget the daily pressures to keep pushing.

Nancy: You act like coming here is a great luxury, like its a country club and you just come and make friends and have fun. I have fun at parties with you and when I come here with you I really don't come here to be with you but to work on myself. Here I can worry about and start to solve my big trouble—my extra 20 pounds.

Betty: But you never let up here, you never relax. You show everybody how you are trying to be so good and improve in your exercise routine. So who cares? You gain a little, you lose a little, so what. I am not going to be a martyr and feel like I am in the military for the rest of my life and stay on a diet and be virtuous and do the daily exercises. So I may come here and work off a little of the chocolate cake. I sort of maintain my weight. I could lose at least 20 pounds, but I am not going to make myself a nervous wreck about it, like you.

Nancy: Sometimes I wish I could be as relaxed and casual and lackadaisical about coming here as you are—not keyed up. Look I hate to exercise and it hurts a lot and I get exhausted. But it is the means to the goal of a better looking me.

Betty: I guess coming here is just an end in itself, a plain old good time when I can do what I want and flop around and move my body fast if I feel like it. I like to just be good to myself here; I take my time bathing and washing my hair and pampering and primping for as long as I want to.

Nancy: Well, here is the time for hard work for me; the little pampering I do I can do in my own bathroom at home. I am scared and panicked when I come here because I realize how easy it would be to let myself go and gain 50 pounds. I need to come here to stop that. I am scared that I am naturally lazy and I would let myself go and eat everything. It is no joy ride here; I have just got to be here to get into shape.

Betty: It is stupid to live so scared—it is sort of like having a policeman to come here but I don't think my body is so bad and I am not going to make myself anxious, so I don't get on the scale more than once a month. Maybe I am more satisfied about my body than you and you really want to change yours.

Nancy: Well, true and the philosophy that I think is right here is that everybody can afford to work on their bodies, and that nobody has a perfect body. Look at how hard some of these fashion model types work out here.

Betty: But let us say you get near to having a perfect body. If you are really a pusher it is never-ending work to keep it so perfect. No let up. If you are a beautiful person, you are always in training and in a rat race. What kind of a life is this constant food deprivation and working out until you are so sore? I come here and gab and I feel like I'm on a vacation. I escape the everyday pressures here—I don't want to add to them or make them bigger, which is what you do.

Nancy: The difference is that you think of it here as time out from everyday living, and I think of it as time in to really pay attention to myself and to my weight problems. I got to the point that if I didn't lose the one and one-half inches from my hips that I did lose here in the past two months, I would have been desperate. Coming here is the court of last resort for me to improve my body—I have tried all kinds of doctors and pills and exercise plans and diets. This is it—it is not play time.

Betty: You are so driven. I am going to try to calm you down and slow you down and get you to relax here. Have fun, take it easy. You are making it like a full-time job or career to come here. You are a nervous wreck. You are healthy and you look O.K., so you are not the biggest glamor puss, so what? Life is too short to push so hard.

In contrast with these two women, each of whom tended to hold to a fairly strong "party line" of either *seriousness* or *playfulness* with regard to coming to the spa, there were a few women who stated that they were both *serious* and *playful* about coming to the spa; on some days, they were more *serious,* and on other days, they were more *playful.* One woman stated:

Sometimes I laugh and lie around the pool here and talk with the girls. It is fun to lie around and gossip. We leisurely dunk in the pool and take a sauna and wash our hair and sometimes then go out to lunch. I am easy on myself those days and I do mild exercises. Then the spa is real recreation, almost like recuperation and a rest cure from daily troubles. There are other days when I don't want to talk to anybody and I won't dare let myself rest in the sauna—I would feel too guilty. Those days I feel I have been bad and eaten wrong and I just want to work hard, I don't want to talk to anybody. I want to be anonymous and come here alone and punish myself by looking at the big number on the scale when I weigh in. That makes me frantic and I exercise to the point of exhaustion, and I sweat out pounds in the steam bath until I nearly faint. I work hard those days—I am too anxious and I don't have the time to be social and playful.

This woman noted that she *seriously* worked hard in the spa when she was alone; she was more leisurely and *playful* when she was with others. Some others commented, in contrast, that they *seriously* worked when they were in the company of others, while they were more *playful* and relaxed when they were by themselves. They stated that they needed others to be an incentive and goad them on—they needed to compare themselves with others in weight-losing or in improving in the exercises. "Others keep reminding me to stick with it." These women stated that they felt more relaxed in going at there own pace and pampering themselves when they were alone relaxing "because it is play alone fun and nobody's pushing you."

A few women said that they thought that coming to the spa was going to be *leisurely play,* but it turned out to be *serious work.* Some of these women said that the spa philosophy and practice were subtly deceptive—spa activities were basically *serious work* under the guise of *playful leisure,* which perhaps some of us feel with regard to sports activities.

So you figure you have some time to kill and you want to do something nice for yourself and you can only buy so many dresses and go out to so many fancy lunches. So you figure you will come here and relax and take a sauna. But then you get here and boy do they work you! And you find bulges you never knew you had, so you better get rid of them. All of a sudden, you realize all the bad parts on your body and you do the exercises until your muscles ache and you can't move. Then you set up an exercise routine for yourself and you figure you're cheating yourself if you don't work hard here. I thought I'd come here to plop in the pool sometimes. But it is not just fun and relaxing—I figure I have got to improve my body and I am working myself to the bone. It is amazing how hard everybody works here—almost as if they're going to get paid for doing their exercises.

Some spa members stressed that in their first few moments at the spa they had to recuperate and rest from their hectic hard work which preceded their spa attendance. "First when I came here, I let out a big sigh to calm down, decompress, and uncork—let myself go." After becoming more relaxed about one's hard work outside the spa, some said that they then became aware of the spa "as a big happy-go-lucky party where all I have to do is enjoy." For some, such a sense of playful enjoyment could only follow "working hard to turn off your mind so your head is free—you have to work hard to relax and have fun at first, and then having fun becomes more natural and you are less self-conscious."

Some women talked about coming to the spa as a *hobby*, which Greenberg has defined:

> . . . as a homeopathic reaction from the purposefulness of serious and necessary work (or acquisition) that takes the form of work (or acquisition) itself. One works at the hobby for the sake of the pleasure in work, and is able to take pleasure in it because its end is not serious or necessary enough to subject its means to the rule of efficiency (though one can make a hobby of efficiency too). The hobby asserts the value of one's time and energy in terms of immediate rather than ultimate satisfactions, and relates the end of work directly to the particular person who performs it. (Greenberg, 1958, p. 41)

Indeed, many women *worked hard at their playful hobby* of spa activities, so showing the *fusion* of *work* and *play*.

Such a *fusion* of *work* and *play* also has been suggested by Wolfenstein who has stressed that fun is obligatory for many contemporary Americans. Some women, indeed, were inclined to feel ashamed if they did not have enough fun in the spas, while a few said that they felt guilty for having too much fun. Women talked about achieving much as well as letting go and "having a ball" in the spas. Some who *worked hard* in the spas said that they did *regret not having fun*—they wondered what was wrong with them if they did not enjoy their spa experiences the way that others did. Many stated that they wanted to do well and also have a good time in the spa. (Wolfenstein, 1958, pp. 86–96)

The spa might start out as a *playful* activity for some, but ended up as very *hard work*, as suggested by Gross in more general terms.

> . . . play itself—the game—becomes a dead-serious activity dedicated to goals outside itself and therefore instrumental and no longer pursued for the sheer joy of it. (Gross, 1963, p. 43)

In the spa, *playfulness* could turn into a kind of *serious* reality, as Goffman has described downkeying, or *playfulness* could turn into even more intensive and extensive *playfulness*, as Goffman has described upkeying. (Goffman, 1974, pp. 359–68) As spa members grew more *serious* or more *playful* in concentrating on their sociable activities, they sometimes displayed role distance from their specific roles as spa-exercisers. (Goffman, 1961, pp. 106-10) They merely carried out the motions of their required exercises as they exchanged multiple conversations of verbal and nonverbal gestures with others.

Kate and Linda talked about their perceptions of the ambivalence of *serious work* and *playful leisure* in the spa, with some summaries of their perceptions of their husbands' attitudes toward the women coming to the spa.

Kate: It is subtle here, because you do have fun and feel so good about how strong you are getting and how fast you can move your body and you are sweating and it is a real high of exhilaration. You forget that you are working real hard. Nobody pushes you to lose inches or weight. It is fun and a great sense of mastering something. The achieving something good for your body is fun, yet you do feel the pressures to change your body.

Linda: My husband asks me so how was the country club today and he feels so sorry for me because I must be so tired from my hard day at the spa and he laughs. Naturally he thinks his day is harder. It is true that the sauna and whirlpool are very relaxing and you practically go to sleep. And you do relax gossiping. But I tell him that he shouldn't make fun of me—the exercises are hard work and it is real tough to stay on my diet. I am stiff and my muscles ache. And it is not easy for me to pass up the lemon meringue pie that I baked. My husband says that he can't feel sorry for me going to the spa—I don't know what work really is.

Kate: Men are that way. My Harry wants me to lose but why do I have to come here and make such a major production out of losing, why not just shut my mouth. He says that I am lucky to have the free time to make a big deal out of getting into shape. He thinks it is a big joke and fun and games for me to come here. The truth is that I really don't have the leisure time to come here but I knock myself out cleaning on Mondays and Thursdays so I can have the time to come here, and I can work hard on myself here and not just work like an employee for all the members of my family. I am entitled to the few laughs with others here—we are all in the same boat. It is no picnic for me to use such self-control. I like to laugh at those clowns here who have a ball when they fall all over each other. I am serious about getting rid of my bulges, but here I can laugh at my fat too and realize it's not the worst thing in the world. So I am playful and serious about myself here.

The intermingling and ambivalent juxtaposition of *playfulness* and *seriousness* was clear in some women's views of the spa as a kind of therapy. Such suggestive data lead to an interesting question for other research settings: are various kinds of therapies *serious work* and/or *playful leisure* experiences? Many women agreed with the following connotation of the spa as therapy: "Therapy here is that you exercise hard, get a lot of anger and hate out, and feel relaxed and relieved, especially when you talk out your troubles with buddies, and then horse around with them." Some stressed that the therapy aspect was "the letting loose and having fun and getting all of your tensions out." Others stated that the therapy component was basically "the talking out of your troubles with others and your helping them with theirs"—so emphasizing a serious connotation of therapy. Many said that after they got their serious troubles out of the way by airing them, then they could forget about them, and "just let loose and have a lot of laughs here." The spa was a place of tension management, with the cathartic and restorative functions of leisure being preeminent. (Gross, 1963, pp. 41–52) One woman stated:

> It is therapy here because you let all your feelings hang out and get rid of your anger. It is fun and painless to do—to let it out. You sweat out all your bottled up tensions and you empty your mind and feel calm and soothed. It is a cheap therapy—you feel so rested just like you had a good night's sleep. You give out a catharsis through your body sweating and moving and through honest words with others. You can tell the people here anything that bothers you, they are all so helpful and friendly. You get everything out of your mind and body and you can be at peace for the rest of the day. The therapy here is sometimes like a tranquilizer. You are dulled and tired out here so you get less hepped up and less intense about your pressures. You use up so much energy here that all you can do is drop off to sleep when you go home. The therapy for me sometimes is to make me passive and to calm me down and it is healthier and cheaper as a pacifier than those drugs on the market.

The spa as a tranquilizer which pacified some seemed to have *serious* and *playful* consequences.

CONCLUSIONS

In many historical and cultural settings, the idea of a spa has often connoted a fashionable place for the upper classes which combines health treatment, luxury, and a mingling of various members of "high society." The intermingling of faith and healing in some spas has shown the mixtures of religion and medicine in the social institution of the spa. Modernity has broken up the leisure class, captured its fragments, and distributed them to everybody. Health spas serve as an example of the spread of a leisure activity from the mark of status of an entire class to becoming a universal experience. Health spas in contemporary America represent a secularization, commercialization, and democratization of body culture. The detailed care of one's body, once the privilege and part of the life styles of primarily the privileged classes indulged in during prolonged periods of spa sojourns, has become a way of life accessible to many people in contemporary America. At fairly low costs, Americans of all social classes can work on their physical fitness in spas for small periods of time, as part of their everyday life styles.

We studied women who attended one spa in particular which has been democratized into an exercise spot. This spa maintained and perpetuated beauty and health values for contemporary women which are preached by the *status quo* cosmetic, clothing, advertising, and mass media industries, as well as by many medical doctors, physical scientists, and workers in the general area of physical fitness.

We observed in particular four types of spa members. *Serious loners* were concerned with the quality and quantity of their own efforts and achievements in the spa. Putting time into concentrating on and improving themselves, they did not want to be distracted by others. *Serious withs,* often comparing themselves with others, were quite concerned about the successes and failures of their bodily shapes and sizes. They reciprocally spoke and listened with each other as they shared many feelings and thoughts about their bodies. The *playful loners* delighted in the sensuality of their bodies, openly enjoying their narcissistic self-caressing and self-pampering. They said that they liked to be selfish and lazy in the spa, which was a soothing diversion from their daily routines. The *playful withs* talked about having fun together in the spa, where they enjoyed gossiping and physically horseplaying with each other. Some were relaxed and light-hearted as they chatted; others let off steam and released tensions in their conversations. Some participants separated while some intermingled the processes of *playfulness* and *seriousness* in the spa.

Spa patrons often struggled with negative and positive body and self images, based upon their sizes and shapes, in a similar manner to group dieters. Many of us feel pressures to try to conform to certain body images. Many of us are as preoccupied with exercise and eating as were some spa participants. In their intensive bodily experiences, spa patrons accentuated quite openly many of our wishes and fears, our positive and negative feelings about our bodies and other parts of our life styles. Some spa patrons wanted to cope with their bodies in a supportive group atmosphere, as do many of us. Others wanted to be by themselves in their exercise workouts, as do many of us. Many of us do seek to be body beautifuls.

SUGGESTED TOPICS FOR
THOUGHT AND PROJECTS

Health Spas

1. Discuss the health spa as a playful leisure as distinct from a serious work activity.
2. Why do health spa participants as well as others engaging in various physical activities or sports have mixed views about being alone or together with others in the scene?
3. Contrast sociability for its own sake with working toward formal specific goals in the health spa and in one other recreational setting.
4. Investigate the differences and similarities between leisure activities reserved for the upper classes and the democratization of leisure activities for the masses. Does the contemporary spa as exercise gym have

anything in common with the spa as total resort in present or past days?

5. In what ways would this study be different if the researchers had conducted a survey of spa participants' attitudes and feelings, instead of observing and conducting open-ended interviews with participants? How did the fact that the researchers were active spa participants themselves affect their research?

6. Why would some people be inclined to go to a health spa instead of a dieting group for weight control? Investigate the differences between samples of people who would or do use health spas or dieting groups as a means of weight control with samples of people who would not or do not use such means.

7. Conduct interviews with people so as to investigate how their bodily careers, as in health spas, are related or are not so related to other parts of their life styles.

8. Investigate how body shape and/or size affects one particular arena of social interaction.

NOTES

[1]For some historical accounts of the development of American spas, see: Leslie Dorsey and Janice Devine, *Fare Thee Well: A Backward Look at Two Centuries of Historic American Hostelries, Fashionable Spas and Seaside Resorts* (New York: Crown Publishers, 1964), esp. pp. 237–321. See also:

"The First Resorts: A Roundup of Vacationlands Preferred by World Leaders," in section, "Spring and the Traveler," *Saturday Review* 52, no. 10 (March 1969): 39–111.

Josephine Robertson, "One Hundred Years of Hot Springs," *American Forests* 82, no. 7 (July 1976): 42–45.

Kathryn Kish Sklar, "All Hail to Pure Cold Water!" *American Heritage* 26, no. 1 (December 1974): 64–69; 100–1.

James Wamsley, "Deserted Spas," *Holiday* 56, no. 3 (April-May 1975): 10–11, 18.

"Where to Take the Waters," *Time Special 1776 Issue* 105, no. 20 (May 1975): 72–73.

[2]Ideas about play and seriousness used in this chapter come from:
Johan Huizinga, *Homo Ludens: A Study of the Play-Element in Culture* (Boston: Beacon Press Paperback edition, 1955).

Kurt Riezler, "Play and Seriousness," *Journal of Philosophy* 38, no. 19 (September 1941): 505–17.

[3]The rest of this section has been informed by my reading of: Marie Killilea, "Mutual Help Organizations: Interpretations in the Literature," *Support Systems and Mutual Help: Multidisciplinary Explorations* ed. Gerald Caplan and Marie Killilea (New York: Grune and Stratton, Inc., 1976), pp. 37–93.

[4]For ideas about laziness and idleness, see: Paul Lafargue, "The Right to Be Lazy," in *Mass Leisure,* ed. Eric Larrabee and Rolf Meyersohn (Glencoe, Illinois: The Free Press, 1958), pp. 105–18; and Bertrand Russell, "In Praise of Idleness," in *Mass Leisure,* pp. 96–105.

[5]For some basic statements about sociability for its own sake, see: Georg Simmel, *The Sociology of Georg Simmel,* trans. and ed. Kurt H. Wolff (New York: The Free Press of Glencoe, Paperback Edition, 1964), pp. 40–57; and David Riesman, Robert J. Potter, and Jeanne Watson, "Sociability, Permissiveness and Equality: A Preliminary Formulation," *Psychiatry* 23, no. 4 (November 1966): 323–40.

Singles Bars 4

with Diane Fishel

INTRODUCTION

Historically and cross-culturally, from the days of ancient Greece and Rome, public drinking houses or taverns have involved commercial group drinking of alcoholic beverages where the ability to buy a drink is available to all as opposed to the bars of private clubs. (Clinard, 1968, p. 402) Taverns in colonial America served as coach stations, places of lodging, schools, courthouses, public meeting houses, post offices, job markets, social clubs, boards of trade, and newspapers. As a result of the Industrial Revolution, thousands of migrants, particularly single men, began to work in factories. The saloon became common in urban areas. The saloon was characterized by strictly *male patronage,* drinking at an elaborate bar with free meals, and a special "family entrance." Saloons helped to relieve the poverty, loneliness, and monotony of city life. Saloons often were workingmen's clubs where men spent many leisure hours. Some were centers of certain kinds of deviant behavior, as drunkenness, gambling, and prostitution. (Clinard, 1974, p. 462)

After the enactment of the Eighteenth Amendment in the United States, the saloon was replaced by the illicit "speakeasy" which had a select clientele, often adulterated alcoholic beverages, and an urban sophisticated setting. After the repeal of Prohibition, the modern tavern appeared. (Clinard, 1968, p. 404) There are now over 200,000 bars and taverns in the United States. (Clinard, 1974, p. 461) *Convenience bars* are adjuncts to daily rounds of activity which are nearby places where people are going to or coming from. In *night spots,* a production or programmed course of activity is provided by performers for audiences. The *marketplace bar* is a center of exchange for various goods and services, especially sex. *Home territory bars* are regarded and used as if they were not public places at all, but rather as though they were the private retreat for some special group. (Cavan, 1966, pp. 143–233)

Studies have found women to be more tolerant of public drinking establishments than men, and that men patronize public drinking establishments more frequently than women. Tavern patrons are more favorably disposed toward taverns than nonpatrons. Although tavern patrons are drawn from all occupational groups, family income, and education are positively related to tavern patronage. Drinking places vary according to social class and personal characteristics of patrons. Many patrons appear to be conventional people without criminal, delinquent, or deviant backgrounds. Age is inversely related to tavern patronage. Single and divorced people go to taverns more frequently than the married or widowed. Some studies have demonstrated that over 60 percent of the men and about 40 percent of the women visit taverns or bars. (Roebuck and Frese, 1976, pp. 23–24)

Historical characterizations and legal statutes have defined all types of bars as borderline with regard to respectability and morality. (Cavan, 1966, pp. 23–45; Roebuck and Frese, 1976, p. 20) Public drinking places have provided a variety of voluntary, time-out, unserious behavior settings where typical behavioral expectations include sociability, playing, and drinking. Social reasons and not drinking *per se* are the primary interests for most patrons in public drinking establishments. (Roebuck and Frese, 1976, pp. 24–25) In these bars, conventional behavior, behavior that counts and has important consequences for real life, may be suspended temporarily for a limited amount of time and space. Time out from work, family pursuits, or one's customary life patterns means the pursuit of unserious activity in the informal setting where one can drop daily routine cares, relax, engage in new experiences with new objects, try out new selves, and take part in a variety of often heterosexual activities. (Cavan, 1966; Roebuck and Frese, 1976)

With the treatment of women on a more egalitarian basis with men than has been the case in many male-centered taverns, the connotations of "single" have changed in after-hours clubs and in singles bars. Such clubs and bars have changed the connotation of single from *exclusively male* to *nonmarried* or *not involved in an exclusive heterosexual relationship*. Singles bars emphasize cross-sex relationships, while many traditional taverns have stressed same-sex male relationships. Singles bars do continue various activities and services of public drinking places, as playful sociability, recreation, an opportunity for tension release, sexual interchanges and a "home away from home." As other drinking establishments, singles bars as limited time-space contexts often stress the immediate here and now, rather than the long-term future consequences of behavior.

The term "single" is used in reference and in contrast to the majority of people—the marrieds. Through the mid-twentieth century, one common American norm was that "normal" human beings were permanently equipped with spouses and progeny. The family was catered to as the consumer unit. (Godwin, 1973, pp. 58, 59) Singleness as a life style became connected to technological advances that led to a sexual revolution in the 1960s. Newer methods of birth control, the breakup of the family and the disenchantment with matrimony, painful experiences in bad marriages, increased mobility, and the need to develop relationships which were adaptable to mobile life styles spawned the sexual revolution. With a philosophy of casual unattached sex with interchangeable sexual partners for both men and women, the media has popularized a sexual revolution that has broken down America's Puritan heritage, making sex without love and marriage not only acceptable but desirable. (Gordon, 1976, p. 221)

In fact, there are over 47,000,000 single, separated, divorced, and widowed men and women over the age of 18 in the United States. (Stein, 1976, pp. 1-2) A more than $40 billion-a-year industry caters to these single people through singles bars, singles resorts, and singles housing complexes. (Stein, 1976, p. 8; Jacoby, 1974, pp. 41-49; Starr and Carns, 1972, pp. 43-48)

Although this singles industry continues to grow, American society has often discriminated against singles. Singles are often stereotyped as "swingers" who engage in much uncommitted sex and as "lonely losers," who have many fears and who are constantly depressed. (Stein, 1976, pp. 2-3; Adams, 1976; Johnson, 1977) Wives may resent and feel jealous of husbands' attractive single secretaries. It is more difficult for some single people to get jobs than married people, since single people are thought to be likely to up and quit a job since they do not have stable commitments. Charge accounts, bank loans, and apartment rentals are hard for some singles to get because they are viewed as unreliable and irresponsible. (Stein, 1976, pp. 25-34)

> Social psychologists are accustomed to referring to singles as 'those who fail to marry,' or as 'those who do not make positive choices.' In psychological and sociological literature, if singlehood is discussed at all, it is generally in terms of singles as being hostile toward marriage or toward persons of the opposite sex, as being homosexual; as fixating on parents; as unattractive, or as having physical or financial obstacles to finding a mate; as unwilling to assume responsibility, or afraid of involvement; as unable to do well in the dating/mating game or having unrealistic criteria for finding a mate; as perceiving marriage as a threat to a career or as being in geographical, educational, or occupational isolation. The possibility that some people might actually choose to be single because they want to be, because they feel it would contribute to their growth and well-being to remain so, is simply not believed possible. (Stein, 1976, p. 4).

Because of such discrimination and stereotypes, the singles industry had to recognize the antipathy of many single people both to publicly identifying themselves as single and lonely for companionship and to be open to congregate socially with other single people. Being single past one's early twenties has connoted the failure of being unable to attract or hold a mate. The singles industry has worked on making singlehood an acceptable and even preferable state so that single people will come out of their hiding places, not feeling angry at and sorry for themselves, and choose to spend their free time with other single people. The singles business has tried to eliminate the loneliness in singlehood—or at least to encourage people to repress their feelings of loneliness and failure behind a facade of cheerfulness. The business world recognized the commercial possibilities present in the loneliness experienced by singles for whom finding a companion for the evening was almost as challenging as finding someone with whom to share the rest of their lives. (Gordon, 1976, pp. 216–18)

Bars labeled "singles bars" were vehicles to transform singlehood from a sad, shameful affair to an "in" status. Men traditionally have been accustomed to go to bars alone and to clandestinely or openly satisfy their sexual appetites, so that male sexual swinging has been endemic to the culture. Singles bars undertook the task of socializing women into the glories of admitting to be unmarried, to be open to engage in premarital and sometimes extramarital sex, and to be on their own in the bars. Women are not made to feel "cheap" if they go to singles bars unescorted which they are made to feel in other bars. In fact, in order to court women, the bars let women in free or offered women reduced rates for drinks. Hugh Hefner's *Playboy* philosophy advertised the completeness and joys of singlehood for men, and Helen Gurley Brown's *Cosmopolitan* philosophy stressed freewheeling love and sexual activities of the independent female loner. (Gordon, 1976, pp. 218–23)

With the advent of the singles bars, male as well as female singles had a place of their own to go—being in the company of other singles made these people not alone. For these single people, marriage was not necessarily the only way to overcome being alone. The bar was a place where both single men and women could go and not feel discriminated against or made to feel sorry for themselves because they were single. The singles bar has been one of the most popular singles establishments, since it is generally the most easily and readily accessible place for most single people in terms of time and energy needed to attend, its geographical convenience, and its relatively low cost. (Irwin, 1977, pp. 32–37)

Perhaps more than many other public drinking places, the singles bars which we visited placed a premium on male-female interpersonal relationships, in both the seeking and avoiding of others. There were not clear-cut beginnings, middles, and ends of evenings for many singles bar patrons, who often did not have a definite focus or purpose in attending the bars— beyond mingling with some people. Drinking, dancing, entertainment, game-playing, and the offering of specific goods and services were often quite minimized in the singles bars. In these bars, the processing of human relationships through the dimensions of *sociability* and *alienation* was paramount, with very little emphasis on props, precise activities, and concrete goals. Most significantly, the singles bars' non-sex-segregated and egalitarian patterns of drinking and talking are a recent development in bar history.

The issue of *respectability* with regard to singles bars leads to the view of such bars as *bastard institutions* as described by Hughes. They are becoming chronic deviations from the established institutions of marriage and the family; as kinds of escapes from such legitimate channels, as protests, they may last throughout many generations. They are gaining a certain stability even though they do not have the support of open legitimacy in all circles. Some singles bars are borderline cases according to the terms of white middle-class *respectability*. (Hughes, 1971, pp. 98–99) Particularly with regard to promoting sexuality and intimacy among the unmarried, such institutions may exemplify some of Hughes' ideas:

> Some of these bastard institutions are directly against the law, or the declared moral values of society. They are in direct conflict with accepted definitions and institutional mandates. Others offer less than a fully respectable alternative, or allow one to satisfy some hidden weakness or idiosyncratic taste not provided for, and slightly frowned on, by the established distributors. Still others quite simply offer a way to get something not readily available to people of one's kind in the prevailing institutional system. They are corrections of faults in institutional definition and distribution. (Hughes, 1971, p. 99)

SINGLES BARS: MAIN THEMES

Self-absorbed singles bar participants focused on their own verbal and nonverbal communication as they calculated how they were making and managing impressions with others. They often perused themselves meticulously in order to face the pressures which they felt to please others. One concentrated on oneself so as to make carefully contrived moves with others, in initiating and in receiving such moves from others. As others approved or disapproved of one's presentation of self, one adjusted one's self image and behavior according to such interactional rewards and punishments. Such self-preoccupation encompassed individual achievement and competition with oneself and others in order to succeed in the setting.

Self-centeredness meant that one concentrated on reinforcing or changing parts of the self as a bar patron. Words, appearances, and gestures were paramount, such as introductory greetings to a new person, the use of clothing, staring, and touching. Often these people maximized sensory experiences. Sometimes feeling alone or lonely, bar participants experimented with various interpersonal communication skills to gain insights into themselves. Some enjoyed the game of playing different roles with different people; others lamented phony affectations and wished that people in the bars would be just plain, down-to-earth, genuine people.

In multiple conversations of body, eye, and speech talk, singles bar participants appeared role embraced and role distant at the same time as they related to quite a few people simultaneously. Bar attenders often experienced themselves as unembodied in their self-consciousness. Attention to one's self and one's body as external commodities often was a main and dominating involvement. In the buying and selling of the self and body in the bars, certain traits, sizes, and shapes were worth more than others, as slimness. Bar patrons searched for concrete, external signs to show that their *self-absorption* was paying off, such as in the possibility or actuality of dates or meaningful relationships. Succeeding in interpersonal relationships could not always be so easily measured, however—much to the dismay of some bar patrons.

Singles bar participants showed *conflicting and contradictory commitments* about how alone and alienated from others they wanted to be on the one hand; on the other hand, how much reciprocal sociability they wished to share with others. Sometimes, quite self-contained, they guarded their privacy. At other times, in openly sharing parts of themselves, they wanted to expose themselves quite publicly. Sometimes they wanted to be quite similar to others; at other times, they wanted to differentiate themselves as distinct and unique individuals.

Bar patrons swung pendulumlike between putting on a happy face which was a cover for their real feelings of the moment, and letting out some of their basic feelings, as fear and anger, with others. Some pretended to be attracted to others and put on a show of being quite attentive to what others were saying. Some more boldly gave off cues that they were not so attracted to others, and were about to move on to different people. They gave out mixed signals of approaching and avoiding others, of being dependent on others as well as independent from others.

Some bar participants defined the setting as playful leisure, a place to relax and let go with others. Others viewed the setting as serious hard work, with many strains and pressures to say and do the right things so as to meet and get along comfortably with others. Singles bar patrons often upheld traditional sex role stereotypes, with men taking the initiative to start and continue acquaintanceships and relationships and women answering on the receiving end to these men. Yet the bars did challenge some traditional norms of behavior in many public places—in particular, those of not looking at or touching others. Over-staring and over-touching were expected behaviors in the bars.

Singles bar participants made many attempts to *authenticate* or *validate* themselves by exemplifying and trying to prove that they were reliable, trustworthy, sincere people, who were enjoyable to be with and who had worthwhile and desirable characteristics to share with others. Getting along with others, receiving praise and compliments from others were ways of *self-validation* for bar patrons. Self-scrutiny and an intense sensitivity to the responses of others, as part of the looking-glass self, led to *self-validation*. Other-consciousness and interaction-consciousness enabled bar participants to play up to others.

Some singles bar patrons had to cope with the fact that they were stigmatized as psychologically disturbed, at the least "mixed up" or "lost," or morally or sexually loose or wild as single people. The self-help offered in the bars countered the isolation that some felt as being alone and different by being single; singles were in the majority in the bars. Singles shared common experiences and problems with each other; they gave and received mutual help and support. Some same-sex and cross-sex singles formed close-knit primary groups in the bars, in which they showed much caring for each other.[1]

Self-validation was aided by the exchange of information and guidance about technical details and practical difficulties which single people had to face with families, friends, employers, real estate agents, and banks. Bar participants *validated* themselves by taking action to meet and mingle with others as singles. Asking a desirable other or being asked by a desirable other for a date could be concrete indicators of achievement.

Singles performances in their *careers* included helping themselves as well as each other cope with and become comfortable in the status of singlehood. People in the bars faced up to the problems of being heard, understood, and cared for, difficulties common in an impersonal and anonymous society stressing secondary relationships. Singles bars as supplementary communities to other communities in which people lived and moved often were microcosms of life styles which people carried on outside the bar—especially, in emphasizing various kinds of achievement, competition, and success in heterosexual relationships. As agencies of social control, practicing resocialization strategies, the bars did teach people how to make it or not make it with a person of the opposite sex through various standardized lines and approaches.

Career performances of singles bar participants were quite expressive, concerning the self-interest and satisfaction of patrons who came with or made friends in the bars. The bars were places where people learned and relearned how to enter and reenter various singles and coupling games and procedures. *Careers* in the bars did exemplify therapeutic strategies and tactics, as catharses of feelings about oneself as single, the working through of emotions and thoughts about oneself in relation to the opposite sex, and varying degrees of resolution about one's life style as a single person.

Verbal and nonverbal patterns of interaction which we observed at the singles bars were not so unusual or exotic or unique. They were not so different from the kinds of interactions which are part and parcel of everyday life. Many processes and activities in the singles bars were merely an intensification or magnification of the ways that many of us are accustomed to feel, think, and act in white middle-class contemporary America, especially in cross-sex relationships.

SINGLES BARS: VALUES AND NORMS[2]

For most bar attenders, single implied the formal and legal status of being officially single—that is, not married, living together, engaged, pinned, or going steady. A constant, steady relationship for these people implied some attachment and "nonsingleness." A few did state that "you really are single until you are married—that contract makes the difference. The band means the end to all the others—you're not available."

Yet, the nature of what "being single" means has become open to question as a result of this study. For some bar attenders, single implied being alone or private in one's head, irrespective of social status—"what counts is whether or not you're single in your head—it doesn't matter whether you're wearing a wedding band or somebody else thinks you're attached.''

For a minority of bar attenders, singleness seemed to be viewed as a wish-fulfillment rather than as a description of their life style behavior or predominant attitudes. Some married men noted that the "steady wife" was at home, but they talked about how nice it was to have a night out "just to look around—it reminds us of the freedom of our college days." Such people seemed to yearn for singlehood and to act out their desires by attending a singles bar.

Because there was such a great range of responses regarding the quality of singleness—be it a state of mind or an actual form of behavior—it seems appropriate to use the phrase *"situational singleness"* to capture the spirit of the varying definitions of single. That is, in the context of the singles bars, in a limited space and for at least a limited period of time, many participants offered verbal and nonverbal communicational cues that they were unattached or alone for at least the moment.

Singleness in the bars for many seemed to mean an openness, even an eagerness, to change or undo one's self-definition of singleness—to become nonsingle in the formation of a relationship. Intense eye gazes at one another, whispering, stroking hair, hugs, kisses, modeling one's body while standing tall with reaching-out arms were some cues of readiness or availability to enter into a relationship with at least one other—to be "coupled" or "unsingled."

This goal to be coupled or unsingled was even shown by the nature of same-sex dyads and triads who entered the bars. People often entered with others, talked with the same or different others, and left with the same or different others. Goffman has referred to the *"withness"* aspect of singles bars.

> . . . while these [singles bars] purport to legitimate pickups . . . individuals nonetheless tend to enter in withs, often single-sexed ones, presumably as a protection against undesired or interminable overtures and being seen as seeking. (Goffman, 1972, p. 24, footnote 32)

"Single" for many bar attenders therefore seemed to connote an actual "withness" and not an "aloneness." Potential "withs" often were available in the bars, with whom one could kill some time, although not choose as a final partner. Standing alone in the room was a temporary process at most. Alone usually meant some minimal eye contact with others, not downcast or closed eyes—if not actual verbal conversation.

Processes of *self-validation* occurring in single and coupling *careers* in the bars stressed that although one acknowledged one's singleness, one was more than open to become *unsingled* and to get together with another, especially another of the opposite sex. Although alone, many bar participants were quite eager to please others so as to become part of a *with*.

Many felt themselves to be *validated* in the bars if they could move from being alone to being coupled, even if only within the limited time and space context of the bar. Sometimes a person did feel *authentic* if he/she managed to become single and uncouple oneself from a with who was judged as undesirable after a short or long encounter. The major point was that bar patrons often felt *validated* if they at least tried to *unsingle* themselves, even if particular couplings were not deemed worthwhile after a certain period of time. *Choosing* to single oneself after a coupling could be a form of *self-validation; being forced* to single oneself from a coupling because of another's choice often led to angry and hurt feelings.

Most women came into the bars with at least one other woman. Entering the bar with female friends, women said that they felt more "secure" or "safer" going to the bar with at least one other woman. They wanted the guarantee of having at least one person with whom they could talk as an assurance that they could ward off undesirable men by talking with a friend and by ignoring those with whom they did not choose to communicate. Being with another made a woman feel less like a "pickup" and gave her moral support.

Men tended to enter singles bars more often by themselves than women did. Some men went to a bar to meet up with their friends, but they did not necessarily enter with them. Some men said that they definitely preferred to go to the bars alone—they "made out" better if they did not have a friend with them. If by chance these men bumped into some friends in the bar, they would of course socialize with them. Yet they did not feel as obligated to socialize with their male friends as if they had come to the bar with these male friends.

Even when men went by themselves to the bars, they did want to be with others once they were in the bars—they did not just want to be alone. Even when men and women came to a bar with friends with whom they stayed during the evening, rather than meeting new people, they still wanted to be with someone. Both men and women wanted to be *unsingled,* even if just for the night. To *be with* seemed to be an important norm in the singles bars. Yet, even as a person *unsingled* him or herself, often he or she did not become *with* or attached to one particular person. *Situational nonsingleness* showed that many bar participants wandered around the room to many others in their eyes and minds—many held some distance and did not focus exclusively on just one other person. A bar patron was not committed totally to a particular other, but was at least partly available for a range of others. Perhaps partial attachment to *many* others minimized intense attachment to just *one* other.

This sense of wandering *multi-focusing* was clearly exemplified when person one at the bar clearly spoke and listened with person two part of the time, while the eyes of person one glanced up and down the bodies of persons three, four, five, six, etc., who stood and sat in the room.[3] Much silent eye communication occurred between two bar attenders, each of whom was located in a different section of the room, and each of whom appeared to be somewhat involved in a verbal conversation with someone nearby. That is, bar attenders constantly seemed to seek out strangers across crowded rooms; some searched constantly to become *situationally nonsingle* even for just a few seconds of eye meetings.

Through the use of focused and wandering stares with person one, jokes with person two, and patting/hugging with person three, the singles bars participants were eager to be *situationally nonsingle* in their multi-focused interactions. Many of us seek to be *situationally nonsingle* in everyday social interactions, especially at parties. Person four might be a participant as to eyes with person five in the sense of a focused stare, with a glance and a blush back as a response from person five. Yet, person four would be a nonparticipant, or a bystander, as to verbal conversation with person five, in the sense that person four might be present near person five's words, but did not exchange words with person five. (Goffman, 1966, pp. 91, 154) The bar scene exemplified varying degrees of role distance and role embracement. (Goffman, 1961, pp. 106–8)

In coupling, that is in joining eyes with bodies, some male participants in particular glanced if they did not outright stare from head to toe at breast and crotch areas of women in different sections of the room. Some women in the bars seemed to ask for such glances; they wanted to be "glancees." Such "glancees" often walked around the room, standing tall, protruding their chests, holding in stomachs, stroking their own arms or hair—they seemed to exhibit themselves on public display. In these nonverbal "sales" and "purchases" of bodies, the publicity of the body as commodity with a price to be sold or to be bargained for was stressed, true in many situations in everyday life. Sometimes out of the corner of an eye, an onlooker would spot another onlooker who looked at the same "glancee-body" as he or she did. The two onlookers sometimes smiled and chuckled as they "caught" each other in this visual communication of "sizing up" and "putting a price" on the same body. Some bar attenders talked quite explicitly about how they arrived at such a price of body detached from whole self—"big breasts make up for a fat ass" and "broad shoulders and a thin waist mean more than a little acne on his face."

In bar patrons' processes of unsingling and approaching others, bodies were viewed as commodities apart from total selves. *Self-absorbed* in their personality and bodily dimensions, individuals experienced themselves as being more or less divorced or detached from their bodies as unembodied selves. One's own body and others' bodies were pieces of objective territories to be observed, controlled, and painstakingly evaluated. (Laing, 1965, p. 69) When do we regard bodies as objective territories?

In approaches toward being with somebody, eyeing and talking about bodies as detached from selves were public gestures in singles bars. The other-consciousness of unembodied selves which Goffman has suggested as in indicator of *alienation* from interaction seemed to be a meaningful involvement obligation in the bars. (Goffman, 1967, pp. 120–24) Other-consciousness with respect to body size and shape, with gradations as to attractiveness, was a step toward unsingling in the bars. Singles bar patrons were extremely conscious of others' body proportions, specific body parts, faces, hair, makeup, clothing, smell, and sound and tone of voice. They became particularly aware of aspects of others' bodies or general appearances which were particularly attractive or unattractive; indeed, the talk about others' bodily attributes often formed the content of many conversations.

In approaching coupling in the bars, another sign of alienation from interaction which seemed to be an involvement obligation for patrons was interaction-consciousness. (Goffman, 1967, pp. 119–20) Many were very involved with the interaction having a smooth flow and going well, and there was often a plethora of positive, affirmative "yes" responses to others, as big, broad smiles, hearty laughter, and very long and rapid nods of the head so as to indicate agreement with another. When agreement with another took the form of a "no," there were many to and fro short jerky shakes of the head, along with frowns, squinted eyes, and a drawing in of the sides of the mouth. Some participants were concerned about keeping their talk with others going at a fairly fast pace, and seemed to have a ready supply of small talk subjects on hand, so as to fill the gaps of painful silences. For some, talking about anything, and even flitting from one topic to another in rapid succession (often with regard to current news events) was better than saying nothing at all. Short and long, old and new jokes, often taken from the mass media, could be convenient fill-ins for awkward pauses and silences. Sometimes the processes and flows of interaction were attended to by nonverbal gestures, as an arm around another, the lighting of another's cigarette or the fingering of another's jewelry or clothing. Many of us are quite interaction- and other-conscious in certain social situations.

Employing such interaction- and other-consciousness, bar patrons were attempting to figure out and size up where and how they stood in relation to another. For many, trying to understand how they were going over with another was much more important than really being involved in the content of conversations. It was amazing that some could keep a rational conversation going at all, since they were also so self-conscious at the same time as they were absorbed in others and in the processes of interaction. (Goffman, 1967, pp. 118–119) Yet, when one stops to think, we all have such multifaceted levels of interaction going on in many occasions of our lives, whether in formal or informal occasions. The singles bar, with its multiple kinds of simultaneous interactions, was in some ways just a heightened microcosm of what many of us do in our daily lives in taken-for-granted ways.

The *self-absorption* in the bars, and with many of us in everyday life, often took the forms of arranging oneself and one's body so as to go over well with others. Speakers and listeners in conversations in singles bars often checked to make sure that their sweaters were on straight and that their hair was in place. Such people appeared to be more preoccupied with how they looked than with what they were saying or hearing. Bar participants demonstrated meticulous concern with their bodies. Rubbing the eyes, smoothing eyebrows, scratching the skin, smoothing the hair with the hands, fingering jewelry, straightening and pulling down sweaters and pants, brushing dust and crumbs away from the body were continual gestures done unto the self while one was verbal and visual with others. First impressions did count—such seemed to be a cardinal principle in regard to one's own body and others' bodies in the bars. We got the impression that some participants were so involved with their own and others' bodies that there was little psychological time or space left for a bar participant to begin to know another fully or to begin to develop empathy with another. Paradoxically, *alienation* from intense interactions in which total selves might grope for rapport was the precise norm for interaction in some singles bars, as people unsingled themselves.[4]

We had an acquaintance who was a very thin, attractive (in contemporary American magazine cover girl terms), large-breasted woman. She often tended to say things that were scatterbrained and she had a nervous giggle. Her talk and her erratic laughter seemed quite secondary in the singles bar, as most men who talked to her were preoccupied with her chest and the way she displayed her chest by twisting and turning. Some men commented to us that they hardly heard what this woman said—or for that matter, even cared what she said. Such men seemed to prefer to look at this woman's chest than to listen to her. Therefore, men's responses to this woman seemed to be very disjointed to the onlooker, as their remarks had very little to do with what the woman might have been saying. It should be noted, nevertheless, that the woman enjoyed the preoccupation with her chest and seemed oblivious to the fact that the conversation might be disjointed. The woman was so preoccupied with her own body that she did not even realize what she was saying or what someone else was saying. She also seemed to enjoy men's preoccupation with her body. Attempts at unsingling or coupling were shown in such eye and body communication, in communication which was not distinctly verbalized.

These ideas of self-, other-, and interaction-consciousness as involvement obligations in the singles bars led us to one basic hypothesis, for which we will continue to offer supporting evidence: *many singles bar participants expressed much ambivalence about how "singled" or "unsingled," "coupled" or "uncoupled" they wanted to be—in their feelings, attitudes, and behavior.* The singles bar scene exemplified aspects of *alienation* on the one hand; on the other hand, different types of *sociability.* (Seeman, 1964, pp. 525–38; Weiss, 1971, pp. 198–205) Such *alienation* and *sociability* were clearly shown even in the names which participants gave to the bars—some called the bars "singles" bars with the expectation that one came to the bars and left as a single person, and others called the bars "dating" bars, with the expectation that one might come to the bar alone but would meet someone to be with inside and perhaps outside the bar.

Alienation and *sociability* were clearly exemplified in word-talk, body-talk, and eye-talk which occurred at the same time between participants. Bar participants frequently gave the impression of "being all over the place" in terms of whom they related to. They related to different people on different levels at the same time. "Body-talk" and "speech-talk" constantly and quickly exchanged positions as main, side, dominant, and subordinate involvements, in Goffman's terms. (Goffman, 1966, pp. 43–44)

An *alienating,* blasé attitude, with which singles bar participants acted *to* and *at* each other, not always *with* each other, often was a permitted and preferred, if not a prescribed, norm of presentation of self in some singles bars. (Simmel, 1962, pp. 151–65) With such *alienation,* singles bar patrons often held themselves at some distance from others as they stressed appearances, placing values on aspects of life according to impressions and effects made on others. Yet *sociability* was another norm for presentation of self, whereby people showed different kinds and degrees of approaches to contact or connect with others. *Sociability* often meant some expression of feelings, a sharing of experience, and a caring for another as one recognized the distinctive, valuable attributes of another.

Cavan has stressed that sociability in bars includes the expectation of *unseriousness* -people in the bar are taking time out from their regularized, hard-working, achievement-oriented routines to be playful in the here and now, in a specific time and place. During such time-out periods, the concern about future effects of immediate bar behavior and the sense of consequentiality are expected to be suspended. (Cavan, 1966, pp. 8–13) Such dimensions are part of singles bar life.

Roebuck and Frese have combined some of the basic dimensions of play and sociability in order to capture the atmosphere in many bars, including singles bars, which are:*

1. *freedom,* both in initiating and terminating interaction and in terms of the latitudes of behavior permissible
2. *equality,* in that all actors are supposed to act as if all are equal in status and thus open for encounters
3. *novelty,* the anticipation that something unusual or out of the ordinary will probably occur
4. *stepping out of the real world* into a play world where behavior is autonomous and consequential only for the here and now
5. *space and time circumscriptions,* i.e., behavior is limited in both location and duration
6. *order,* which though more problematic here than in more conventional settings, is generated by actors in their behavioral routines

*Reprinted with permission of Macmillan Publishing, Co., Inc. from *The* Rendezvous by Julian B. Roebuck and Wolfgang Frese. Copyright © 1976 by The Free Press, a Division of Macmillan Publishing Co.

7. *permanency,* which refers to the sometime anticipation of actors that their play group will endure over time
8. *secrecy,* i.e., an air of secrecy may obtain among members within such a setting demarcating their setting and their membership. (Roebuck and Frese, 1976, pp. 48–49)

Some of our data do exemplify the thrusts in Roebuck and Frese, and in Cavan, with respect to bar experiences stressing time-out periods, and here and now with consequentiality held in abeyance, and "not really counting unserious behavior" ". . . connoting an anticipated discontinuity between the immediate present and the foreseeable future." (Cavan, 1966, p. 235) Yet some singles bar patrons we observed were somewhat more serious than these descriptions suggest—at least some were "serious players" in the game of "making it" on a superficial or meaningful level with other human beings in the struggle to become unsingled or coupled. Some bar participants in our sample were taking time out from their regular daily routines to attend the bars, but some were putting much effort and hard work into putting *time in* to "score" in various human relationships. Many were not merely having fun, relaxing and enjoying themselves—they were working hard with the arts of impression management to "sell" themselves or "come across successfully" to others; others worked hard at being "bought." (Goffman, 1959, pp. 208–37) Quite a few females and some males were quite future-oriented; they talked about meeting others they could be friends with, date, or form serious relationships with in the future outside the bar settings. Many said that their immediate mixing and mingling might have future payoffs, in terms of ongoing, long-term, steady relationships in the future.

It is our belief that Cavan, and Roebuck and Frese, did not emphasize enough the multiple kinds and degrees of *alienation* which go on in bars, hand in hand with the *sociability.* Perhaps there was simply not so much *alienation* in their bar settings in the midst of lighthearted joviality. It is our impression that the approaches and the avoidances, the pushes and pulls, toward and away from such relationships of *alienation* and *sociability* captured some central dynamics of the ambivalent interactions of singles bar participants, and some of the rest of us as well.

Such approaches and avoidances via *alienation* and *sociability* have been discussed by Goffman in the framework of *"open"* occasions, ". . . where participation itself confers the right to initiate talk with anyone present and to be received in a friendly manner." (Goffman, 1972, p. 207) The strategic designs and tactics in sizing up the other occurred in the singles bars as Goffman described them:

The initiator exposes himself to rejection and to the judgment that he is undesirable, which judgment anyone who keeps his distance is allowed to avoid; the recipient exposes herself to providing personal evidence of another's desirability without obtaining the relationship that is the usual safeguard of this admission. (Goffman, 1972, p. 207)

The strategic answer is that the initiator undertakes to be tentative and discourageable enough so that if he/she is to be rejected, the rejection can come delicately as if by indirection—allowing the initiator to maintain the line that no overture has been intended. When the recipient desires to encourage an overture, he/she does so in a manner that can be viewed as mere friendliness should the need arise to fall back on that interpretation. Therefore, what might be an overture ". . . is effectively put off with what might be a declination or effectively encouraged with what might be a show of interest." (Goffman, 1972, p. 207)

It appeared that such protective covers to maintain an integrity of a *valid* self which was not threatened by actively intruding upon or passively receiving the attentions of another operated within the bar context. One showed *sociability,* but need not be defensive about becoming *alienated* from others. One could have the strength to stand alone if a particular acquaintanceship did not work out. Many singles bar participants appeared to be civilly *alienated* so as to be able to deal with semi-rejections and to be able to shrug off such negative cues as more neutral "mere" lack of interest. Civil *alienation* was one *career* pattern in the bars. (Hughes, 1958, pp. 62–67)

Singles bar interaction exemplified quiet and loud testing out of one to another to check out mutual interests in *sociability.* Eyes were longingly glancing but relatively silent. Touching and fast one-liners were more aggressive, noisier shows of interest. Eyes and words still could show a sense of tentativeness and casual friendship to ward off feelings and thoughts of nonmutual or one-sided acceptances or rejections of *sociable* overtures. Hesitations, noncommittal statements, wandering of eyes all over the room allowed for a "comfortable" feeling of *alienation* to defend against "too close for comfort" *sociability.* Goffman has spoken of the quiet and loud invitations to *sociability* which can exist in a tentative and constrained manner:

> . . . readiness on the part of an individual to engage in pairing with a particular other, this not necessarily having led to any show of interest at all—a state of checked desire sometimes called 'having eyes for.' An individual can also give the impression that he is more than ordinarily open to pairing, sometimes called 'being on the make.' (Goffman, 1972, p. 207, footnote 16)

THE SINGLES BAR SETTING

The eight singles bars which we visited in a large metropolitan area in the northeastern United States were broken down into two specific categories: neighborhood-based bars and metropolitan-based bars. We found that the three neighborhood-based bars which we attended were frequented primarily by people who lived in the immediate area, although their popularity was beginning to spread. Originally these bars attracted only people living within about a ten to 15 block radius. At one time they were

FLOOR PLAN OF A SINGLES BAR

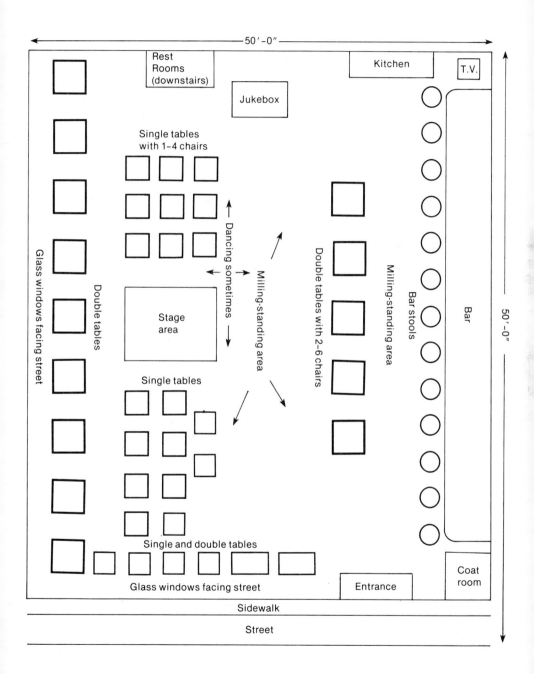

barely even heard of by people who did not live within that vicinity. Since these bars were generally not so well-known, they were not so crowded and people did not run the risk of needing to wait to get in. The people one met at these bars were likely to live nearby and so the chance of meeting someone who was "geographically undesirable" was minimized.

The atmosphere in the neighborhood-based bars was generally very relaxed and casual—participants spoke of "being down to earth" and "taking it easy" in these bars. The people who went to these bars dropped by for a couple of hours to pass some time with neighbors and friends, had a couple of drinks, and then went home for the night. The dress was very informal, often jeans and T-shirts, except for one bar which required men to wear ties and jackets on Friday and Saturday nights.

The names and locations of the five metropolitan-based bars which we visited were well-publicized right and meet other singles. The metropolitan-based bars were much larger than the neighborhood-based bars. People came from all over one large urban area to go to these bars; often they were the only singles bars which people knew about. The fact that these bars were always crowded and that one might have to wait in line to get in was not a deterrent for those people who attended these bars.

The people who went to the metropolitan-based bars liked the idea that so many people were attracted to these bars—they talked about liking "the crowded live action where there was never a dull moment." They preferred to meet a cross section of people rather than just those who lived near their residences. Some said that it was very exciting never to know what kind of person one "might be pushed into or shoved into next." Often people who went to the metropolitan-based bars said that these were the best bars to meet people in—they did not know which other singles' bars were considered "good." This evaluation was especially true for those people who had recently moved to the large city where the bars were located or who did not live in the large city. Some stated that they liked the fact that the metropolitan-based bars were high-pressured; they thought that the neighborhood-based bars were too low-keyed and too informal.

The entrance fees of some bars did not seem to deter people from going to the bars. Some of the bars had dancing. It was a matter of individual preference as to whether or not to go to a bar with dancing. Some people thought that it was easier to meet someone if you could just go over and ask her/him to dance rather than be forced to think of a clever introductory line. Some said that they just liked to dance, and they wanted to kill two birds with one stone—to be able to dance and also meet people. Others said that it was hard to meet and carry on a conversation with someone with the loud music blaring. In our study, no significant factors were found to differentiate the bars with dancing from those without dancing.

Although no significant differences were found in the times when people went to the singles bars, it was apparent to us that Wednesday and Friday nights were more popular and that the bars generally were more crowded on these nights. People in the bars accepted the fact that Wednesday and Friday nights were "the nights" to go to the bars, but they could not explain why or how this information was common knowledge. Some believed that since Wednesday was the middle of the week, it was a good night to go out and a good night to meet someone to go out with that weekend. Others said that Friday was the beginning of the weekend. Since Saturday was generally thought of as "date night," when one should already have a date and not show in public that one did not have a date, Friday was a good night to go out as a single to meet people.

Many singles bars were dimly lit, with hanging lamps over the bar and throughout the room. Often there were hanging plants scattered throughout the room. Windows often surrounded many sides of the bar from the floor to the ceiling, so one could see the street from inside the bar, and one outside the bar could see inside the bar. Often tables which were located near the bar and had a seating capacity for from two–six people as well as chairs were removed from the floor when the bar got crowded. Many bars tended to require the removal of this furniture when they got quite crowded after 8:30 or 9:00 P.M. on Wednesday and Friday nights. People stood at or near the bar area, milled around within less than 20 feet of the bar, and sometimes in between tables and on or around a stage area if there were such an area. Sometimes they glanced at a television program; sometimes they danced. The table areas in the bar, around which two–six people usually sat, took up between one-third to one-half of the public space in the singles bars. Since many more people stood in the bars than sat at the tables, one easily got the impression that most of the space in the bar was taken up by standing people. Often the tables, however, occupied more physical space in the bar than did the standing around, milling areas. The bars were quite public arenas; one had to leave the main room to go to a rest room, which was often up or down a flight of stairs.

Often there were between three–six waitresses in distinctive, brightly colored uniforms, one–three young men called busboys, two bartenders, one bouncer and one manager. Sometimes entertainers performing in the bar mingled with the patrons. One or two guitarists sometimes provided live entertainment after 9:00 P.M. for approximately 20 minutes each hour. There was jukebox music the rest of the time.

The numbers of people who came to the bars varied at different times. Some bars got as many as 150 to 225 people at peak hours. The most crowded nights were Wednesday and Friday, when people were elbow-to-elbow as they milled around in the standing areas and at the bar proper. The least crowded nights at the bar were Sunday and Monday, when there were often between 25 and 50 people present in the bars. On these "slow" nights, most people sat at the bar and at tables, although a few always remained standing. Some bar patrons told us that Tuesday and Thursday nights were nice "middle of the road" times to come to the bars in terms of crowds. On Tuesdays and Thursdays, there might be 75 to 100 people who would come to a bar during the evening, and as one woman said: "There are not so many of us then to be elbow-to-elbow, but it's not so empty that we can hear an echo across the room." Saturday nights at some bars which were quite crowded were rather distinctive times. Mainly couples attended some bars on Saturday nights. Most of the couples sat at tables, and a few couples sat at the bar. Very few couples stood and milled around in the standing areas of the bars. Occasionally singles would sit or stand close to the bar— mostly dominated by men, with just a handful of women.

Many of the bars which opened at the latest in the afternoons were virtually empty before 7:00 P.M. The singles bars did not appear to attract the after-work cocktail crowd. The time between 7:30 and 9:00 P.M. seemed to be dinner hour at the bar. There were only a few people at most at the bar proper, and between one-fourth and one-half of the tables were filled with diners. At about 9:00 to 9:30 P.M., the crowd who milled around in the bars started to come. Often this crowd made up a full house by 10:30 to 11:00 P.M. On most weeknights, many people started to leave the bars at about midnight. On Friday nights, the bars started to empty out about 1:00–1:30 A.M.

The spring and the fall were the most popular seasons for frequenting the bars; patrons said that the nice weather drew people out to come to the bars. The winter was the next most popular season, with sometimes small crowds on Friday nights, as people went skiing over the weekends. Quite a few regular bar patrons rented or owned ski lodges. A significantly smaller crowd of people frequented the bars in the summer; sometimes the bars were even quite empty on Friday nights. Many of the regular bar patrons had summer houses and took vacations in the summer, and had singles bars in summer resort areas. Sometimes Sunday nights were popular times to come to the bars in the summer, after people returned from long drives from summer houses where they spent their weekends. Sometimes people would go to the bars for dinner on Sundays, as their weekends were ending and they were getting ready for a week of work.

Often conversations did seem to take place between people sitting at tables which were next to each other, especially at times when the bars were not so crowded. However, when the table area was very crowded, people tended to talk only to one or two people at their particular table. People sitting at the bar did interact with each other and with those people standing near the bar at all times, whether there were many or few people in the bars.

Often entertainers performed in the midst of much noise. No one in the scene encouraged the crowd to be quiet, to stop what people were doing, and to pay attention to the performers. The small percentage of regular bar patrons sometimes seemed to pay a little more attention to the performers; some of the regulars became acquainted with or already knew performers. Others who seemed to be paying attention to the performers were those who did not seem to know what else to do. In order to look like they were doing something purposeful, these latter patrons would sometimes take a sudden interest in the performers, sitting at the edge of their seats, jutting their chins forward and opening their eyes wide. The music of the performers or the jukebox was sometimes moderately, sometimes minimally audible on crowded nights over all the voices, clicking glasses and dishes of those drinking and eating. Often if an intense listener was approached by someone, or if someone caught the eye of the listener, the sudden interest in the performers quickly diminished. Many bar patrons seemed to flit back and forth between talking to each other and listening to/watching the performers.

CHARACTERISTICS OF PARTICIPANTS

Sex Ratio

The eight singles bars which we visited in a large metropolitan area in the northeastern United States seemed to have a clientele ratio of 65 percent male and 35 percent female. Since many of the bars that had entrance fees dropped these fees to encourage more females to come, there was an inducement for males to come. Since females usually drank less than males, women often objected to having to pay to get into the bars, or paying for a two or three drink minimum.

One woman discussed the sex ratio as follows:

There are definitely more males than females in the singles bars. Men drink more than women and are more apt to go to a bar just to drink, to mingle or be with their friends, and maybe meet a few new females to date, but not necessarily. Females will almost never go to a bar just to drink—they go primarily to meet men, and if they're not in the mood to meet new people, they won't go at all, whereas men will.

A man described the sex ratio as follows:

There are still many women who believe in the old-fashioned traditional concept of women not belonging in bars unescorted despite the fact that singles bars are for both men and women and encourage both to come freely. Men will go to a singles bar to hang out, bullshit, and drink, whereas females won't—it's not considered nice.

Age

The age range in the singles bars was about 22 to 30 for females; 25 to 40 for males. The mean age was about 25 for females, 28 for males.

Religious, Racial, and Ethnic Background

The neighborhood-based bars were approximately 65 percent Christian and 35 percent Jewish, whereas the metropolitan-based bars were about 80 percent Jewish and about 20 percent Christian. Both types of bars were 100 percent white and about 95 percent American-born. The Christian population included quite a few Italian, Irish, and Polish Americans.

Social Background, Education, and Occupation

The overwhelming majority of the people at singles bars came from middle-class backgrounds, that is, their parents' incomes were classified as middle-class. Exactly what those incomes were were not identified to us. However, the 150 people we spoke to at some length referred to themselves as being from middle-class backgrounds. While some of them probably were upper-middle-class, they all tended to say middle- rather than upper-middle. (We did not delve into what the bar participants' parents did for a living, so this evidence is somewhat inconclusive and/or based on the interviewees' self-perceptions.)

Most of the men had completed college and slightly less than half had had some graduate school training in either business, education, psychology, sociology, or social work, or were taking graduate courses at night. Most of the men had white collar jobs; there were few professionals (medical doctors, lawyers, or accountants).

Not only were there few professionals in the singles bars, but bar participants apparently did not even anticipate meeting such professionals there. The following conversation exemplified this idea:

She: What do you do for a living?

He: I'm studying to be a rabbi.

She: Don't put me on. What do you really do?

He: Honestly, I'm studying to be a rabbi.

She: I don't believe you.

He: O.K., if you really want to know, I'm a cab driver.

She: Wow, that's great. Whats it like to drive a cab in a city like this?

We knew the man and he was, in fact, studying to be a rabbi. The interesting thing was that the girl rejected the idea that the man was studying to be a rabbi and openly accepted the man when he said that he was a cab driver. Interesting phenomenon. The same kind of remark could and would have been made had the guy said that he was studying to be a doctor, since people rarely expected to meet medical students in the singles bar either. People in singles bars would accept certain identifications of self and reject others. Although a cab driver essentially is thought of as a bum (especially young cab drivers) by some people in American society, and a rabbi is often thought of as an upstanding professional, in the singles bar, the cab driver was more positively evaluated than was the rabbi.

Slightly more than half of the women had completed college; most had at least attended college for a little while. Many of the women were teachers, secretaries, or administrative assistants. We also observed quite a few stewardesses.

The consensus among the women was that they wanted to meet men who had at least a college degree or better. The women said that the first thing that they wanted to find out when they met a man was where he went to college and what his occupation was. The women seemed concerned about finding out facts that might affect their future. They seemed to have very definite future goals in mind. One woman stated:

> I want to meet a man with a good education who has a steady, stable job, and is financially secure. These things are very important to me when I think about getting involved with someone. It's tough enough to meet someone who wants to settle down. If he's having trouble making ends meet or changes jobs frequently for whatever reasons, you haven't got a prayer in getting him to stop running and start a family.

The men, on the other hand, wanted to know if the woman lived alone and where she lived. They generally wanted a woman to have at least some college, but a college education for a women was not terribly important to most of the men. A man said:

> If I meet a girl and I'm attracted to her so long as she's got a good head on her shoulders, a little common sense, then I don't really care if she went to college or not. A college degree really isn't a panacea you know. I want to know will I have to travel very far to see her, am I going to have to hassle with roommates or parents—that's what I want to know for the moment. I'll worry about the other things later when I know her better, like how educated she is—first I want to see if we even like each other and want to start a relationship.

Here we began to see certain conflicts emerging in terms of the ideologies of the men and women. Many women were much more future-oriented than men and quite obviously interested in finding a man whom they would want to date steadily and perhaps marry. They did not seem to want a fly-by-night relationship or a passing affair. Most men, on the other hand, were living strictly in the present. They were concerned only about now, today, not tomorrow. According to many men, what would happen tomorrow would be dealt with tomorrow. Many women were going to deal with tomorrow almost before they dealt with today.

Marital Status

At the start of this study, it was originally and incorrectly assumed that anyone who was in a singles bar was single in formal status. This assumption was made for two reasons: (1) Anyone in a singles bar was playing out aspects of a single role, conforming to the norms and mores of the singles bar while he or she was there. (2) Since the ones who were married played their roles as singles so effectively, giving off cues of singleness and no signs of being attached outside the bar, it was almost impossible to tell for sure if they were in fact married.

Most married people in the singles bars which we observed were very careful not to make statements that might give them away as married. They were vague about where they lived or what their activities were outside the bar. A common topic of conversation in the singles bar was what people did in the summer, where they went. Did they have homes in certain singles communities? A person who was married would generally try to stay clear of these conversations. Yet, such conversations were no sure fire way to tell if someone were married or not, as there were many singles who did not have summer homes, who did not make specific summer plans, and who played it by ear in the summer months. A few married people did wear their wedding bands, but most did not—they either never wore bands or they took them off while they were in the bars. We were generally forced to accept all in the singles bars as single. We did find 12 people who admitted that they were married, ten men and two women. We suspected that others were married, by somewhat rather undefinable qualities, sometimes connected with a rather mysterious withholding of various kinds of information about everyday life styles.

Most of the women we spoke with agreed that they were aware of the fact that many married men were in singles bars, trying to "put one over on us." One woman said:

> I can't know for sure at first if a man I meet is in fact married. I may have a feeling that he is though. Call it female intuition. Until he asks me out and I find myself going out at odd hours during the week, either right from work or for lunch, never on a weekend. I can't know for certain. If I have a strong suspicion, I may mention it but they generally deny it and in such a way to make me feel foolish and then I don't know whether I was right or wrong. So I just wait and see—it's a chance you have to take coming to the bars.

Some men and women admitted to having been married before. Most of the time, however, both men and women (but mostly the men) were skeptical about admitting former marriages. They would hesitate and look taken back when we asked them about having been married. We took such reactions to mean that they had been married before and we wanted to find out why they reacted in this manner. Many of them said that they were bothered by preconceived notions that they felt their never-married peers had about divorced people being unstable or poor risks for future involvements. They were quite anxious about such stereotyping and told us that they almost never admitted to someone whom they just met that they had been married before. Men stated:

> Even if I'm asked right out I may try to get around it and change the subject. Sometimes it works. Often my being evasive is taken to mean I am trying to hide something. It depends on how astute the girl is. I don't feel it is necessary to tell this to somebody right away. It is a personal thing with me and I don't always want somebody to know about my past experiences so soon.

> It's not that I care if a girl knows I'm divorced but I don't like the idea of being thought of as emotionally unstable or a poor risk just because I had a bad experience and made a mistake in my life. I don't want to get involved again right now but the divorce has nothing to do with that. I have my reasons. I am a stable, together person and I don't want people to start questioning me about

my past history and making rash judgments when they don't even know me or the circumstances.

Some men who said that they did not care if women knew if they were divorced because they really did not want to get involved again, in fact, did care a lot. In fact, they did want to get involved again, involved at least on some level. Such men liked to feel that they were just as eligible for a mate as anyone else, and they resented being written off as unstable.

Some women who were divorced and had no children stated that they felt fine about telling men that they had been married—"since nobody is supposed to be a virgin anymore, some men are turned on to divorcees because we've been ripened by experience." "Some men think we are less naive and know the score more having knocked around than women who have never been married." Some women who said that they did not tell men that they were divorced did so because they did want to get involved again—and they were afraid that men would shy away from a divorced woman with a child.

Many women who had never been married were not so opposed to meeting or getting involved with a divorced man, even if he had a child. "Usually the mothers take care of their kids, and it is good for my maternal instincts to take care of these kids once in a while." The men who were never married said that they were not against dating a divorcee without any children, but were a little hesitant to get involved with one who had children. "It is an extra burden to worry about somebody else's kid and even to lay out money on the kid when you're not sure how much you like the girl—it's too complicated."

SOCIAL MOTIVATIONS FOR GOING TO SINGLES BARS

The following descriptions of social motivations for going to singles bars are listed in the order in which they were most frequently cited to us. They progress from the most often cited to the least often cited. It should be kept in mind, however, that these categories are not mutually exclusive. There are numerous instances where the categories overlap in live experiences, but for clarity and analytical purposes, it was necessary for us to separate the categories from each other.

Companionship: From Self-Estrangement to Any Form of Sociability

Bar participants had a strong need and desire for *companionship.* They were *self-estranged* and unable to find self-rewarding activities in which to engage themselves. Just being at the singles bar helped to overcome this *estrangement* through one of the forms of *sociability* available to him or her there. One was never alone in a singles bar. Just walking inside the door was a self-rewarding experience for one who sought *companionship* through any form of *sociability*.

Some bar participants felt quite *self-estranged* in the midst of other bodies. They could act *sociably,* but they felt *alienated.* Indeed, some were confused and ambivalent about how *alienated* and how *sociable* they felt—they sometimes attempted to deny one or the other response. Some bar attenders seemed to feel that *alienation* was even necessary in the bar in order to attain the goal of *companionship. Self-estrangement* was mentioned as a prerequisite to *companionship* by many participants and so seemed to be an acceptable form of *alienation* in the bar setting. This kind of *alienation* was shown in a rather insecure sense of other-direction, in the sense of attaching paramount importance to the effect one had on others (Riesman, Glazer and Denney, 1950)

Women in particular were concerned with the importance of clothes as a significant presentation of themselves.

> You are really dressing to make a killing—it is calculated, and it is all in the image. You have got to keep up with the fashions so they won't call you passé. I really wowed the last guy with my new platform shoes—I had them before almost anyone else did.

We found that women were more concerned with their overall appearance, clothing styles, hairdo's, etc., than the men were. Many women said that they went home from work before going out to the bars to do a "whole revamping": often, they would take a bath, wash their hair, put on fresh makeup and go through three changes of outfits before they went out to the bars. Women said that if they did not actually go home from work to change their clothes, they at least washed and freshened up their makeup before going to the bars—"primping for us counts more than for the guys—they don't need to worry about their looks so much." Women often said that they would bring a change of clothes to work if they anticipated going out to a bar on a particular evening. One woman said:

> Women here have got to look with-it and still stand out from the crowd—we have to be distinctive, but still go by the current fashions—how we first go over with a guy is what really counts. They care about what we look like, not what we do for a living.

Many men said that they changed their clothes after work before going to singles bars only because they did not want to go to the bars in a business suit, and they were merely changing into something more comfortable. Some men said that women could go to work dressed more casually than men could. Some men mentioned that they might go home and shower after work before going to a bar but mainly because they were hot and smelly from working all day—"to be clean, not to get dressed up for a bar." Men added that if they did not have time to go home after work to change their clothes, that it was O.K. for them to go to the bars dressed as they were at work.

Women were much more *self-absorbed* in their bodily appearances and perhaps were much vainer than were men at singles bars, quite true in other aspects of everyday life as well. Women often talked about "making a super first impression." The men felt that they would be or that they should be accepted as they were. Men often did say that they did care if a woman showed a lot of concern about the way she looked—"I like a girl to be all done up but if she has on jeans, she better at least be neat and well-scrubbed." Some men added that appearance and clothing were not so important for men. A number of women did comment of the fact that men seemed sloppily dressed, and they wished that the men would wear something beside jeans and T-shirts. "They should at least wear a nice pair of slacks and a turtleneck sweater—they look so much better that way."

Such other-direction, often based on *self-absorption,* beside being shown in attitudes about clothing, was also exemplified in the handling of one's body nonverbally. *Body-Comparers* would stare or glance at a particular body area of someone else of the same sex. Breasts, crotches, hips, rear ends, and legs often were perused. Then the *Comparer* would look over this same body area of his or her own body. Slight smiles or frowns resulted from such comparisons. *Body-Smoothers* rubbed their cheeks down to attain that "sunken-in-cheek look," pulled down sweaters to get rid of excess clothing bulges, and tucked in shirts and blouses to make the body tight and firm—to make body parts stand out.

Some "overweight" participants (more than 20 pounds to lose according to some life insurance charts—indeed, only a few singles bar participants appeared to be as much as 25 or more pounds overweight) were *Snugglers,* who wore loose-fitting garments, wrapped sweaters around them, "shivered," hugging themselves or their arms in such a way as to "cover" bulges—whether by crossing the arms in front of the stomach, or holding arms at one's sides to minimize hip size. Thin participants tried to look even thinner by sucking in their stomachs so that their stomachs would appear even flatter than they already were. Some large-breasted women tried to look even chestier by taking occasional deep breaths and holding their breath for a while to accentuate their breasts. The body norm in the bars was to appear as slim as possible, while mildly or strongly acknowledging the development of the sexual organs.[5]

While seeking for *companionship* in bodily presentations of selves, bar participants stated that *companionship* connoted all kinds of *sociability.* (Weiss, 1971, pp. 198–205)

> *Intimacy.* I'm here because I'd really like to find a man to love, to get married, and settle down. I am really ready to give and receive feeling, and I'm not looking for the flaky types. I'm lonely just being with any old guy. I want trust and understanding. (Woman)
>
> *Social Integration.* I'm just looking for a gal of similar interests—a buddy. Sure, we both might enjoy sex—it's fun. But I like sports and all kinds of music. It's fun to do things with somebody who likes your thing too; she's not

just putting up with it. It's a long life and you might as well be with somebody who likes to kill time like you do. (Man)

Opportunity for Nurturant Behavior. I really feel that I want a kid and I sure want the right father for it. I know I need a father sometimes too, so I want a strong man who knows who he is. He can help me be a better mother. But I want him to take care of me and I want to take care of him. (Woman)

Reassurance of Worth. I want a gal who'll build me up, pat me on the back. She can do her own thing too, but I'm not a woman's libber. So if I have a hard day at work she'll understand—at least I know I have a good little woman who thinks I am worth something. (Man)

Assistance and Guidance. Sure, people can help each other out by getting rid of tensions in bed. But I'm looking for a guy who will help me find myself—help me figure out what I want to do with my life and maybe even lend me some money to go back to school. I can get a better perspective on finding myself by finding a guy I really like who has constructive suggestions for me. (Woman)

Whatever kind of *sociability* singles bar participants were seeking, most admitted to being lonely as sometimes many of us are. Those desiring *companionship* wanted to be with other people, preferably of the opposite sex. Some wanted temporary *companionship;* some were looking only for "the one night stand." Some sought short-term but steady *companionship.* Others were looking for somebody to date occasionally or on a long-term basis. Others wanted to begin deep, viable relationships that might lead to marriage. There was much pressure and tension in working for such *companionship* in the bars. *Alienation* and *sociability* seemed to operate hand-in-hand.

Sometimes the simultaneous demonstration of *alienation* and *sociability* was clear in discussions of the pros and cons of minimal commitments of people to each other and of casual affairs. Bar patrons stated that minimal commitments had the advantage of "giving you some good times so you don't feel lonely, but letting you be as free as a bird to do what you want with your life." Others said that such minimal commitments only allowed for superficial relationships "where you don't get to know the other person." Some said that their series of minimal commitments were frightening, "because they really leave you high and dry with nobody you can count on in a real crisis." Some bar patrons stressed that the merits of casual affairs were that "by knowing many different people in many different ways, you get to know more about what you like and don't like, sexually and emotionally." Some added that they liked the exciting variety of casual affairs where they could go to different people for different reasons—"no one person can fulfill your every need." Some said that one problem was that one person usually did not remain casual and got more serious about the relationship. A few stated that they were getting worn out having many casual affairs, and "you're really hung up about deep intimacy with somebody if you have to have casual affairs, and you should straighten out your head by therapy, or whatever."

We both sensed that the atmosphere in most bar settings was very strained and forced as people were showing mixed feelings about casual relationships. Others as well as ourselves could feel this pressure in the moments of walking in the door. The main cause of this pressure seemed to be that many people in the singles bars were trying so hard to meet people that we as observers could sense their effort. People constantly fussed with themselves, making sure that they looked O.K. They seemed to smile all the time so that no one would think that they were bored or disinterested. They nervously lit cigarette after cigarette, and clasped their drinks for dear life. Many seemed ill at ease. Some people tried to overcome their discomfort by acting very blasé. They seemed to be asking: who needs this? They did not want anyone to think they were losers or that they really needed or wanted to meet people. Everyone was trying to impress each other. Guys fumbled for matches to light women's cigarettes so as to impress women that they had good manners and knew the right thing to do. There was a lot of competition in the singles bar, and that made people very "uptight." This kind of atmosphere is often present in everyday cocktail and social parties.

> I get very nervous before I go into a singles bar. I know I'm relatively attractive and have a good figure, but so do so many other girls there that I worry whether I'll ever be noticed in the crowd. I always try to wear something a little flashy so I'll be noticed. Sometimes I wish I had blonde hair. Blondes always stick out in a crowd. (Woman)

> I'm always on my guard in a singles bar. I watch what and how I say things, 'cause I don't want to come across as being obnoxious or stuck-up. Some guys do, you know. They try so hard not to be that way that they come across even worse than they are. All the tensions can get to you so you start to brag about how great you are and that you are a real catch. Girls get turned off by this bragging. I try hard to stay cool, but it is really hard work to come off as a low-pressured or soft-sell when you're so keyed up inside. (Man)

All this pressure tended to cause people to act very phony and put on various acts for others. They tried to overcome or even deny the pressure and tension, and they ended up putting on a show. By such shows, people could *validate* themselves in the bars.

> Everyone knows why you're here; you want to meet people. But at the same time, no one wants to seem over-anxious. You have to act very cool about it and the tougher you act the cooler people will think you are. (Man)

> I really don't need to go to the bars. I know enough people. I just happened not to be doing anything tonight, so I thought I would drop by for a few laughs. I tell people I don't need to be here. (Man).

> I do want to meet new men to go out with, but I don't want them to think I'm hard up for a date. I try not to seem too excited if a guy asks for my number or asks to take me out. I want him to think he's only one of many, even if he's not. Keeps them on their toes too. Guys can be real smart-asses especially if they think you really want them. (Woman)

Few people ever admitted to each other that they would really like to meet new people. As a matter of fact, many almost went out of their way to tell each other how "undependent" they were on the singles bar for meeting new people. They talked about where they had been on dates lately or where they and their friends went together to pass the time when they did not come to the bars. Many wanted to be sure that everyone knew that they had an abundance of dates and friends. "I don't come here too often, I'm usually pretty busy" was an often overheard comment.

Even the "regulars" (in our data, the participants who went at least once a week to a certain bar and sometimes more often) seemed to have and state justifications for being at the bars. "I come to have a few drinks with my friends—that's all." And if someone would ask, "Haven't I seen you here before?" a fumbled, nervous answer or explanation was usually given, as "I can't remember—maybe I came here for a little while with a friend, but I don't make it a custom." Many were defensive and on their guard, showing much pressure and tension. Few were "natural" in the bar. As a matter of fact, a number of people told us that they were very surprised to see how different someone they met in a singles bar was when they went out on a date with him or her.

Sometimes the regulars developed known histories as to their philosophies and styles of dealing with members of the opposite sex. These regulars became known in various friendship networks that developed within the bar or that were brought to the bar from outside settings. In particular, women warned their female friends or female newcomers to the bar about such male regulars who were known to: "make a big play for you and then dump you;" "make sexual demands on you all the time;" and "be a total long-winded bore—he never stops talking about himself." Some regular female bar patrons also had certain reputations and were pegged by males as: "going down with anybody—she's an easy make;" "leading you on and on and never producing;" and "wanting to get heavy and serious right away." Quite a few people known for their past relationships with others were known to the people in the bars. Negative flaws usually were found in such past histories, with the person considered as not a good "bet" to get together with. Occasionally people with known histories were praised and pitied because of having put up with undesirable and sometimes sadistic cross-sex relationships in their pasts.

With known and unknown pasts, many tried to be pseudo-secure in a singles bar. It was not easy to do, and while many might appear secure on the outside, they were quaking in their pants inside. Often we saw people taking a deep breath so as to relax themselves, relieve the tension a little.

The fear of being rejected or put down seemed to cause a lot of tension. No one wanted to be made to feel like a fool in public. So people seemed to be very careful about what and how they said things, and they tried to size others up beforehand to attempt to get an indication of whether or not their overtures would be accepted. Careful testing out of oneself and others was a basic part of bar patrons' *careers.*

I feel a girl out—give her a little wink or smile and see if she react back. She may not know I'm smiling at her, but I'll try that before walking over to her. I am cautious and I don't want some chick getting snooty and putting me down. Nobody enjoys being rejected with all those people watching—can bring you down. (Man)

You have to be careful about what you say and your tone of voice. The first introductory statement will make it or break it for you. But you are never home free—you have to keep watching it—guys like you to listen to them but have your ideas too. (Woman)

Many women told us that they were very uptight about guys making advances at them or suggestive statements about going to bed with them.

I don't appreciate a guy making comments about sleeping with me when he just met me. I don't think it's necessary or cute but they seem to think so. I never know what to say when a guy says things like, 'you look delicious,' and then rubs his tongue across his lips. I don't know how to deal with it—but the bar is not the time or the place to say those things. It is no compliment for a guy to make those remarks, though many guys think girls will eat it up, no pun intended.

There was much pressure in the bars to approach and avoid others almost at the same time—to be *sociable* and *alienated* almost simultaneously. The idea of jumping in and keeping one's distance was shown clearly in some greeting approaches; some bar patrons were teachers and others were learners with regard to appropriate approaches between the sexes. Very seldom was the old-fashioned method of just walking over and starting a conversation by introducing oneself used. There was very often some product exchanged, be it a physical entity such as a cigarette or a match lighting a cigarette. Public relations jokes also were exchanged, as "Did you hear the one about?" Such interchanges seemed to be very successful introductory approaches.

Some of the other introductory greetings which we heard were initiated by men to women, such as "You're kind of cute, I really can't explain it. What's your name?" "Want to sit at one of the tables and have a drink where we can talk away from this crowd?" "You look like my kind of girl—I've been trying to get over to you for the past half hour." "Do you have one of those Biblical names like Rebecca?" (In this last case, it appeared that the guy was trying tactfully to find out the woman's religion.) Affirming *traditional sex role stereotypes,* men usually initiated such questions and comments to women, searching for common rapport.

There were also the Jewish geography lines used as introductory greetings. "Don't you know so-and-so?" "Aren't you a friend of so-and-so?" If it turned out that the person did in fact know such people, the two generally continued talking along these lines for a while, trying to see how many people they knew in common. Other similar introductory greetings included, "Don't I know you from somewhere?" or "You look very familiar." We once heard a guy make very clever use of these somewhat trite introductions. The guy walked over to a girl across the bar, pointed at her for about ten seconds, and then said "Paris 1970."

One "deviant case" of an aggressive woman who came on strong to a guy stood out in our data. The woman walked over to the man and told him that she was very attracted to him and inquired as to whether he thought he could be attracted to her. She did ask the man in various ways to go to bed with her, for about ten minutes. The guy stood there with a baffled, "what's going on here" look on his face, very ill-at-ease. He occasionally glanced around the room trying to appear very removed from and disinterested in what the woman was saying. He said nothing to the woman. Finally, he turned to us, shrugged his shoulders, as if to say, "What do I do to get rid of her?" We just smiled at him. Then obviously having thought of nothing that would get him out of this situation very gracefully, he said, "Excuse me, I have to look for a friend of mine," and walked off, never turning around until he got to the other side of the bar. People around this man and woman capitalized on this occurrence and began to discuss what had just taken place. It was a good opportunity to start a conversation. The fuss made over this incident emphasized how rarely in the singles bars women took assertive sexual initiatives. Aggressive bold come-on *careers* did not work for women, in terms of attracting men. According to bar norms, women should not approach men in such a fashion, but it was a commonly accepted, everyday occurrence for men to approach women in similar ways—as is the case in many situations in everyday life.

In many of the common greetings, including the pseudo-recollections from the past, there was a taken-for-granted assumption of familiarity. One need not become familiar. One already knew the other. The basis for a relationship started in the real or fake past—one need only continue, and not initiate, the relationship. The same principle applied to the Jewish geography or the "do you know so-and-so" lines. The two people assumed that they knew each other by association indirectly with a third party. They both knew at least one person in common, and therefore they were not really strangers to each other. They had in a sense already been introduced by this commonness.

Indeed, the bar scene capitalized upon the making or renewing of acquaintances. Simmel has said:

> Under the rubric of acquaintance, one knows of the other only what he is toward the outside, either in the purely social—representative sense, or in the sense of that which he shows us. The degree of knowledge covered by 'being well acquainted with one another,' refers not to the other *per se;* not to what is essential in him, intrinsically, but only to what is significant for that aspect of him which is turned toward others and the world. (Simmel, 1964, p. 320)

When such acquaintances in the bar pretended that they have met before, they seemed to be operating within a "pretense awareness context." Glaser and Strauss have defined the *awareness context* as the ". . . total combination of what each interactant in a situation knows about the identity of the other and his own identity in the eyes of the other." (Glaser and Strauss, 1964, p. 670) Some bar acquaintances who operated within the "pretense awareness context" were fully aware that they had never met before one particular evening, but they pretended to rely upon a past introduction as a way to emphasize the continuity of the relationship. Maybe through the assumption of knowing each other already, they could "get down to business" and eliminate the nervous stammerings and gropings of the very newly acquainted. Bar patrons *validated* themselves in initiating *careers* with others by having something in common with others.

Whether greetings were carried out through such *pretense* or more *open* awareness contexts where unfamiliarity between ego and alters was assumed, introductory greetings or lines in the bars served as kinds of imitiation rites. The introductory line was a rite of separation from others who were both outside and inside the bar. In focusing on a dyad, the introductory line also might serve as a rite of preparation for an ego-alter relationship to begin. (van Gennep, 1961, pp. 15–25)

In such rites of preparation for a coupled *career,* many stressed that they did not want to initiate sexual overtures at the outset of meeting someone. Most women and men interviewed said that they did not go to the bars to score. They said that if they wanted to have a sexual relationship, they would call up someone whom they already knew. At the same time, they admitted that it was probably possible to find someone in the bar who would sleep with them that same night. Many stated that if they met someone and left with him/her from the bar and they ended up sleeping together, fine—but the end result of sleeping together was not the reason for going to the bar.

> If I want to have sex, I'll call up a girl I know. If I go to a singles bar, it's because I want to meet new people as buddies or friends. I may or may not sleep with a girl I meet that night—it doesn't make any difference to me. I don't think about it one way or the other—I don't come here for that reason. (Man)

Both men and women said that they went to singles bars to meet new people to go out with. The bars were part of a supportive social movement to help people cope with being single or alone. The women used the terms "to date" more often than the men did. The men generally used the terms "take out" or "go out with." Apparently "to date" sounded too committed as a stance to many men.

> I just want a casual, easy-come, easy-go thing—I want to go out with somebody to have a good time, share some laughs. I don't want to really date somebody. If somebody says they're dating so-and-so, they're implying that they're girl friend and boy friend and that's a heavy trip. (Man).

> Guys think that when we talk about dating, we have big ideas up our sleeves and we're going to nail them down. Dating is a hot and big deal thing—but I do use the term dating to some people, because that is what I am looking for. (Woman)

Many men said that they did not want to meet a woman to see more than occasionally. They did not actually say that there was no possibility of a more permanent relationship with a woman—but they were not looking specifically for that kind of relationship. "I want to find a girl to go out with off and on—I'm not making an effort to find the right girl, but maybe she'll come along."

Many men were not inclined to say that there was even a possibility of having anything more than just a casual relationship or an occasional date with a woman. Some said that they were "a little scared of" long-term relationships. As best as we could discern, for their *self-validation,* many men were going to play hard-to-get, no matter how much they might or might not have wanted to get caught. They did not want to let any woman know that they were ready to settle down, even if they were. The men's norms in the bars held that women should go after a man they wanted and do everything in their power to catch him.

In terms of male *careers* in the bars, a man was never supposed to let on that it was easy to catch him—that was not a part of the game. A man would finally succumb and would admit that he really liked a woman—the woman would feel very self-satisfied that she had hooked a guy who was so hard to conquer. Such a woman might have caught the ladies' man, who no one ever thought would settle down and be content with one woman. *Traditional sex role stereotypes* were actualized in the bars. The men tried to give the impression of being real run-arounds, while the women tried to get men to stop running, according to the men. Many women agreed that a main focus of their *careers* in bars was to work hard at catching a man.

> It is not cool for a guy to say he wants to settle down—that is a faggy idea. Most wouldn't even admit that to their friends or themselves. We like to give the impression of being men-about-town—we can have our pick of girls—we do not like to think of our inevitable fate of getting hooked. But let a girl work hard to catch me and I will see if the time has come for her to be Miss Right and for me to settle down. It will take one hell of a girl to stop me from running. (Man)

Many men admitted that other men in the bars did want to get married, but they did not want to admit this fact for themselves. "It is not so cool to give in to the idea you are going to get married—better to show you are an independent playboy." Men said that they did not want to get married, but stressed that many women came to the bars to find husbands.

Many women did say that they would like to meet a man and get married. Many said that they were getting tired of the bar scene. Why did the women continue to go to the bars? Women stated:

> You are not going to meet anyone sitting home watching TV. You never know what might happen and who you might meet, so like it or not, you keep going—there is always the chance that you will find the one-in-a-million guy. There aren't that many places to meet new people so you just hang in there, trying.

It is hopeless here because I want a serious thing, but I push myself. It gets to be a matter of luck and timing. You have to catch him when he is getting unsure of his playboy image—when he has decided he may be ready to settle down. That is the name of the game and it is a game of chance.

Women were *validating* themselves by at least trying to act constructively by coming to the bars to meet desirable men. They were not just waiting for men to find them.

Not only were many women bored with running around, but they added that such running made for a very lonely life after a while. Not having someone for themselves was an empty existence. Women said that while they had been very selective at one time about the type of man they wanted to marry, they had become more open-minded, and no longer insisted that a man have all the qualifications of their childhood dream man. Their singles bar *careers* had taught them that they would have to reconcile themselves to a man with some limitations.

Women stressed that if a man said that he did not want to get involved, it was a good idea to believe him. One woman stated:

Most of them don't know what they want—they want to settle down and don't want to settle down at the same time. But if a guy tells you at the outset he's not ready for settling down, you are a fool to have false hopes and to think you are the great woman who will make him change his mind. Don't ever think you are the great crusader to change a man—or you will get a broken heart. It is hard enough to get a guy who says he really likes you to stop playing around, and if he says he really doesn't want to stop playing around, move on.

Escape Boredom: from Meaninglessness, Isolation, and Powerlessness to Social Integration

Many participants sought to *Escape Boredom* by going to a singles bar. They did not like having too much free time on their hands. They did not know what to do with themselves during such time. These people seemed to assign a low reward value to something which many people cherish dearly—having time to oneself. They felt that they had few personal controls over events which took place in their lives (*powerlessness*) and little understanding of these events (*meaninglessness*). By going to the bars, these people sought to find others who were in the same situations as life styles, or others who were striving for the same objectives as they were (*social integration*). One's sense of *alienation* perhaps could be overcome by some sense of *social integration* offered at the singles bars.

Escaping boredom was the second most often cited reason for attending singles bars, with feelings of anxiety and restlessness about "how to kill time" or "what to do with all the extra time on my hands after work." Some said that when they were not sure what they felt like doing, they would attend a singles bar. People who talked about *boredom* seemed vague in their views about what they wanted from cross-sex relationships—they were unclear in their beliefs. They had hopes and wishes, but they did not expect that they, or anyone, could make satisfactory predictions about future outcomes of behavior. By going to the bars, they seemed to want to fill in some vaguely defined *meaningless* void in their lives—they were at least looking for some short-lived temporary meaning.

> Who really knows what a relationship is about? I don't know what I am looking for, because it is all so unique to two people. So I go to the bars, and who knows, I may find the perfect girl who will change the course of my life—I hope I know her when I see her. I'll go to see what's happening. If the girl is rich, maybe I won't have to work as a glorified Boy Friday any more, called a manager. But maybe I will be uptight if a woman has more money than I can make. What is love? It's all chance. But you come here and you can have some laughs and love for the night—that counts, because it makes you feel good. (Man)

Some stressed that bars inspired them to enjoy the playful pleasures of the immediate moments.

Some who wanted to *escape boredom* expressed a kind of *alienated isolation* besides *meaninglessness.* They assigned low reward value to goals and beliefs that are often highly valued in contemporary America. Some complained about "big deals" being made about people who made a lot of money or had much prestige. They were bored with the dull routines of their daily lives in which they felt very cut off from other human beings. They wanted to *escape* such *boredom* at night in the bars—and maybe find a less boring, less *alienated* life. Some were looking for relaxing leisure at the bars so as to escape the pressures of daily work.

> I now make a lot of money and so I've made it, but I am restless. You can only buy so much with money and I see it means nothing. So maybe I will find a nice girl here and we'll move to a commune in the country and get other values. The rat race is hectic and boring, and here maybe I'll find somebody who thinks the same way and we'll leave the scene. (Man)

This sense of *isolation* as a basis for *boredom* sometimes was coupled with a feeling of *powerlessness* and the wish to prove some sense of personal power in the bars.

> What I say or how I vote doesn't matter in the running of this country—it is all for the elites and the big brass on top. These guys can even buy the girls they want. But on a more personal level, even though I can't control my country at all, I can make it with a girl. I have a good gift of gab and a nice chest. If I play my cards right at the bar, I can get a girl with all the right words and touches. I can be in control with a girl, even if all I do is follow orders as a citizen and on my job be a 'yes man.' (Man)

Although some of the bar participants felt *powerless* in some parts of their lives—they felt that their behavior could not determine the outcomes which they sought—they seemed to look for a greater sense of personal power and *self-validation* in the bars. Many men, especially, wanted to escape the dullness of their daily work and talked about "making it with a girl to give me some cheer for the next dreary day of pushing buttons at work."

Many stressed that they felt *isolated* and *bored* on their jobs where they had superficial and fragmented relationships with others. In the bars, they looked for at least some kind of *social integration* of the moment, whether they were the common concerns of drinking, eating, "having some laughs," or looking at other people. The territory of the singles bar threw people together as captive performers and audiences to each other—they were in the same boat, in the same location, for a certain period of time. For some, there were similar objectives—be it in passing the time through talking about life experiences, offering information about places and times of social gatherings, or in sexual banterings. Some people arranged to fix up their friends on dates in the bars—whether with present participants in the bar or with outsiders. By alleviating *boredom* the singles bar scene often was labeled by the participants as recreation, entertainment, and fun. The bar scene was looked at as a "good time killer" and as an "enjoyable way to get out of the house."

People came to the bars looking for *sociability* as a general motive to alleviate *boredom* in their lives in general; many tried to create and enforce *sociability* so as to discount *boredom* in the scene itself.

> I try to have a few laughs here so at least I'll be less bored than at home in front of the TV. With some people, you have a naturally good time—it is jokes all the way, and time passes so fast. With other people it can be a drag, but if you keep trying to make it amusing, it isn't boring, because you are working hard. You can meet lots of people in just a single night with just a few friendly hellos—so you never are bored and have nothing to do at the bars. Even if you just look at people, there is so much to see, it is like a live museum or a live stage show with some real characters, like dressed in these tight clothes to attract attention. (Woman)

The participants expressed various reasons for *escaping boredom.* Many singles wanted some diversion from the daily humdrum of the work-a-day world. They wanted to get out of the office, go somewhere and relax, let out all the pent-up pressures and tensions of the day. Many did engage in a catharsis of various feelings and a working through of their emotions in their singles bar *careers.* Some stated that they wanted to "let loose" or "let my hair down." Some talked about "Just getting out and away from all the shit and having a few drinks for kicks." While many admitted that they could have gone to a quieter place to relax, they chose to go to a singles bar to release their tensions so that they "could kill a few birds with one stone."

> I can have a couple of drinks here to mellow me, relax, talk to my friends, and maybe meet some new people at the same time. Even though I want to take it easy after a hard day at the office, I still want to be in a place where there will be some action. It is a diversion and entertaining to come here, and you can

really let go of your cares and have an ego-trip if somebody likes you who you like too. (Man)

Some people said that they went to singles bars to break up dull, uneventful evenings.

Coming here is a good way to end the day—it is a nice change of pace. I come home from work, have dinner, watch a little TV or read the paper, and then I get bored. I want some action or I will fall asleep at 8:00 P.M. It really wakens you up and livens you up to go to the bar. (Man)

I hate to stay home all evening, even if I am on the phone all night. It is so useless to keep gossiping with the same old friends about the same things over and over again. So since I am a friendly person, I can go to the bar and meet some new people and get into some new topics of conversation and there is always the chance that some night will be my magic night to meet a dynamite guy. At least I can keep hoping for this new kind of excitement in my life by going to the bar—if I always stayed home, I would get more and more bored. (Woman)

Find One's Self: from Powerlessness and Meaninglessness to Social Integration, Opportunity for Nurturant Behavior, Reassurance of Worth and Assistance.

The third most cited reason for attending singles bars was that of *Finding Oneself.* Those who said that they wanted to *find themselves* felt *alienated* in the senses of *powerlessness* and *meaninglessness*. They sought more than just finding someone who was in a similar situation or who had similar objectives. They also wanted to find *meaning* for their lives which seemed unfulfilled and empty of purpose. They needed relationships that would increase their self-esteem and make them feel that they were competent in some role (*reassurance of worth*). They sought *assistance,* or at least the assurance that *assistance* would be available to them should they need it in any way so as to relieve their feelings of anxiety. They were searching for various signs of *self-validation*.

Some singles bar participants seemed to feel helpless—out of control about what kind of work they did and about what happened to them (passive form) or what they did (active form) to lead to the downfall of human relationships. Such a person was not sure about what he or she did right or wrong, but there was often problems in relationships with the opposite sex. Such people seemed *powerless* in controlling the outcomes of relationships: "I wanted it to work, but I had no say."

Others were not sure about what to feel or believe about forming or continuing relationships—many conflicting cues made individuals very confused as to their sense of values. Their predictions about relationships often came out wrong.

It really is a joke—you never know. I think something will be perfect and it falls flat. Or it starts dull and then it gets to be beautiful. I give up. Predictions are meaningless. I am really turned on at first and think this is it, and then I get so bored with the guy that I fall asleep when he talks. Predictions are meaningless. (Woman)

Those who felt such senses of *meaninglessness* and *powerlessness* were looking for almost anything which they could get out of relationships—they dared not go so far as to hope for or to expect *intimacy*. Indeed, *intimacy* might be too threatening for some because of its great intensity, openness, and at least its expected ready access. But sharing concerns, goals, and ideas in relationships of *social integration,* wanting to have or care for a child, to *nurture* another as if this other were a child or to be as if a child oneself in relationships offered the *opportunity for nurturant behavior.* Bar participants wanted to find and *validate* themselves through such *nuturant* behavior.

Such participants also wanted to feel competent in cross-sex relationships—they wanted to make up for their low self-esteem that was damaged or lost in other relationships. They looked for *reassurance of worth, to authenticate* themselves. *Assistance* to gain such worth by sexual attention and interest on the part of somebody of the opposite sex could be found in the singles bars. Whether it was through a sexual relationship *per se,* or through the exchange of goods and services, some singles bar participants sought specific *assistance.* A person of the opposite sex might be a sexual partner, money lender, source of occupational or housing information, or a sympathetic ear who functioned as a "lay psychiatrist," as in the case in many everyday situations. Specific *guidance* and suggestions about the directions for one's life were sought by some participants who searched to find themselves.

More often than not, these searching participants were recently divorced or separated people. Many divorced and separated men and women in the bars were married right after college in their early twenties, and now they were eager to see what they missed by getting married so young.

> I never did these things before I was married. I have to find out more about how people get into relationships before I get married again—I have to learn more about what I want and don't want by forming relationships in the bars. I missed sowing my wild oats when I was younger, because I got married too fast, and now I want to get it out of my system. I can test out different parts of myself here. You don't wallow in self-pity here and you get back into circulation. You get the whole picture of yourself by seeing how different people like different parts of you. (Man)

> It is a real learning experience here—I was very naive and inexperienced when I got married. I have to meet a lot of different men and date different types of men before I get married again. I got locked into one person so early—when I was 19—that I never let myself develop and now I feel like I am about 14 again—open for surprises and to learn everything. (Woman)

Some of the divorced and separated people in the bars told us that they were bothered by the preconceived notions which they felt many of their never-married peers had about divorced people being unstable or poor risks for future involvements. Many said that because they had been married, they felt that they were more self-aware and more involved in really *finding themselves* than their less experienced nonmarried friends. "We really are on the way to find ourselves the most, but we don't like to admit we were married here, because of the loser image of divorced people." Some said that if they were asked right out if they had been married, they would try to be evasive and change the subject. Many continued to stress that their "making a mistake" in a "bad marriage" had made them aware of what they wanted and did not want out of a relationship. Many stated that they were eager to *find themselves* in viable relationships.

Security: from Normlessness, Isolation, and Self-estrangement to Reassurance of Worth

The fourth most often cited reason for attendance at singles bars was that of *Security.* Those who sought *security* by going to the singles bars seemed to have suffered a loss of commonly-held standards and had feelings of personal inadequacy. They seemed to be confused about values—about how to define right and wrong (*normlessness*). There was a feeling of apartness from society or a low degree of commitment to popular cultural values expressed by these participants (*isolation*). These people also expressed feelings of *self-estrangement* and sought *reassurance for their worth* and recognition of their competence.

Participants often talked about how there were not definite standards or values for behavior. "You just have to meet somebody and work it all out in the individual relationship—there are no rights and wrongs." Yet, participants said that they wanted to lean on others for *security,* and that "you can't always have it your own way." "You really have got to compromise a lot of yourself and what you have been taught to make it work." The need to compromise was a lesson learned by many in their *careers* as bar patrons.

A few females talked about how they wanted somebody to "hang on to," although they felt squeamish about the "guys who seem to be involved in shady business deals." Also, "You can wind up with a hippy who's in the clouds at these bars, and your dreams of money gotta go if you think he's worth it." Many women realized that they automatically would give up the virginity-before-marriage preachings of their parents in order to find some *security* in a man.

Indeed, some bar participants seemed to see discrepancies between the end of a *secure* relationship and the means of compromises in order to reach such *security.* Such people dealt with *normlessness* on the social-psychological level in the sense that they very much expected that some socially unapproved attitudes and behaviors (illegal activities, making only a little money, "premature" sexual relationships) were required to achieve the goal of *security*.

In a somewhat different version of this *normless* form of *alienation,* some bar participants went further and seemed to feel *isolated*. They not only expected that *security* as a goal might depend upon some illegitimate means, but they assigned low reward value to some beliefs that were valued highly by many contemporary Americans. Some said that in a relationship of personal *security,* one might be living with a white collar criminal—making his money by so-called illegitimate means. Or, one might find *security* in a few or multiple sexual relationships rather than in one marriage partner. Extramarital sexuality and/or living together unmarried had elements of *security* for some bar participants who said:

> It is better to have someone who is really involved, there with you, than no one—or somebody whose mind and feelings are in another world—who is away from you. I think there is a lot of hypocrisy about marriage. The only really together relationships are the nonlegal ones. It is false sense of security to have a piece of paper. There is a real internal commitment when you don't have a piece of paper. (Man)

Another kind of *alienation* voiced by bar participants looking for *security* was that of *self-estrangement*. Some people in the bars anticipated future rewards from the attitudes and behaviors which they gave off at the bars. Bar interactions were not looked upon as rewarding in and of themselves, but for the *security* of specific payoffs. Such payoffs might come in the forms of compliments about one's body or clothing, asking for or getting asked for a date, or a sexual proposition. Such *secure* payoffs were forms of *self-validation* for bar patrons, sometimes in the form of dinner and ski weekend invitations.

Many people in the bars who were *self-estranged* exemplified their *alienation* as the degree of dependence of their attitudes and behavior upon anticipated future rewards. A woman zipped down her body suit through the "valley" in between her breasts. A man put his thumbs in his pants pockets, twisted his hips, and rocked back and forth on his heals. Such actions did not always seem to be performed for the here-and-now show, but for the sake of developing relationships which would go into the future, beyond a particular night. Also, such relationships would develop outside the context of the bar. The *self-estranged* bar attender often seemed to look forward toward time and space extensions of relationships beyond the bar of the moment. Such come-ons in anticipation of future relationships occur in many situations in everyday life.

Indeed, such "future-outside anticipators" seemed to look to prove their worth in the bar. They would become *secure* in proving their worth to another by receiving "worth points" by others. *Reassurance of worth* could come in giving lip or eye service approval to one's appearance or daily routine of life. Sexual compliments and laughter to another's jokes were other means to *reassure worth*. Often-used phrases to affirm another's worth were: "I really like you for yourself, not just what's on the outside," and "I really want to get to know you as a person with all your interests—not just this superficial chit-chat." *Careers* of some bar patrons stressed getting to know others below the surface.

Bar participants gave off and received *security* with such *reassurances of worth*. Some said that the lines were obviously "bullshit," but in the singles bar scene, the idea was to buy such lines as real, even though they might not be. "You have to put on a show that you really care, but how the hell do you know after talking to somebody for ten minutes?" "How is it possible to tell somebody you just met how much you really want to get to know them when you know absolutely nothing about them to base such a desire on?" However, such lines were bought by both men and women and did serve as concrete methods of *reassuring one's worth* in the bars, as they often do in everyday life cross-sex relationships. Participants said that in searching for *security,* their show of sincere interest in another was often a kind of contrived play-acting. "Everyone knows it is a big show and a big game here, but it makes people feel secure because you know that every night the show will go on here." The repetitious show was predictable and consistent.

Excitement: from Normlessness and Isolation to Assistance

The fifth most often cited reason for attendance at singles bars was that of *Excitement*. Those who were looking for *excitement* sought *assistance* to overcome feelings of *normlessness* and *isolation*. They wanted to know that someone would be in the bar to help them "make it" through the night or longer. The singles bar provided a service for those who sought *excitement*—they could be stimulated with and by others, through verbal and nonverbal conversations and communications.

The response of *excitement* showed that the singles bar was a mildly contracultural phenomenon. Attitudes and behavior at the bars seemed to magnify and intensify some contemporary American values, sometimes so as to distort them as caricatures; some orientations at the bars seemed to turn upside down some white middle-class norms of everyday interaction. One example of such a distortion and a turning upside down starts with what Goffman has called "civil inattention."

> What seems to be involved is that one gives to another enough visual notice to demonstrate that one appreciates that the other is present (and that one admits openly to having seen him), while at the next moment withdrawing one's attention from him so as to express that he does not constitute a target of special curiosity or design. (Goffman, 1966, pp. 131–32)

Some singles bars' participants seemed to reverse this process and practiced what might be labeled "civil overattention." That is, bodies often become targets of special curiosity, intricate body-persuals from head to toe took place quickly and frequently. Eyes stared at other eyes or bodies with almost no diversion for as long as five to 15 minutes, while mouth-conversations might be occurring with entirely different people.

Civil overattention as a means toward the goal of forming some kind of relationship with another often indicated a kind of counter-norm or even *normlessness* regarding the means to the goal of a relationship. That is, the often socially unapproved *over-stare* was viewed not only as a permitted and legitimate means to the initiation of a relationship, but as quite a preferred means. Staring seemed "civil" in the bar in the sense that it was restricted to the eyes—staring eyes often accompanied a poker face. One was noncommittal with a straight-lined mouth, yet quite involved in an *over-stare*—thus often giving off mixed cues. This *over-look* complied with the recognized social amenities of the subcultural scene of the singles bar. Singles bar participants dared to stare for as long as fifteen minutes at one person. Perhaps some of us wish that we could carry out this kind of behavior on an everyday basis, but we have been socialized into its impropriety.

Staring was a kind of game people played with each other's eyes. Staring often was used as a ploy to meet someone. People would stare at each other for approval before approaching one another. Often women would stare when they saw a man whom they wanted to meet. Rather than approaching him, a woman would stare at a man, and usually he would come over to her. Certain *traditional sex role stereotypes* became evident to us. Many women seemed to feel that men should be the initiators of relationships. A woman would show her interest in a man by staring at him, but she would not actually approach him and begin a conversation. One woman said:

> He should come over to me. I don't think it's right for a woman to go over to a man and just start to talk to him. If a guy is really interested in me, he'll come over—and maybe he sees I've been looking him over and smiling at him. A girl shouldn't appear over-anxious.

A man often would stare at a certain woman to single her out of the crowd. Then, when he finally went over to this woman, she would know that the guy wanted to meet her and not any number of other women around her. Staring often seemed to work as an initial device for meeting another as is the case in everyday life. A person really had to look someone straight in the eyes for at least a few minutes or else the person would not really know that one was staring at him or her and not someone else. Indeed, staring was a basic singles bar cue that a person wanted to initiate a relationship. Mutual staring connoted that a man and a woman wanted to start their own party—each wanted to be host/hostess and guest for the other in beginning sociable gestures.

In stressing the significance of eye contact, Simmel has said:

The union and interaction of individuals is based upon mutual glances. This is perhaps the most direct and purest reciprocity which exists anywhere. . . This mutual glance between persons, in distinction from the simple sight or observation of the other, signifies a wholly new and unique union between them. (Simmel, 1969, p. 358)

In the singles bar, *excitement* seemed to come through staring—this behavior which was not approved of in other parts of society often led to the reward of a relationship in the bar. Selves were *validated* by others staring at them.

What good is it just to stay home night after night staring at the TV? Here I may stare and get some kicks in return—whether laughs or an actual date. It is fun to stare, and you can't do such in your ordinary life.

Civil overattention pointed to the idea that the often illegitimate behavior of staring became a most legitimate means to connect to another in the bar. Bar participants disregarded the inattention norm of many social gatherings and magnified an overattention norm. As a kind of reaction formation to other public places, it was difficult to decide if civil overattention through staring was a mere magnification of one side of a continuum of interaction rituals, and thus a *subcultural* phenomenon, or a reaction strongly against culturally common interaction rituals, and so, a *contracultural* phenomenon. Interactional strong reactions as the *over-stare* stressed cultural norms as well as variations and deviations from such norms.

People who went to the singles bars expected not only to be stared at but expected to stare themselves. Bar participants were in fact on display for all to see. Staring was taken for granted. If one were not stared at in the bar, one might wonder what was wrong with one that nobody was looking at him or her. The competition and *excitement* in the bars bred staring.

Outside the bar, staring is hardly condoned as it is in the bar. Mothers will turn to their children and tell them not to stare at people who in certain ways appear physically odd. In white middle-class society, "it is not nice" to acknowledge peculiarities of a person by staring at him or her. A man who stares at a woman on the street is often called a voyeur or a lecher. The construction worker who stares at the girls passing by often is thought of as crude. The man who stares at another's wife at the country club can be labeled as a "dirty old man." People outside the bar are not public territory. No matter how strange or beautiful or ugly they may be, their intent is not to have other people stare at them. In the bar, in contrast, the intent is to give and receive stares.

What the bar participants have done was to take a phenomenon that was condemned, and thought of as not only useless, but distasteful and crass by many white middle-class people, and turned it into an acceptable means of meeting others and a symbol of *excitement*. Outside the bar, we are not supposed to stare at someone we may think of as eccentric, or one may not rightfully stare at another's wife. In the singles bar, however, everyone might be said to be eccentric in some way (at least in the wish to stand out from the crowd), and as for staring at another's wife, or husband, if such people were in the singles bar, then they were there to be stared at.

Staring in the singles bars was somewhat of a contracultural phenomenon—perhaps even the acting out of a wish fulfillment that one would like to be able to do whenever he/she wanted to and not be condemned for doing so. Outside the bar, the stare is not thought of as an innocent gesture or as a mere aesthetic commentary, but often as something that has sexual—in the sense of immoral or crude—overtones. Stares in the singles bar might have crude and lecherous overtones, but such stares were either overlooked or accepted. There was a time and place for everything, and the singles bar was the time and the place to stare—not on a public street or in a private country club. When one left the bar, in terms of polite white middle-class society, one must return to a non-staring state of being, but inside the bar, the non-staring norms could be reversed dramatically.

This problem of classifying *sub* or *contracultural* phenomena as in the example of staring existed within the stress of mutual openness in the singles bar. *Alienation* in the sense of *isolation* meant assigning low reward value to goals or beliefs which were highly valued in contemporary America, such as the privacy rights of the person. In the singles bar we saw the value of privacy of person constantly challenged. Indeed, extreme *publicness* and very permissive *tangibility rights* as part of close geographical proximity to others were part of the *excitement* of the singles bar atmosphere.

The singles bar was an example of "mutual accessibility." In an atmosphere of informality and solidarity, bar patrons recognized each other as being of the same special group. People were mutually accessible to each other in that they were in positions which were both exposed and opening. The "open regions" around the bar were physically bounded places where any two persons, acquainted or not, had the right to initiate face engagement with each other for the purpose of extending salutations. (Goffman, 1966, pp. 131–32)

The singles bar as an open region of mutual accessibility has been described clearly by Cavan in her general references to bar interaction.*

> Public drinking places are 'open regions': those who are present, acquainted or not, have the right to engage others in conversational interaction and the duty to accept the overtures of sociability proffered to them. . .
>
> The physical door through which one enters a drinking establishment is a symbolic door as well, for those who come through it declare by entering that unless they put forth evidence to the contrary, they will be open for conversation with unacquainted others for the duration of their stay. Whatever their age, sex or apparent position, their biographical blemishes or physical stigmas, all who enter are immediately vested with the status of an open person, open both in having the right to make contact with the others present and the

---

*"Bar Sociability" in *Liquor License: An Ethnography of Bar Behavior* by Sherri Cavan. Copyright 1966 by Sherri Cavan, Aldine Publishing Company. Reprinted by permission.

general obligation of being open to others who may contact them. To decline the status of being open, to demand that one remain uncontacted requires work of a particular kind, for the assumption that one will not be contacted by another without good reason is unfounded within the bar. Those who desire to avoid the overtures of others must be able to distinguish themselves from the others present, for the general rule of civil inattention is held in abeyance, and not only idle glances at other patrons but also idle glances at features and fixtures of the establishment all convey one's openness. There are no protective goods, no newspapers, letters and books to serve as an alternative form of involvement. If such props are used, they may themselves serve as grounds for initial overtures of sociability. . .

Not infrequently, what would pass for civil inattention in other settings is taken as an invitation for interaction in the bar. Thus in most cases entering patrons are either completely ignored, remaining entirely unacknowledged by those already present, or they are gazed at in such a way as to be extended an invitation to join or at least to respond to the gazer. (Cavan, 1966, pp. 49–50)

Cavan mentioned that perhaps the only way to avoid such sociability in the bars was to seat oneself away from the physical bar at a booth or table that was available for that purpose (Cavan, 1966, pp. 50–51) In the singles bars, however, such seating might or might not be a way for one to avoid contact and sociability with others. Often bar participants seated at tables would begin a conversation with those seated at the table next to them, especially as they ate as well as drank (which many did at all the bars which we visited). Many singles bar participants whom we observed went to the bars for dinner as well as to meet and mingle with others. Bar participants would frequently walk over to those seated at a table and sit down and begin a conversation.

It was almost impossible not to be an *open region* whenever one placed his/her body in the bar. It was assumed that anyone who was there was there to meet and be with other people—sitting down at a table was not thought of as an indication to the contrary. People who did not sit at the tables in the bars did so only because they were not as accessible to as many others by sitting down, not because they were totally inaccessible. Most people did stand at the physical bar because it was easier to move around and mingle, but such mingling could be done and was done from the tables too.

I don't know why those three girls standing there bothered to come here at all. Numerous guys have gone over to them, and each time they have stuck their little noses in the air at them. If they didn't want to meet anyone or they didn't want people to talk to them, then they shouldn't be here. If they want to be cold, snotty bitches, then they should go do it somewhere else. If they think they're so above all this, then why are they here? (Man)

Those two guys over there have been sitting talking to each other all night. Haven't moved once to try to meet or speak to anyone else. Wonder why they came here instead of staying home or going to a quieter place if they only wanted to talk to each other. Very unsociable. Why go to a singles bar, if that's all they wanted to do? I have tried to get their attention a few times, but to no avail. It is a real downer, and they should just go home if that's how they're going to be about it. (Woman)

We did sit down at tables or booths in the bars a few times to see if in fact we could be "closed off" in the bars. We found that we were in fact expected to be just as open sitting down as we were standing up. Some said that if people wanted just to have dinner and not talk to anyone else beside their friends, they should go to a "regular restaurant." "Bars aren't the place to go if you're not in the mood to be sociable." Those sitting at tables were considered to be open to others, especially if they were seated facing the bar. The only ones who were thought to be slightly unsociable perhaps were those who had their backs to the physical bar and, of course, such seating was not necessarily by choice. At a table, at least, someone had to sit facing away from the bar—not everyone could have the choice seats.

We overheard two girls arguing as to whose turn it was to sit facing the bar while they ate dinner. Neither one wanted to be with her back to the bar. First, they both said that they wanted to be able to see what was going on, and second, they said that they thought that they would look unsociable if their backs faced other people—they would be less attainable, but not inaccessible. A man from the bar might walk over to a woman facing him, but he was not as likely to walk over to a back when he could not see the face that went along with it. We did observe one instance where a woman with long, straight, jet black hair was sitting with her back to the bar, while her friend was facing the bar. More men walked over to see what was in front of the Polynesian-type hair than walked over to the girl whom they could see from where they were standing.

Some participants commented upon why the bar as an *open region* was so *exciting:*

> Forget privacy—at the bar, your body is not your own. You don't know who is going to touch you where next. Every touch is a surprise—not really expected. It is fun and scary to see who will handle you next—there is always someone new to turn you on in a body part that you never knew was so sensual. (Woman)

We observed that many people in the bars had a constant habit of always touching each other. (Montagu, 1972) They could not talk to one another or walk by each other without touching each other. It could be a hand on a shoulder, a pat on a head, a hand steadying a hand to light a cigarette, or a touch on many parts of the body. Touching did not just happen when it was crowded—often, touching could be avoided. There was much touching when there was plenty of room to pass without having body contact. People seemed to go out of their way to rub up against others. Often people would just move others aside with their arms on others' shoulders as they passed. Many seemed to touch quite automatically and unconsciously. There seemed to be more people touching each other in the bars than on crowded subways and busses in the height of rush hours. Our data confirmed the comic line which we heard: "A singles bar is like a massage parlor where everyone stands up."

In the bars, touching could be a simple gesture to start a conversation. "What an attractive necklace you're wearing," one man went over and said to a woman, while picking the necklace up to get a better look at it and stroking her neck as he did so. "It must have taken you years to grow your hair that long," another guy said as he ran his fingers through the hair of a woman who was standing next to him. Both comments could have been made just as easily without the physical contact. Still, the touching reinforced what the people were trying to say in initiating relationships. The touching established a greater closeness or *intimacy* than just words alone. Such approaches do occur in everyday dating situations.

Touching often was a sign of approval or a gesture of affection. "You're really nice" one man said as he patted a woman on the head. "Thanks for the drink," said one woman while caressing the man's hand as she took the drink from him. "You're really very cute," one man said, while hugging the woman very close to him. "You have strong hands," said one woman as she stroked the man's fingers. In some cases, it seemed evident that the touch had certain direct sexual connotations—through touching, people were trying to say that they really wanted to get to know each other better.

Touching also could be a pompous, "superior-to-thou" gesture. Touching could be a way of assuring oneself that one would be noticed and that one was worthy of recognition. The tall, good looking man (by contemporary American playboy "cover-boy" standards) walking across the room who pushed women past him as he came through often was saying "Watch out—I'm coming through." This man wanted to be sure that every woman noticed him. He wanted recognition for his virility and body potency.

Touching also was carried out very often for lack of words to say. Two people have just met, they have finished the necessary introductions to establish a relationship, they have made all the small talk they could think of—so one or the other touched the other one. He might put his hand on her shoulder as much to ask, what next? She might stroke his thigh, not knowing what to do with her hands, or exactly what she should say or was expected to say. Whenever there was a lull in the conversation, touching somehow seemed to fill the void until new words came out of the mouths of the two people. Often, after someone had told a joke, while laughing the participants would hug or fondle each other—they shared the enjoyable common experience of the joke which was reinforced through touching each other's bodies. Having established some credentials of having something in common, people felt that they could touch each other. Touching could fill in the voids of stutterings, hesitations, and silences to indicate a feeling of rapport which need not depend on the logical usage of words.

Touching might be meant as a direct sexual proposition. A man took a woman's hand in his, squeezed it, and motioned with his head to leave the bar. No words were said. The touchings and motions said it all.

The territory of the *public* body as an *open* region was stressed in touching as a most viable way to relate to others in the bar:

> To be in touch with others, you really have to feel their skin. If you start on the outside, then you can feel on the inside, both in terms of affection and sexual feelings. I go to a bar and touch a girl's shoulder, and I feel her tingle and quiver and that is great. We are nice to each other at the bar because we hug and kiss each other a lot, and usually we are sincere about making each other feel good by touching—it isn't phony. (Man)

Was this constant hugging and kissing in the bar a real sign of or desire for *intimacy?* Or, were such continuing public shows of touching at the singles bar a mere indication of an intense, "out of touch" *pseudo-gemeinschaft* kind of relationship, one of feigned caring? Singles bar touching showed both sincere and feigned gestures of caring for another person. At the least, some kind of momentary sensual *excitement* was available at the bars for many. The provision of the available body through the service of the touch or the contact of the eyes showed that sexual *assistance* and *guidance* were offered for and received by some in the bars. Our data have suggested that participants who were oriented to the *excitement* of touching and being touched might be looking for some very specific and limited sexual *assistance* in the scene, but they did not seem to seek deeper levels of *intimacy* or *social integration,* as such terms have been defined in this book.

Indeed, superficial social *excitement* in terms of heightened sensual *publicness.* Invasions of personal space were expected behavior. "Respecting" the privacy of a person's body territory seemed to be a sign of rejection or at least a mild insult. Small group experiments have indicated the many verbal and nonverbal defenses which a person might use in claiming his/her personal territory: in contrast, in the singles bar, many bodies appeared to be nonprivate, free regions upon which to make multiple claims. (Sommer, 1969) *Careers* in singles bars often involved touching and staring gestures of communication. Newcomers were immediately socialized into these nonverbal gestures.

Goffman has discussed how many social settings make clear the privacy rights which an individual has to his or her own sheath (skin and clothes), possessional territory (personal effects as gloves, matches, parcels, jackets, handbags), and information preserve (set of facts about oneself). (Goffman, 1972, pp. 38–39) Stares and tactile examinations of the body in the singles bars claimed that such usually private body territories were in the domain of public jurisdiction over which many participants could legitimately rule. Violations of self-territories were norms of singles bar interactions.

Indeed, superficial social *excitement* in terms of heightened sensual awareness was rampant in the singles bars.

You can eat or drink or both. You can mingle in a crowd or go off by yourself for a while. You can sit or stand and be part of it or just observe. I get lots of kicks just watching what goes on around me—the games and all the impression points. Listening to all these conversations is more fun than going to a Broadway show. You get restless and there is always a change of pace here. (Man)

The crowd did change from minute to minute. Often, the bar scene was like an ongoing open-house party. People came and went. New faces and personalities were constantly emerging. There was never a dull moment. Despite the fact that many considered the scene to be hectic, crowded, and tense, the scene was also very *exciting,* with many sights and sounds.

You never know what's going to happen next here in the bar. Never dull and you are always on edge, waiting and wondering what is just around the corner. Something is always happening. It is never quiet and peaceful. If you start to get bored, all of a sudden there is a new look or a new touch and it wakes you up from your lethargy. (Woman)

Uncertainty about the meanings of affection bred excitement in bar, as suggested by one woman, stressing her "open" approach.

I'm always excited to find out whether some sweet-talking smoothy likes me for me or because he thinks I'm an easy make. It's exciting to have all kinds of affection available to you and you can give hints about which kinds you want. There's always somebody to hold your hand, put an arm around you, kiss you, hug you, make love to you, even if it's just for the evening. They will tell you any endearments you want to hear. Choose to believe them or not—it's up to you. The atmosphere makes you on edge and excited.

CONCLUSIONS

Historically and cross-culturally, bars have been temporary and voluntary unserious behavior settings, stressing drinking and sociability, and borderline with respect to respectability. The single status in the singles bars has changed the connotation of single from exclusively male, which has been characteristic of many public drinking establishments, to nonmarried or not involved in an exclusive heterosexual relationship. Singles bars have attempted to legitimize and encourage single females' presence in the settings, without male escorts, as distinct from bars which have catered to males or heterosexual couples.

Singles bar participants expressed much ambivalence about how "singled" or "unsingled," "coupled" or "uncoupled" they wanted to be in their multi-focused word-talk, body-talk, and eye-talk. Ambivalent approaches and avoidances, pushes and pulls, toward relationships of *sociability* and *alienation* captured some central dynamics of the interactions and motivations of singles bar participants. Such orientations, which are a microcosm of many of our everyday interactions, were captured in social motivations cited by participants for going to singles bars: (1) *Companionship:* from self-estrangement to various forms of sociability; (2)

Escape boredom: from meaninglessness, isolation and powerlessness to social integration; (3) *Find one's self:* from powerlessness and meaninglessness to social integration, opportunity for nurturant behavior, reassurance of worth and assistance; (4) *Security:* from normlessness, isolation and self-estrangement to reassurance of worth; and (5) *Excitement:* from normlessness and isolation to assistance.

Men and women in the singles bars seemed to conform to traditional stereotyped sex roles. Men lit women's cigarettes, bought women drinks, offered women their bar stools. Women expected men to do these things. Often women blushed, giggled and strutted, putting their body-commodities on display. Women in the bars did act "cutesy," weak and helpless. A woman expected that a man she met would take her phone number or ask her out—if he did not, she would not ask him out. A man did not expect that a woman would call him or ask him out. When a woman in a singles bar said that she was liberated, she generally meant sexually liberated only. Many women were very traditional and they did not want to be thought of as "feminists"; they went out of their way to be sure that they were not labeled "female power" or "women's libber" types. Women enjoyed using feminine wiles to get what they wanted, as complimenting and idolizing men. Men liked these wiles.

Many men tried to be quite virile, because that was what women liked. Men did not want women to think that they were in any way effeminate. Some men deviated from traditional sex roles in the bar when it was convenient for them to do so—some did not want to bother lighting a woman's cigarette or buying a woman a drink. Or, they were in their own way mocking "women's lib." If you're so liberated, do it or buy it yourself; you can't have it both ways, they seemed to be saying. Despite the lack of "women's libbers" in the singles bars, some men seemed to feel threatened by the spirit of women's liberation.

Generally men approached women, and women did not approach men. If a woman did initiate a relationship, she usually used an "excuse" to do so—i.e., asked for a match or the time. Most singles bar patrons seemed to like sex role definitions just as they were and made no attempts to try and change them. The bar appeared to be a definite *subcultural* reflection of *traditional sex role stereotyping,* with distinctive expectations for men and women's roles.

While the singles bar accentuated some societal norms about sex roles, it deviated from some societal norms about nonverbal communication. The *over-stare* and *over-touch* were very legitimate processes in the singles bar, although they are not preferred, permitted or tolerated behaviors in much of everyday American life. Such informal and casual sensory publicness meant that invasions of personal space were the expected behaviors in the bar, contrary to many facets of contemporary American life. Ambivalent cues were given off in such nonverbal communication, expressing on the one hand, sincere, honest, genuine unaffected gestures of caring for another person; on the other hand, feigned, artificial, affected, hypocritical, and deceitful gestures, merely pretending caring for another person.

The singles bar highlighted the simultaneity of sincere and cynical orientations to others which are part of contemporary American life. We believe that the singles bar scene is an intensive microcosm of many everyday interactions between the sexes in America, even with its exaggeration of the differences between the sexes. By going to the singles bar, the opportunity to let loose inhibitions restricted by some socialization norms was provided. Certain tensions could be eliminated, if only temporarily. Don't we all wish that we could just reach out and touch someone whenever we want to and not be thought of as weird or strange? Or stare at anyone who catches our eye and not be looked upon as a voyeur who is invading someone else's privacy? Or to be able to make up stories and be as phony as we want to and get away with it—and to have people believe you, or at least go along with you temporarily? Some singles bar interactions fulfilled the wishes of many of us.

SUGGESTED TOPICS FOR THOUGHT AND PROJECTS

Singles Bars

1. How are singles bars similar to or different from some other life situations, in terms of people's sensitivity to the impressions they make on and receive from others?
2. Discuss how body talk and speech talk reinforce each other or conflict with each other in the singles bar and in other informal social occasions.
3. Discuss how alienation and sociability operate together in one sphere of interpersonal communication familiar to you. When do people prefer to be alienated from, rather than sociable with, others?
4. Discuss how the singles bar is both a reflection of mainstream white middle-class urban America as well as a subculture or contraculture.
5. How are aspects of sex roles in singles bars the same as or different from sex roles in other parts of everyday life?
6. How could one use a formal or structured interview questionnaire as a researcher in a singles bar? How can a researcher establish the validity and reliability of her/his data gathered in such a bar or a similar setting?
7. What are some implications of institutions as singles bars for changing orientations about singlehood, couples, married life or leisure time?
8. Compare the phenomena of staring or touching in two different social environments.

NOTES

[1]The rest of this section has been informed by my reading of: Marie Killilea, "Mutual Help Organizations: Interpretations in the Literature," *Support Systems and Mutual Help: Multidisciplinary Explorations,* ed. Gerald Caplan and Marie Killilea (New York: Grune and Stratton, Inc., 1976), pp. 37–93.

[2]Some of the ideas in the rest of this essay have been pointed out or discussed in our unpublished paper, "Urban Courting Patterns: Singles Bars," presented at the American Sociological Association meetings in August 1975, and in our article, "Urban Courting Patterns: Singles Bars," in *Our Sociological Eye: Personal Essays on Society and Culture,* ed. Arthur B. Shostak (Port Washington, New York: Alfred Publishing Co., Inc. 1977), pp. 8–26.

[3]I am using the term multi-focused to imply that each person carries on different types and degrees of interaction simultaneously with different people. Goffman uses the term "multifocused gathering" to apply to situations where there are more than three persons present, and so there may be more than one encounter carried on in the same situation. See: Erving Goffman, *Behavior in Public Places: Notes on the Social Organization of Gatherings* (New York: The Free Press of Glencoe, Paperback Edition, 1966), esp. p. 91.

[4]We are suggesting that certain situations as singles bars prescribe a level of alienation or distance from interaction which is quite appropriate and even desirable as a kind of involvement. One is correctly involved in such situations if one is so alienated. We, therefore, are questioning some of Goffman's view of involvement and alienation as quite opposite processes; rather, we suggest that these two processes can be simultaneous and complementary. See: Erving Goffman, "Alienation from Interaction," in *Interaction Ritual: Essays on Face-to-Face Behavior,* Erving Goffman (Garden City, New York: Doubleday & Company, Inc., Anchor Books, 1967), pp. 113–36.

[5]For some classical discussions of fashion being used as a means of equality with as well as differentiation from others, see: Georg Simmel, "Fashion," no trans., *International Quarterly* 10 (October 1904): 130–55; and William Graham Sumner, *Folkways: A Study of the Sociological Importance of Usages, Manners, Customs, Mores, and Morals* (New York: The New American Library, Inc., 1940), pp. 166–78.

For some meanings of clothing, see:

John Carl Flügel, *The Psychology of Clothes* (London: L. and V. Woolf at Hogarth Press and The Institute of Psychoanalysis, 1930).

Paul Schilder, *Image and Appearance of the Human Body* (New York: John Wiley, 1964).

Conclusions 5

The three settings of singles bars, health spas, and dieting groups exemplified a trend toward focusing inwardly upon the self in America in the 1970s, away from an extension outward into larger political and social issues of the day. The settings showed specific ways to put into practice new kinds and degrees of self-awareness. Such awareness stressed the self-interests and satisfactions of members who concentrated on self-expression. The settings applied therapeutic strategies of mental, emotional, and physical self-consciousness which are palatable to a broad range of white middle-class people. Such social movements based upon intense *self-absorption* catered to diverse people alienated, atomized, and fractionated in a pluralistic society. Such mutual help settings were vehicles toward the reconstruction of a close-knit primary group.

Such relatively innocuous pleasure-seeking and self-improvement environments kept people quiet, concentrating on themselves in their own little worlds, with little interest, time, or energy left to question or criticize the wider society. In such a manner, the plethora of settings which cater to one's narcissism and to one's interpersonal relationships are functional for the ongoing social system. In particular, most of the people in the three settings desired to conform to the societal image of what white middle-class media and advertising preach to us is a happy, healthy, attractive, and morally good person. The three settings worked on both reinforcing and changing aspects of the individual to fit into *status quo* America, rather than stressing macro-societal change.

As types of social movements, the three settings aimed to produce changes mainly within their members rather than in society. Within a community of membership, the settings collectively promoted individual change. The individual's efforts to deal with her/his own problems became part of her/his efforts to solve an individualistically-based social problem with which she/he was intimately familiar—be it overweight, lack of physical fitness, or the difficulties of people being alone in a society.

As diversions and escapes from difficulties of life, often placing a premium on *sociability for its own sake,* such settings sometimes provided causes worth fighting for with intense involvement—causes based upon quite narrowly selfish foci. Some participants viewed the settings as enabling them to cope with some of their real difficulties of life, which they viewed as based upon bodily and interpersonal problems. In America's nation of joiners with an endless variety of causes in the midst of social and political anomie, perhaps some could seek self-growth in viable ways in such self-centered environments.

For some participants, dieting, physical fitness, or groping to connect with others seemed to be a partial involvement of their life styles. For others, circumscribed institutions catering to such interests as well as the interests themselves seemed to comprise an all-encompassing absorption, a major part of adult socialization processes. Ambivalently *alone* or *together* with others, *playful* or *serious,* tradition- or change- oriented, group dieters, health spa, and singles bar patrons went to settings which both *reinforced* and *mitigated against* participants' perceived *stigmas* of bodily and interpersonal flaws. Partaking of the rituals of rather enclosed, safe, protective settings, many participants tried to confront themselves and solve some of their personal problems outside the settings. They lived amidst impersonal mass urban society based upon a standardization of the rules through bureaucracies, not catering to individual uniqueness.

The fact that participants in group dieting, health spas, and singles bars shared common experiences meant that all had a common base of *mutuality* of problems with each other. Caregivers as leaders had the same central foci and problems as carereceivers as followers, so that recipients of a service could change roles to become caregivers. Helpers often increased their sense of interpersonal competence as a result of making an impact on another's life. The common experiences of coping with the body and/or interpersonal relationship meant that participants realized that they did not have unique experiences. They realized the universality of their interests and problems and found a safe arena in which to face their common concerns.

Participants in each setting offered each other *mutual help* and *support.* Individuals were members of groups which met regularly in order to provide acceptance of each other and mutual aid as they showed concern about the condition and progress of others. The group felt helped by an individual's success as measured by group standards of bodily improvement or interpersonal rapport, or harmed by an individual's failure. The groups' support systems consisted of enduring patterns of continuous or intermittent ties which played a significant part in maintaining the psychological and physical integrity of the individual in dealing with short-term and long-term challenges.

Sociability as a basis for such emotional support and bonding solidarity evolved from a particularized focus upon a common interest or problem to a more generalized reciprocal caring for the welfare of the whole person. Participants enjoyed each other's company as steady, predictable acquaintances and friends to count upon as companions. Such comrades accentuated people's positive and minimized people's negative self images. Participants grew more aware of themselves as people with complex emotions and motives and also enjoyed themselves in the settings as fun-filled recreation, full of juicy gossip, which made one forget one's cares.

Dieting groups, health spas, and singles bars offered an atmosphere of collective willpower and belief. Part of each setting's philosophy was that everyone could be successful in some endeavor, be it to lose weight, become physically fit, have a meaningful life as a single person, or find fulfilling relationships with others in a singles bar. Participants watched over each other, corrected each other, and helped each other recommit herself/ himself to values of the setting when an individual wavered in resolve. Each setting was a kind of concentrated pep rally in which participants both stated and showed by their own behavior that many ideologies and programs of the groups worked.

Concrete information, suggestions and guidance about common concerns were available in the three settings. Through educational strategies, members often arrived at new definitions of their problems as they shared specific information about practicalities learned through experience. Sharing belief systems, participants carried out constructive actions toward shared goals, including physical and mental socializing and working. Concrete indicators of achievement for doing existed in each setting, as weight-measurement charts, and asking someone or being asked for a date.

Careers in the settings exemplified kinds of inspirational, spiritual movements, and secular religions. Group dieters and health spa participants explicitly discussed how they had been conditioned to worship and revere ideals of thinness and physical fitness. Sinning was a common word used in the settings, whether in regard to cheating on a diet or in social relationships. Members called themselves saints or angels if they considered themselves pure and good in eating, exercising or in dealing with others. Cycles of *confessionals, testimonials,* and *redemption/reformation* as well as *guilt-atonement* patterns occurred in all groups as participants exposed the errors and virtues of their ways, measured by formal and informal norms. There was a sense of an esoteric exclusiveness of a privileged elect in the three settings where insiders in a kind of secret society with their own special ways of conceptualizing and behaving could be quite distinguished from outsiders. Such socio-religious aspects of group dieting, health spas, and singles bar stressed the primary goal of the good life here and now. Participants wanted to maximize aspects of a fulfilling life in the *present;* they were very much embedded in the details of their day-to-day, here-and-now existence.

Singles bar participants seemed to show less faith in ideals and less acceptance of regulations handed down by authorities considered wise than did group dieters and health spa patrons. The dieters and health spa members often showed a missionary zeal in advocating their partial or more total life styles; they proselytized to many about the goodness of their chosen paths. Many singles bar patrons had rather mixed feelings about the pros and cons of their life styles based at the bars. They were not as committed to definite faith or belief systems as were many in dieting groups and health spas.

As examples of the service society which has markets for the distribution of intangibles, the three settings showed the active participation of consumers in the production and management of many services. The settings were an outgrowth of the increasing participation of the American public in matters of physical and emotional well-being. These voluntary associations for consumers were caregiving systems which paralleled, complemented, and competed with other more professionalized systems. Perhaps the settings were solutions to the shortage of professional personnel in the areas of body and interpersonal care.

The three settings constituted definite subcultures, with mores and norms about eating, exercising, and interacting with others. Recognizable and predictable patterns of life styles emerged which showed much mutual dependency of people on each other. Networks of social support in a substitute world of sometimes stable quasi-families existed with demonstrations of altruism, care, help, wisdom, and self-knowledge as participants protected each other as well as themselves. The settings of mutual help were supplementary communities to other communities in which people lived and moved. For some, the settings were permanent communities to which people became attached for a long time. For others, the settings were temporary, transitional communities which intensified, scaled down, or occasionally challenged competitive conventional society. Group dieting, health spas, and singles bars, with a premium placed on achievement and competition, and succeeding in bodily or interpersonal goals, were intense microcosms of many values in contemporary America. Participants merely accentuated in the three temporary settings parts of their lives which existed outside the three settings.

The three settings were agencies of social control which used various strategies of resocialization. Quite a few discussed their processes of conversion to the particular philosophies and practices of each setting. Group dieting and health spas were a microcosm of a more general public concern over excess pounds and flab. Such settings were training and social control agencies to help many lose and keep off pounds and flab. In such contexts, overweight people were indoctrinated into the assets of thinness and the liabilities of fatness so that they would conform more with standardized beauty and health ideas pushed in contemporary America. Singles bars standardized lines and approaches between the sexes so that certain kinds of behavior were socially approved of and others were not; the bars offered hard core in-house training experiences about how to make it or not make it with a person of the opposite sex. The philosophy and tactics of "scoring" with another were part of a real learning experience for some idealistic newcomers at the bars.

The issue of total/partial *career* commitment was complicated. Quite a few people talked about dieting, exercising, or meeting people of the opposite sex as their core life involvement—even if they did not carry out such activities for many hours a day. Being very much of an advocate for or a convert to a particular setting often did not depend upon the amount of time put into that setting. The quality of involvement or commitment rather than the quantity of time was the crucial factor. Many aspects of conversion and resocialization of the settings were in the minds and hearts of participants, and only secondarily had to be shown by behavior. Such internalized commitments were carried beyond the concrete settings, in which participants might spend only a few or several hours a month.

The three self-help settings were vehicles toward coping with long-term deficits and deprivations. Continual psychological boosts and helpful information were part of the long-term support and encouragement offered. Coping meant facing and working through shame and fears about problems; it led to a willingness to admit and be open about problems with others. The ultimate goal reached by some participants was the development of a more positive, constructive attitude about themselves as persons. Often modest but attainable goals for modifying the body and interpersonal relationships were stressed. More ambitious and relatively unattainable goals were not emphasized: as reaching ideal bodily dimensions, employing perfect sociability strategies and tactics, or curing once and for all one's interpersonal difficulties or bodily deficiencies. Modest and realistic goals in the settings meant that the settings were likely to continue and satisfy their members, because high expectations which were frequently not realized were not set. Placing a premium on continuing participation and trying to minimize disillusionment and dissatisfaction, the settings attempted to make activities and goals workable and realistic for members.

Sometimes the three settings were vehicles to aid in coping with life-cycle transitions, as becoming an adult, becoming a parent, marital separation and divorce, and widowhood. Letting out tensions and shaping up the body were common concerns of new mothers, separated and divorced women, and widows in group dieting and health spas. Singles bars provided access to new social roles, new networks of social relationships for the never-married, separated, divorced, and widowed people. Involvement in the settings was a turning point for some, leading toward the development of a new life style bringing self-satisfaction as well as care for and commitment to others. Participants in all three settings began to reexamine and redefine the roles which they performed in many of their social networks.

Quite importantly, all three settings showed aspects of a therapeutic method, where there was a catharsis, a working through, and varying degrees of resolutions about certain feelings and thoughts. This therapeutic model included the letting off of steam, sociability for its own sake as a means to face tensions, expressing specific fears and worries, the giving and receiving of practical knowledge, and constructing helpful solutions to emotional problems. Participants began to accept themselves to a greater degree as they became quite aware of their strengths and limitations. The three settings built upon individuals' needs for attachments to group systems which involved a laying bare of crises, conversions and cult formation, often leading to significant attitudinal change. Many of us seek out such therapeutic strategies and support in various groups.*

Although dieting groups, health spas and singles bars do exemplify some useful and constructive therapeutic orientations, there is another viewpoint of such therapy. Lasch has stressed that much of the contemporary narcissistic climate is therapeutic, not religious. People hunger neither for personal salvation, nor for the restoration of an earlier age, but for the feeling, even if only a momentary illusion, of personal well-being, health, and psychic security. Such therapy is based on a view that there is no historical continuity in modern society which has no future and need not think of anything beyond its immediate needs. People have no hope of improving their lives in important ways. Therefore, people have convinced themselves that what matters is psychic self-improvement in getting in touch with their feelings, learning how to "relate," eating health foods, and jogging. Such pursuits are harmless in themselves—yet elevated to a program and wrapped in the rhetoric of authenticity and awareness, they signify a retreat from the political turmoil of the recent past. (Lasch, 1976, p. 5) Warlike conditions pervade American society, many dangers and uncertanties surround people as many have lost confidence in the future. The poor have always had to live for the present, but now the middle-class is desperately concerned about personal survival, sometimes disguised as hedonism. (Lasch, 1976, p. 10)

The ethic of self-preservation and psychic survival which are clear in group dieting, health spas, and singles bars are rooted not only in the objective conditions of economic warfare, rising rates of crime and social chaos, but also in the subjective experiences of emptiness and isolation. Does such an ethic reflect the belief that envy and exploitation dominate even the most intimate relations—indeed, a projection of inner anxieties as well as a perception of the way things are? Does the cult of personal relations in such settings become increasingly intense as the hope of political solutions recedes, and does such a cult conceal a thorough-going disenchantment with personal relations? Does the cult of sensuality in such environments imply a repudiation of sensuality in all but its most primitive forms? Does the ideology of personal growth, superficially optimistic about the power of positive thinking, basically radiate pessimism as the world view of the

---

*The conclusion up to this point has been informed by my reading of: Killilea, Marie "Mutual Help Organizations: Interpretations in the Literature," in *Support Systems and Mutual Help: Multidisciplinary Explorations,* ed. Gerald Caplan and Marie Killilea (New York: Grune and Stratton, Inc., 1976), pp. 37–93.

resigned? (Lasch, 1976, p. 11) Although the settings stress many manifest and latent social services for members, do they basically reflect the spirit of resigned pessimism of many Americans who turn into themselves for fear of understanding and changing American society?

Some Personal Reactions to My Research

INTRODUCTION

As we analyzed our fieldwork data, we realized that the content of what and whom we chose to see and emphasize was an endemic part of the process of our participant observation and open-ended interviewing. Indeed, the themes which we as researchers focused upon were a basic part of our research methodologies. Our personal involvement with others in the field were a most basic part of our research.

I have found that I am virtually incapable of using terms as "subjects" or "objects" with regard to people in the fields with whom I shared life experiences. I was as much a "subject" or an "object" to others as they were to me. I do not want to degrade or depersonalize others or myself by such categories. Therefore, when appropriate, when we have discussed the human beings with whom we have interacted, we call them "people," or "women" or "men." My inspiration for my personal approach toward my field experiences comes from my most memorable learning and human experiences with Dr. Everett C. Hughes and Dr. Samuel E. Wallace, two of my dissertation advisors at Brandeis University.

The four basic themes of this book: *self-absorption, conflicting and contradictory commitments, authenticating and validating oneself,* and *construction of performances,* the processing of *careers* through social settings, can be directly related to our research processes in each of the three settings. In particular, the theme of a *self-absorption* can point to notions about the researcher's *control* or *lack of control* over her/his study. The theme of *conflicting and contradictory commitments* can highlight the researcher's position of marginal fence-sitting in her/his study—to what degree and in what ways is the researcher a *participant* or an *observer.* The theme of *self-validation/self-authentication* can suggest the researcher's struggle for the discovery, formulation and testing of *hypotheses,* with regard to valid and reliable data. The theme of *construction of performances/careers* illustrates the concrete ways in which the researcher moves in and out of *relationships* with people in the field, with a concern for *reciprocal relationships* between the researcher and the people whom she/he studies.

GROUP DIETING

My basic role was that of participant observer in Trim-Down (pseudonym) group dieting meetings. I went to only one meeting of each of 41 different Trim-Down groups. I attended these different groups on a "one-shot" basis in order to grasp a sense of the breadth of the Trim-Down organization and to get a feeling for some differences between Trim-Down groups. I attended 25 meetings held by one Trim-Down group and 24 meetings held by another Trim-Down group. I went regularly to the weekly meetings of these two Trim-Down groups to try to understand in depth some of the meanings of the group process.

Rightly or wrongly, I decided to *control* part of my behavior as participant by not abiding by a formal rule of the group—that of weighing in on the scale at the weekly meetings. Executives who had given me permission to do my study said that I need not weigh in if I did not want to. I did not want to be held accountable for my weight changes or stabilization, and so intensify my own bodily preoccupations and perhaps thus impair my observations of others' concerns about their bodies and weight. After all, I was really there to study the groups—not to worry about my own weight—or was I?

Trying as hard as I could to define myself as a graduate student interested in overweight, I found that Trim-Down lecturers and members pegged me into certain roles beyond my *control*. For example, they viewed me as: a close business colleague with whom they could share business problems; a research and management consultant who could help improve the quality of the groups; a potential Trim-Down customer who needed a salespitch; a sisterly-friend-therapist who provided an open ear to listen to their interests and personal problems; a daughter or the daughter of a close friend who did or did not remind them of their own children; and a snoopy intruder or spy, who worked for Trim-Down executives or for a competing weight-losing organization or who would tattle on their cheating on the diet to group leaders.

Because of my position in the group as a graduate student researcher as well as a woman who was concerned about my 15–20 excess pounds, I found that others as well as myself had ambivalent conflicts about how *involved with* or *detached* I was from group members. Some women with whom I spent much time did seem to accept me as one of them, since I was open about my dieting doldrums. However, every now and then they did point out that I really was not one of them as I was doing research and I did not weigh in on the scale each week. They stated that they better not discuss their cheating on the diet around me, as I might tattletale on them to the group leader or give my professors a bad report about them.

As I did not feel quite valid as a group member, I tried to *authenticate* myself as a researcher. I gathered many pages of field notes of direct quotations, paraphrases, appearances and impressions of people as I openly took notes on the scene. Indeed, I *validated* myself in my role as a researcher by my voluminous note-taking in the scene so as to prove to myself that I was not just an ordinary Trim-Downer with a weight problem. I became very anxious about what to do with all this information. Gradually after rereading my notes many times and devising four or five qualitative coding schemes, I began to see the quasi-religious rituals of group dieting, manifesting reverence to thinness ideals—based upon the way Trim-Downers themselves perceived their experiences and acted in the groups. I saw repeated instances of such rituals. When I asked many Trim-Downers about the idea of secular-religious rituals, they agreed with me.

My own *career* in the groups made me very conscious of wanting to give members and leaders something back for giving me the opportunity to study them. Some leaders laughed and said that my relationship with them was one of "mutual exploitation"—they would give me the opportunity to watch if I would tell them what they were doing effectively or not so effectively. I refused to offer such judgments and labeled all the groups with the ambiguous word of "interesting." Most honestly, I could offer lengthy stories about my own dieting problems and I could empathize with others' struggles to lose weight. Some expected that I was somewhat of a nutritional expert, and they asked me questions about foods and diets. If I had any knowledge about their questions, I shared such knowledge with them. Sometimes I felt like an intermediary spokeswoman for the Trim-Down program: I was in a position somewhere between that of a group lecturer and a group member, and I found myself speaking on behalf of the Trim-Down diet plan.

In order to give of myself to the members, I kept my notebook very open to their views so that they could read my handwriting and would not think that I was writing something against them. I assured the members that any information which I was gathering would be confidential and that I would not identify people by their names and I would not reveal any personal information that would give away the identity of a person. Also, I honestly answered any questions which members asked me about my personal and educational life. When I noticed that some members intricately perused me up and down and then whispered to each other, I felt glad that they were getting even with me and casting judgment on my body since they seemed to suspect that I was casting judgment on their bodies.

My group dieting study was limited because of my minimal use of quantitative and statistical data which perhaps could have shed some important light on weight-losing patterns of different types of members. Also, I had only limited interviews with many participants in the contexts of meetings: I did not gain much knowledge about group dieters' lives outside the groups which could have been related to their dieting and weight. I only captured a part of the dieting life style. More studies need to tap individuals' motivations for joining such weight-losing groups so as to distinguish such persons from so-called "overweight" people who are not predisposed to join the groups. I believe that my study has capitalized upon the richness of data gathered in the group meetings *per se,* although perhaps I missed out on an insider's understanding by not weighing in at the weekly meetings.

HEALTH SPAS

My colleague, Dr. Hannah Wartenberg, and I were actual participants in a health spa. We were regular, paying members of a spa. We told some members and employees that we were doing some vaguely-defined research on physical fitness. When asked, we usually said that we were teachers. Sometimes we said that we taught on the college level or that we were sociologists. We did not state our clearcut research purposes to some members and employees in the spa, as we believed that marking ourselves out as different from others would lead others to treat us differently than ordinary spa members. We gathered our data by an active and changing use of our own bodies in the foreground, not by sitting still and reflecting and watching in the background.

I clearly realized that I was not completely in *control* of my role in the spa as soon as young female exercise leaders told me exactly what to do, in terms of what kinds of exercise clothing to wear, how many pounds and inches on various parts of my body to lose, and how to carry out correctly many specific exercises. I felt angry about being told about my body inadequacies, and I resented the young exercise leaders who were not at all experts lecturing to me about dieting and weight. After all, I was a professional Ph.D. sociologist who had been studying weight-losing.

I had lost about 15 pounds in studying group dieting, but I always felt that I had missed out on some important experiences by not weighing in in the groups. In my spa study, I was less defensive than in my group dieting study and I was prepared to expose my body to public view in order to experience my reactions' to others' overt judgments. I was angry in the spa. I was angry at myself for not having perfect-sized and perfect-shaped body parts. I was angry at the two very well-proportioned (according to contemporary American white middle-class standards) young holier-than-thou models who had the nerve to point out crisply my bodily flaws. And I was jealous of such young beauties.

I gathered *control* over my anger by frequenting the bathroom, where I simmered down as I wrote down elaborate field notes about verbal and nonverbal conversations and about the physical layout of the setting. I realized that I was not a researcher in *control* in terms of asking the leading questions, taking the initiative. To really experience the spa, I had to be at the mercy of the environment. I had to let myself be led, be open to correcting and improving my exercise routines and my body shape. I needed to conform to the spa environment if I wanted to fade into the background and be inconspicuous as a researcher. The real price which I paid for my research included many nights of moaning and groaning with strains and aches in my muscles and joints.

I had almost immediate rapport with many spa members, based upon our common experiences of exercising and relaxing in physical activities. I did *not* feel like a *marginal participant observer* so much in this study, because for all practical purposes of overt deeds, I was not so different from regular spa members in external appearances. I did not have many *conflicting and contradictory commitments* as a researcher, because I did not need to work hard to show that I was at least a partial insider.

In fact, although I was angry at the so-called experts for judging my body at the beginning of our study, I began to be sold on the spa as a valuable and worthwhile activity after my first six times at the spa. In fact, I became a compulsive fanatic about attending the spa regularly, as did many members—and not only to gather data. If I did not go to the spa at least three or four times a week, I really felt that I was missing something and depriving myself of definite self-improvement.

After I went to the spa regularly for a few months, my initial high-spirited enthusiasm wore off. In fact, as I began to feel more at ease and casual about my spa routines, I began to rather automatically carry out the mechanics of the exercises in the spa, without hardly thinking about anything at all. I felt so exhausted from exercising, and I began to take the spa routines so for granted that I had to pinch myself in order to remain an alert observer and listener. Such experiences contrasted with the times when I went to the spa deliberately to gather information and I really resented exercise leaders paying close attention to me and criticizing my body shape and my exercise movements.

Hannah Wartenberg and I did not want to prematurely close our minds to the richness of our abundant data by organizing our data into categories at too early a stage in our research. As some people approached us about writing up our research, such external pressures goaded us into thinking about spa activities as leisure time pursuits. We reread our field notes many times to find that spa patrons worked very hard on their bodies as well as let themselves go and had a good time at the spa. I recalled some of my readings about play and seriousness. I also remembered some of Goffman's ideas about "withness." In the middle of one night, I literally woke up and started to think about serious/playful and loner/with as important frameworks with which to analyze our data. Hannah and I reread our field notes and went back to the spa many times to have such basic typologies confirmed. We found many examples of serious loners, serious withs, playful loners and playful withs in the spa.

Our *careers* as totally involved spa participants often made us feel that we did not owe spa participants anything, and that we were literally paying our pound of flesh for the sake of our study. As regular members, we gave of our bodies and of our money, feeling exhausted, in pain, and judged by others. We received information about others' similar bodily offerings. We were weighed and measured, used and did not use exercise equipment, as stationary bicycles and weights, dressed and undressed in locker rooms, swam, sat around the pool, took whirlpool, sauna and steam baths, showered and washed our hair. Perhaps as researchers we listened more and talked less than regular spa patrons. Because we were so involved as insiders in the spa, only occasionally did we feel guilty about not discussing the details of our research interests with participants. We talked with people about their spa experiences in quite a similar manner to the way in which such people talked with each other about the spa.

In our preliminary, exploratory study carried out for the purpose of generating ideas, we did not seek out random or representative samples of spa patrons. Because our study was carried out solely on the premises of the spa, we did not discover people's feelings and attitudes about the spa when they were not at the spa. People's reactions about the spa might have been different when they were away from the spa than when they were actually at the spa. Because of our experiential and sometimes disguised roles as researchers, we did not have access to the hard facts and figures of the health spa organization. We did not believe that we could probe employees too much about their work without being perceived as nosy intruders, so we gathered little data about the spa staff, which has limited our study. We did not investigate or compare different kinds of spas, which could be another research focus. Future studies might concentrate on men's use of health spas and compare similar or different orientations to the spa held by men and women. We focused on women, and not on cross-sex relationships which sometimes did occur in coed swimming pool and whirlpool areas, and in occasional exercise classes. Perhaps more fully visible researchers, using systematic interviews and questionnaires in a broad sample of spas, can gain a different perspective on various dimensions of spas which we missed out on by choosing to pass sometimes as total spa members in only a few spas.

SINGLES BARS

One of my undergraduate students, Diane Fishel, in a university in the northeastern United States, undertook as her senior year project a study of singles bars in a large northeastern metropolitan area. At that time in 1972, Diane was an active participant in some of the bars as part of her own personal life style. Diane also had a keen analytic eye in interpreting some of the attitudes and behaviors in the bars. Diane was an insider in the bar scene. At that time, I was an outsider to the bar scene, but as Diane's teacher, I became very enthusiastic about some of Diane's field notes and general ideas. I involved myself directly in Diane's study, attending some singles bars and doing library research. Diane and I were both participant observers and we conducted open-ended interviews in various bars, often telling people that we were doing research. We were also quite open about our feelings and thoughts about ourselves as fairly young single women.

We employed snowball sampling techniques. That is, one bar participant would lead us to another bar participant to talk with. When we attended the bars, we often chose the interviewees at random from the people in attendance at the bars, "sizing up" people who looked like they would be open to talk with us. Some of Diane's acquaintances and friends were among our key informants—they pointed out some basic aspects of bar behavior and led us to various people to chat with and interview.

I found that calling myself a "sociologist" in the bars put off some people who became defensive around me. The label of "sociologist" seemed to be an inappropriately fancy and formidable title to use in the bars. I learned to call myself a "teacher" rather than a "sociologist" from some experience in which men and women rather quickly walked away from me when I said that I was a "sociologist," but more people stayed to talk with me when I stated that I was a "teacher." Some bar patrons in fact were teachers, although few were "college professors."

Diane and I soon realized that our personal characteristics, especially aspects of our appearances and clothing, and our conversational styles— quite unrelated to our research skills—were decisive factors in the tolerance and openness granted to us by bar patrons. How bar patrons sized us up was similar to how they sized up each other. We realized that we could not have complete conscious, rational *control* over our research, because much of our ability to do our research depended upon being accepted as ordinary bar comrades.

Quite a few male and female bar patrons laughed us off when we tried to be honest about our intellectual and research interests in the bars. They said that such a story was about the best "line" that they had ever heard, and they were eager to use such a "line" with new people whom they met. They added that we had a sophisticated, protective defense if we did not wind up meeting men whom we liked and who liked us. Whether or not we met men, we would be successful in collecting our information. When we fulfilled others' expectations in acting like full-fledged participants, even when others knew that we had somewhat "other purposes," we were able to relax and gain more insights into the bar scene than when we persistently pushed our research goals.

As researchers, we tried to keep our mouths shut and listen to others; as regular bar participants, we might have been prone to talk more. We realized that to do our research, we had to engage in some sharing of drinks, jokes and quick one-liners with others. To avoid slipping into becoming "ordinary" bar patrons, we brought ourselves back to our roles as researchers by walking outside the bar for a breath of air, going to the ladies' room and changing conversational partners.

Diane and I had quite a few *conflicts* about our *participant observer roles of marginality*. We were reluctant to focus upon one or two cross-sex relationships in an evening at a bar, for fear of missing out on many important happenings of others in the bar. Yet when we held ourselves aloof as detached observers, engaging in multiple snatches of conversations with quite a few people, we felt that we were missing out on what the beginning of a relationship meant at the bar.

We were concerned about being too alienated and *ethnocentric* as researchers, imposing a foreign, uncongenial perspective on the bar scene, over-categorizing and over-generalizing about bar patrons. We were also concerned about being too sociable and *going native* as we sought personal rapport with bar patrons. In order to discover the lines of men's approaches to us, we were rightfully reproached by some guys as being hypocritical come-ons when we refused to leave the bars with them. We grew restless when we let ourselves be used by some females as sympathetic ears to hear the intricacies of their love lives so that we were not free to be with others for portions of some evenings. We had conflicts about continuing relationships beyond the time and place setting of the bar, for purposes of our research, and for our personal interests.

At the beginning of our study, Diane felt quite comfortable in the bars as part of her personal life style. I was a snobby elitist who was glad that I did not need to depend on the bars for my social life. By the end of our study, Diane became more critical and questioning about the merits of the bars as she observed superficial interpersonal gimmicks. I began to enjoy the bars more throughout the study, meeting some warm, sincere and humorous bar patrons, and I realized how I had wrongly stereotyped singles bar participants as certain types of people.

Sharing our autobiographies as fairly young single women with bar patrons was a basic way for Diane and I to *authenticate* ourselves as worthwhile human beings and researchers. At first we wanted to capitalize upon the uniqueness of the singles bar as a setting by noting the rich empirical details. When Rita Seiden Miller encouraged us to present a paper on our findings at the American Sociological Association meetings in August 1973, we began to reread our data many times in order to capture some basic themes. Diane talked a lot about why she went to the bars. Diane's reasons paralleled those of many bar patrons with whom we talked—wanting to socialize with others and not be lonely.

From my background in sociology, the themes of alienation and sociability seemed quite appropriate as conceptual frameworks to make sense of some of our data. We coded our field work notes in terms of these ideas, and we went back into the field to investigate the validity and reliability of our hunches. We spoke about our conceptual ideas to some bar participants, who were quite enthusiastic about the accuracy of our perceptions. We found many instances of alienation and sociability as we defined such terms in the singles bars.

When we entered the bars, we either bought ourselves drinks or stood around the bar and looked around; sometimes we started talking with others. Sometimes we let guys buy us drinks. We soon learned that according to bar norms, we as women were supposed to wait for men to talk to us first, and so we stopped initiating conversations with men. Also according to bar norms, we learned that we could get guys to come over and start talking with us if we looked at or slightly smiled at them. With some bar patrons, we simply exchanged introductory greetings and some superficial chatter and then moved on to others; often we did not state our research intentions to such people. We often did state our research interests to people with whom we spoke for more than 10 or 15 minutes.

We did feel that we could not pay back many patrons for all the valuable insights which they gave us; the only way in which we could *reciprocate* was to discuss our own feelings and thoughts about being single and some aspects of our lives. Such an offering did seem to induce quite a few to speak with us. We did constantly over-anticipate resistance and rejection by others, mainly because of our own guilt about spying into the lives of others, without being sure about what we were giving or could give to these others in return.

We needed to conform to norms of the setting to carry out our research, such as quietly standing or sitting and eavesdropping into others' conversations, sipping drinks, and smoking cigarettes. We were only slightly irregular as singles bar patrons in that we tended to say less than many others. We tried to inconspicuously jot down notes on paper napkins, paper tissue containers or in small notebooks which we carried in our purses. Often we frequented ladies' rooms and took notes in toilet stalls. Sometimes we took notes as people talked with us, if we felt that others were comfortable with us writing in front of them. We assured them that their responses would be anonymous and confidential—we would not identify people by name or reveal personal information that would give away the identity of a person.

We did not strive to obtain a representative sampling of any defined population in our preliminary and exploratory field research project on singles bars. We hope that we have gathered some suggestive data and offered some useful analyses which may be referred to or elaborated upon in future more systematic research which more clearly tests some hunches and hypotheses which we have struggled to discover. We chose bars which were familiar to us and in which we felt fairly comfortable. A more representative sampling of different kinds of bars which cater to different kinds of people should be undertaken in future studies.

Our study was done almost solely on the scene. None of our in-depth interviews were done outside the singles bars. People might have had quite different reactions to the bars when they were not actually on the premises of the bars. We visited only a limited number of bars in one section of a large metropolitan area. We, therefore, could not speculate on differences or similarities of the bars in our sample with those in other parts of this urban area or outside this urban area. We thus were restricted to a limited time and space sample. Most of the people whom we saw were middle or upper-middle class, white and young (below 35 years old). Our study did not stress relationships among same-sex companions because the singles bars which we visited put a premium on opposite-sex relationships, and some antagonistic cooperation between same-sex associates was visible. No comparative study was made of other singles establishments, such as singles-only apartment houses, country clubs, organizations, summer retreats, or resorts holding singles' weekends. Singles bars are only one aspect of what we sense to be increasing options for life style choices by singles.

CONCLUSIONS

I believe that the processes of much research are intertwined with the content and findings of the research. I have related some dilemmas in my own field research, which I believe are intimately related to the basic themes of my research. As I focused on the theme of *self-absorption* or preoccupation with self, I was sensitive to the researcher's *control* or *lack of control* over one's study. Concentrating on *conflicting and contradictory commitments,* I thought about the marginality of some researchers' roles, in terms of being a *participant* and an *observer*. With the theme of *self-validation, self-authentication,* I pondered many researchers' struggles to gather *valid* and reliable data. Focusing on the theme of *construction of performances: the processing of careers through social settings,* I reflected on the researcher's concern about *reciprocity* in field relationships. I believe that it would be useful for more researchers to share with others their personal feelings and thoughts which significantly shape their research so that we can have a more thorough and deeper understanding of the complexities of research processes.

References

Abraham, Sidney. *Preliminary Findings of the First Health and Nutrition Examination Survey, United States, 1971-1972: Anthropometric and Clinical Findings.* Rockville, Maryland: U.S. Department of Health, Education, and Welfare, Public Health Service, National Center for Health Statistics, April, 1975.

Adams, Margaret. *Single Blessedness: Observations on the Single Status in Married Society.* New York: Basic Books, Inc., Publishers, 1976.

Aldebaran. "Fat Liberation—A Luxury? An Open Letter to Radical (and Other) Therapists." *State and Mind* 5, no. 6 (June-July 1977): 34-38.

———. "Uptight and Hungry: The Contradiction in Psychology of Fat." *RT: A Journal of Radical Therapy* 4, no. 8 (November 1975): 5-6.

Allon, Natalie. "Group Dieting Interaction." Ph.D. dissertation, Brandeis University, 1972.

———. "Group Dieting Rituals." *Transaction/Society* 10, no. 2 (January/February 1973): 36-42.

———. "Latent Social Services in Group Dieting." *Social Problems* 23, no. 1 (October 1975): 59-69.

———. "The Stigma of Overweight in Everyday Life." In *Obesity in Perspective.* Fogarty International Center Series on Preventive Medicine. Volume 2, Part 2, edited by George A. Bray. Washington, D.C.: U.S. Government Printing Office. October 1-3 1973a, pp. 83-102.

———. "Tensions in Interactions of Overweight Adolescent Girls." *Women & Health* 1, no. 2 (March/April 1976): 14-15; 18-23.

Allon, Natalie, and Fishel, Diane. Urban Courting Patterns: Singles Bars." In *Our Sociological Eye: Personal Essays on Society and Culture'* edited by Arthur B. Shostak. Port Washington, New York: Alfred Publishing Co., Inc., 1977, pp. 8-26.

Aubert, Vilhelm and Messinger, Sheldon I. "The Criminal and the Sick." In *Medical Men and Their Work'* edited by Eliot Freidson and Judith Lorber. Chicago: Aldine/Atherton, Inc., 1972, pp. 288-308.

Bates, Marston. *Gluttons and Libertines: Human Problems of Being Natural.* New York: Vingage Books, A Division of Random House, 1971.

Becker, Benjamin J. "The Obese Patient in Group Psychoanalysis." *American Journal of Psychotherapy* 14, no. 2 (April 1960): 322-37.

Becker, Howard S., and Carper, James W. "The Development of Identification with an Occupation." *American Journal of Sociology* 61, no. 4 (January 1956): 289-98.

———. "The Elements of Identification with an Occupation." *American Sociological Review* 21, no. 3 (June 1956a): 341-48.

Becker, Ron. "Your Own Beauty Spa." *McCall's* 102: 11 (August 1975): 88-89, 118, 128.

Beller, Anne Scott. *Fat & Thin: A Natural History of Obesity.* New York: Farrar, Straus and Giroux, 1977.

Berland, Theodore, and the Editors of Consumer Guide. *Rating the Diets.* Skokie, Ill.: Publications, International, Ltd., 1977.

Bloy, Jr., Myron B., ed. *Multi-Media Worship*. New York: The Seabury Press, 1969.

Bossard, James H. S., and Boll, Eleanor S. "Ritual in Family Living." *American Sociological Review* 14, no. 4 (August 1949): 463–69.

Bruch, Hilde. *Eating Disorders: Obesity, Anorexia Nervosa, and the Person Within*. New York: Basic Books, Inc., Publishers, 1973.

———. *The Importance of Overweight*. New York: W. W. Norton & Company, 1957.

Buchanan, Joseph, R. "Five Year Psychoanalytic Study of Obesity." *American Journal of Psychoanalysis*. 33, no. 1 (1973): 30–41.

Cahnman, Werner J., ed. *Ferdinand Tonnies: A New Evaluation: Essays and Documents*. Leiden, Netherlands: E. J. Brill, 1973.

———. "The Stigma of Obesity." *Sociological Quarterly* 9, no. 3 (Summer 1968): 283–99.

Cavan, Sherri. *Liquor License: An Ethnography of Bar Behavior*. Chicago: Aldine Publishing Company, 1966.

Chelminski, Rudolph. "Surviving Spas of Europe Evoke Past Gilded Age." *Smithsonian* 5. no. 5 (August 1974): 58–65.

Clinard, Marshall B. *Sociology of Deviant Behavior*. 3rd ed. New York: Holt, Rinehart and Winston, Inc., 1968.

———. *Sociology of Deviant Behavior*. 4th ed. New York: Holt, Rinehart and Winston, Inc., 1974.

Cooley, Charles Horton. *Human Nature and the Social Order*. New York: Schocken Books, Inc., Paperback edition, 1964.

Coser, Rose Laub. "Laughter among Colleagues." *Psychiatry* 23, no. 1 (February 1960): 81–95.

Craft, Carol A. "Body Image and Obesity." *Nursing Clinics of North America*. 7, no. 4 (December 1972): 677–85.

Csikszentmihalyi, Mihaly. *Beyond Boredom and Anxiety: The Experience of Play in Work and Games*. San Francisco: Jossey-Bass Publishers, 1975.

Davis, Fred. "Deviance Disavowal: The Management of Strained Interaction by the Visibly Handicapped." In *Illness, Interaction' and the Self*, Fred Davis. Belmont, Calif.: Wadsworth Publishing Company, Inc., 1972, 130–49.

de Tocqueville, Alexis. *Democracy in America,* edited by Richard D. Heffner. Abridged. New York: The New American Library, Mentor Books, 1956.

Dorsey, Leslie, and Devine, Janice. *Fare Thee Well: A Backward Look at Two Centuries of Historic American Hostelries, Fashionable Spas and Seaside Resorts*. New York: Crown Publishers, 1964.

Duguid, John. *Pleasures of the Spa*. New York: The Macmillan Company, 1968.

Durkheim, Emile. *The Division of Labor in Society,* trans. George Simpson. New York: Free Press of Glencoe, 1964.

———. *The Elementary Forms of Religious Life,* trans. Joseph Ward Swain. New York: Collier Books, 1961.

Dwyer, Johanna T. "Psychosexual Aspects of Weight Control and Dieting Behavior in Adolescents." *Medical Aspects of Human Sexuality* 7, no. 3 (March 1973): 82–108.

Dwyer, Johanna T.; Feldman, Jacob J.; and Mayer, Jean. "The Social Psychology of Dieting." *Journal of Health and Social Behavior* 11, no. 4 (December (1970): 269–87.

Dwyer, Johanna T., and Mayer, Jean. "Potential Dieters: Who Are They?" *Journal of the American Dietetic Association* 56, no. 6 (June 1970): 510–14.

Fat Liberation Front. Box 342. New Haven, Connecticut, 06513.

The Fat Underground. Box 5261. Santa Monica, California, 90405.

"The First Resorts: A Roundup of Vacationlands Preferred by World Leaders." In section, "Spring and the Traveler." *Saturday Review* 52, no. 10 (March 1969): 39–111.

Fishel, Diane, and Allon, Natalie. "Urban Courting Patterns: Singles Bars." Paper presented at the American Sociological Association meetings, August 1973.

Flügel, John Carl. *The Psychology of Clothes*. London: L. and V. Woolf at Hogarth Press and the Institute of Psychoanalysis, 1930.

Flythe, Jr., Starkey. "New Life in the Old Spas." *Saturday Evening Post* 244, no. 2 (Summer 1972): 88–89, 129.

Freidson, Eliot. *Profession of Medicine: A Study of the Sociology of Applied Knowledge.* New York: Dodd, Mead & Company, 1970.

Freud, Sigmund. *Jokes and Their Relation to the Unconscious,* trans. James Strachey. New York: W. W. Norton & Company, Inc., 1960.

———. *Totem and Taboo,* trans. James Strachey. New York: W. W. Norton & Company, Inc., 1960a.

Friedman, Abraham I. *Fat Can Be Beautiful: Stop Dieting, Start Living.* New York: Berkley Publishing Corporation, 1974.

Garfinkel, Harold. "Conditions for Successful Degradation Ceremonies." *American Journal of Sociology* 61, no.5 (March 1956): 420–24.

Glaser, Barney G., and Strauss, Anselm, L. "Awareness Contexts and Social Interaction." *American Sociological Review* 29, no. 5 (October 1964): 669–79.

Godwin, John. *The Mating Trade.* Garden City, New York: Doubleday & Company, Inc., 1973.

Goffman, Erving. "Alienation from Interaction." In *Interaction Ritual: Essays on Face-to-Face Behavior.* Erving Goffman. Garden City, New York: Doubleday & Company, Inc., Anchor Books, 1967, pp. 113–36.

———. *Behavior in Public Places: Notes on the Social Organization of Gatherings.* New York: Free Press Paperback edition, 1966.

———. *Frame Analysis: An Essay on the Organization of Experience.* New York: Harper & Row, Publishers, Harper Colophon Books, 1974.

———. "On Face-Work." In *Interaction Ritual: Essays on Face-to-Face Behavior.* Erving Goffman. Garden City, New York: Doubleday & Company, Inc., Anchor Books, 1967, pp. 5–45.

———. *The Presentation of Self in Everyday Life.* Garden City, New York: Doubleday & Company, Inc., Doubleday Anchor Books, 1959.

———. *Relations in Public: Microstudies of the Public Order.* New York: Harper & Row, Publishers, Harper Colophon Books, 1972.

———. "Role Distance." In *Encounters: Two Studies in the Sociology of Interaction.* Erving Goffman. Indianapolis, Ind.: The Bobbs-Merrill Company, Inc., 1961, pp. 83–152.

———. *Stigma: Notes on the Management of Spoiled Identity.* Englewood Cliffs, N.J.: Prentice-Hall, Inc., A Spectrum Book, 1963.

Goldwyn, Eileen Nancy. "Weight Watchers: A Case Study in the Negotiation of Reality." Ph. D. dissertation, University of California, Berkeley, 1970.

Goodman, Norman; Richardson, Stephen A.; Dornbusch, Sanford M.; and Hastorf, Albert H. "Variant Reactions to Physical Disabilities." *American Sociological Review* 28, no. 3 (June 1963): 429–35.

Gordon, Suzanne. *Lonely in America.* New York: Simon and Schuster, 1976.

Graves, Vivian, and Graves, Charles. *Enjoy Life Longer: Guide to Sixty of the Leading Spas of Europe.* London: Icon Books Ltd., 1970.

Greenberg, Clement. "Work and Leisure under Industrialism." In *Mass Leisure,* edited by Eric Larrabee and Rolf Myersohn. Glencoe, Ill.: The Free Press, 1958, pp. 38–43.

Gross, Edward. "A Functional Approach to Leisure Analysis." In *Work and Leisure: A Contemporary Social Problem,* edited by Erwin O. Smigel. New Haven, Conn.: College and University Press Services, Inc., 1963, pp. 41–52.

Gross, Edward, and Stone, Gregory P. "Embarrassment and the Analysis of Role Requirements." *American Journal of Sociology* 70, no. 1 (July 1964): 1–15.

Grosswirth, Marvin. *Fat Pride: A Survival Handbook.* New York: Jarrow Press, Inc., 1971.

Grotjahn, Martin. *Beyond Laughter.* New York: McGraw-Hill Book Company, 1957.

Hafen, Brent Q., ed. *Overweight and Obesity: Causes, Fallacies, Treatment.* Provo, Utah: Brigham Young University Press, 1975.

Hodges, Jr., Harold M. *Conflict and Consensus: An Introduction to Sociology.* 2nd ed. New York: Harper & Row, Publishers, Inc., 1974.

Hoffer, Eric. *The True Believer: Thoughts on the Nature of Mass Movements*. New York: Harper & Row, Publishers, 1951.

Holt, Herbert, and Winick, Charles. "Group Psychotherapy with Obese Women." *Archives of General Psychiatry* 5, no. 2 (August 1961): 156–68.

Hughes, Everett C. "Bastard Institutions." In *The Sociological Eye: Selected Papers on Institutions and Race*. Book One. Everett C. Hughes. Chicago: Aldine/Atherton, Inc., 1971.

———. *Men and Their Work*. Glencoe, Ill.: The Free Press, 1958.

Huizinga, Johan, *Homo Ludens: A Study of the Play-Element in Culture*. Boston: Beacon Press Paperback edition, 1955.

Hyman, Herbert H., and Singer, Eleanor, eds. *Readings in Reference Group Theory and Research*. New York: The Free Press, 1968.

Irwin, John. *Scenes*. Beverly Hills, Calif.: Sage Publications, 1977.

Jacoby, Susan. "49 Million Singles Can't All Be Right." *The New York Times Magazine*. 17 February 1974, 41–49.

Johnson, Paul F. *Psychology of Religion*. Rev. ed. New York: Abingdon Press, 1959.

Johnson, Stephen M. *First Person Singular: Living the Good Life Alone*. Philadelphia: J. B. Lippincott Company, 1977.

Jordan, Henry A., and Levitz, Leonard S. "Behavior Modification in a Self-Help Group." *Journal of the American Dietetic Association* 62, no. 1 (January 1973): 27–29.

Jordan, Herbert. *Baederbuch der Deutschen Demokratischen Republik: Im Auftrag des Ministeriums fuer Gesundheitswesen*. Leipzig: G. Thiemo, 1967.

Kalb, S. William. "A Review of Group Therapy in Weight Reduction." *American Journal of Gastroenterology* 26, no. 1 (July 1956): 75–80.

Kalisch, Beatrice J. "The Stigma of Obesity." *Journal of the American Dietetic Association* 72, no. 6 (June 1972): 1124–27.

Kaplan, Max. *Leisure: Theory and Policy*. New York: John Wiley & Sons, Inc., 1975.

Karp, Stephen A., and Pardes, Herbert. "Psychological Differentiation (Field Dependence) in Obese Women." *Psychosomatic Medicine* 27, no. 3 (May-June 1965): 238–44.

Kelley, Kitty. *The Glamour Spas*. New York: Pocket Books, 1975.

Kenyon, Gerald S. "A Conceptual Model for Characterizing Physical Activity." In *Sport, Culture, and Society: A Reader on the Sociology of Sport,* edited by John W. Loy, Jr. and Gerald S. Kenyon. New York: Macmillan Publishing Co., Inc., 1969, pp. 71–81.

Kiell, Norman, ed. *The Psychology of Obesity: Dynamics and Treatment*. Springfield, Ill., Charles C. Thomas, Publisher, 1973.

Killilea, Marie. "Mutual Help Organizations: Interpretations in the Literature." In *Support Systems and Mutual Help: Multidisciplinary Explorations,* edited by Gerald Caplan and Marie Killilea. New York: Grune and Stratton, Inc., 1976, pp. 37–93.

Kinzer, Nora Scott. "The Beauty Cult." *The Center Magazine* 7, no. 6 (November/December 1974): 2–9.

Kotkov, Benjamin. "Experiences in Group Psychotherapy with the Obese." *International Record of Medicine* 164, no. 10 (October 1951): 566–76.

Lafargue, Paul. "The Right to Be Lazy." In *Mass Leisure,* edited by Eric Larrabee and Rolf Meyersohn. Glencoe, Illinois: The Free Press, 1958, pp. 105–18.

Laing, R. D. *The Divided Self: An Existential Study in Sanity and Madness*. Baltimore, Md.: Penguin Books, 1965.

Lasch, Christopher. "The Narcissist Society." *New York Review of Books* 23, no. 15 (September 1976): 5, 8, 10, 11–13.

Laslett, Barbara, and Warren, Carol A. B. "Losing Weight: The Organizational Promotion of Behavior Change." *Social Problems* 23, no. 1 (October 1975): 69–80.

Levine, Jacob, ed. *Motivation in Humor*. New York: Atherton Press, 1969.

Lévi-Strauss, Claude. *Totemism,* trans. Rodney Needham. Boston: Beacon Press, 1963.

Lichtenstein, Grace. "A Nation of Fat Heads." *Esquire* 80, no. 2 (August 1973): 94–95, 138.

Louderback, Llewellyn. *Fat Power: Whatever You Weigh Is Right*. New York: Hawthorn Books, Inc., Publ., 1970.

Maddox, George L.; Back, Kurt W.; and Liederman, Veronica R. "Overweight as Social Deviance and Disability." *Journal of Health and Social Behavior* 9, no. 4 (December 1968): 287–98.

Maddox, George L., and Liederman, Veronica. "Overweight as a Social Disability with Medical Implications." *Journal of Medical Education* 44, no. 3 (March 1969): 214–20.

Manning, Peter K., with Zucker, Martine. *The Sociology of Mental Health and Illness.* Indianapolis, Ind.: The Bobbs-Merrill Company, Inc., 1976.

Marty, Martin E. *Varieties of Unbelief.* Garden City, New York: Doubleday & Company, Inc., Anchor Books, 1966.

Matthews, Victor, and Westie, Charles. "A Preferred Method for Obtaining Rankings: Reactions to Physical Handicaps." *American Sociological Review* 31, no. 6 (December 1966): 851–54.

McCannell, Dean. *The Tourist: A New Theory of the Leisure Class.* New York: Schocken Books, 1976.

Merton, Robert K., and Barber, Elinor. "Sociological Ambivalence." In *Sociological Theory, Values, and Sociocultural Change: Essays in Honor of Pitirim A. Sorokin,* edited by Edward A. Tiryakian. New York: Harper & Row, Publishers, Harper Torchbooks, 1967, pp. 91–120.

Mills, C. Wright. *The Sociological Imagination.* New York: Grove Press, Inc., First Evergreen Edition, 1961.

Modigliani, Andre. "Embarrassment and Embarrassability." *Sociometry* 31, no. 3 (September 1968): 313–16.

Monello, Lenore F., and Mayer, Jean. "Obese Adolescent Girls: An Unrecognized 'Minority' Group?" *American Journal of Clinical Nutrition* 131, no. 1 (July 1963): 35–39.

Montagu, Ashley. *Touching: The Human Significance of the Skin.* New York: Harper & Row, Publishers, Perennial Library, 1972.

Moustakas, Clark E. *Loneliness.* Englewood Cliffs, N.J.: Prentice-Hall, Inc., 1961.

National Association to Aid Fat Americans, Inc., Box 745, Westbury, New York, 11590.

O'Dea, Thomas F. *The Sociology of Religion.* Englewood Cliffs, N.J.: Prentice-Hall, Inc., 1969.

"On Gym Nests and Spa Spots." *Mademoiselle* 79, no. 6 (October 1974): 86.

Orbach, Susie. *Fat Is a Feminist Issue: The Anti-Diet Guide to Permanent Weight Loss.* New York: Paddington Press, 1978.

Oursler, Fulton. *The True Story of Bernarr Mac Fadden* (1868–1955). New York: Lewis Copeland Co., 1929.

Park, Robert E., and Burgess, Ernest W. *Introduction to the Science of Sociology.* 3rd. ed. rev. Chicago: University of Chicago Press, 1969.

Park, Robert E.; Burgess, Ernest W.; and McKenzie, Roderick D., eds. *The City.* Chicago: University of Chicago Press, 1925.

Powdermaker, Hortense. "An Anthropological Approach to the Problem of Obesity." *Bulletin of the New York Academy of Medicine* 36, no. 5 (May 1960): 286–95.

Pruyser, Paul W. *A Dynamic Psychology of Religion.* New York: Harper & Row, Publishers, 1968.

Radcliffe-Brown, A. R. *Structure and Function in Primitive Society.* London, England: Cohen & West, Ltd., 1952.

Reichman, Stella Jolles. *Great Big Beautiful Doll: Everything for the Body and Soul of the Larger Woman.* New York: E. P. Dutton, 1977.

Richardson, Stephen A.; Hastorf, Albert H.; Goodman, Norman; and Dornbusch, Sanford M. "Cultural Uniformity in Reaction to Physical Disabilities." *American Sociological Review* 26, no. 2 (April 1961): 241–47.

Riesman, David, with Glazer, Nathan, and Denney, Reuel. *The Lonely Crowd: A Study of the Changing American Character.* New Haven, Conn.: Yale University Press, 1950.

Riesman, David; Potter, Robert J.; and Watson, Jeanne. "Sociability, Permissiveness, and Equality: A Preliminary Formulation." *Psychiatry* 23, no. 4 (November 1966): 323–40.

————. "The Vanishing Host." *Human Organization* 19, no. 1 (Spring 1960): 17–27.

Riezler, Kurt. "Play and Seriousness." *Journal of Philosophy* 38, no. 19 (September 1941): 505–17.

Robertson, Josephine. "One Hundred Years of Hot Springs." *American Forests* 82, no. 7 (July 1976): 42–45.

Roebuck, Julian B., and Frese, Wolfgang. *The Rendezvous: A Case Study of an After-Hours Club.* New York: The Free Press, 1976.

Room, Robin. "Ambivalence as a Sociological Explanation: The Case of Cultural Explanations of Alcohol Problems." *American Sociological Review* 41, no. 6 (December 1976): 1047–65.

Rudofsky, Bernard. *The Unfashionable Human Body.* Garden City, New York: Doubleday & Company, Inc., 1971.

Russell, Bertrand. "In Praise of Idleness." In *Mass Leisure,* edited by Eric Larrabee and Rolf Meyersohn. Glencoe, Illinois: The Free Press, 1958, pp. 96–105.

Sagarin, Edward. *Odd Man In: Societies of Deviants in America.* Chicago: Quadrangle Books, 1969.

Sarton, Edgar. "Where Bad Is Good." *Holiday* 50, no. 3 (December 1971): 30–31, 56, 68.

Schachtel, Ernest G. *Metamorphosis.* New York: Basic Books, Inc., 1959.

Schachter, Stanley. "Obesity and Eating." *Science* 161, no. 3843 (August 1968): 751–56.

————. "Some Extraordinary Facts about Obese Humans and Rats." *American Psychologist* 26, no. 2 (February 1971): 129–44.

Schachter, Stanley, and Rodin, Judith. *Obese Humans and Rats.* Potomac, Md.: Lawrence Erlbaum Associates, Publ., 1974.

Scheimann, Eugene, with Neimark, Paul G. *Sex and the Overweight Woman.* New York: New American Library, Signet Book, 1970.

Schilder, Paul. *Image and Appearance of the Human Body.* New York: John Wiley, 1964.

Schur, Edwin. *The Awareness Trap: Self-Absorption Instead of Social Change.* New York: Quadrangle/The New York Times Book Co., 1976.

Seeman, Melvin. "On the Meaning of Alienation." In *Sociological Theory: A Book of Readings.* 2nd ed., edited by Lewis A. Coser and Bernard Rosenberg. New York: The Macmillan Company, 1964, pp. 525–38.

Simmel, Georg. "Fashion." *International Quarterly* 10 (October 1904): 130–55.

————. "The Metropolis and Mental Life," trans. H. H. Gerth and C. Wright Mills. In *Man Alone: Alienation in Modern Society,* edited by Eric Josephson and Mary Josephson. New York: Dell Publishing Co., Inc., A Laurel Edition, 1962, pp. 151–65.

————. *The Sociology of Georg Simmel,* trans. and edited by Kurt H. Wolff. New York: The Free Press of Glencoe, Paperback edition, 1964.

————. "Sociology of the Senses: Visual Interaction," trans. Robert E. Park and Ernest W. Burgess. In *Introduction to the Science of Sociology.* 3rd. ed. rev. Robert E. Park and Ernest W. Burgess. Chicago: University of Chicago Press, 1969, pp. 356–61.

Sklar, Kathryn Kish. "All Hail to Pure Gold Water!" *American Heritage* 26, no. 1 (December 1974): 64–69, 100, 101.

Slater, Philip E. *Microcosm: Structural, Psychological and Religious Evolution in Groups.* New York: John Wiley & Sons, Inc., 1966.

Smith, Roger W., ed. *Guilt: Man and Society.* Garden City, New York: Doubleday & Company, Inc., Anchor Books, 1971.

Sommer, Robert. *Personal Space: The Behavioral Basis of Design.* Englewood Cliffs, N.J.: Prentice-Hall, Inc., A Spectrum Book, 1969.

"Spa at Home." *Sunset* 151, no. 2 (August 1973): 60–61.

Spykman, Nicholas J. *The Social Theory of Gerog Simmel.* New York: Atherton Press, Athel-ing Edition, 1965.

Starr, Joyce R., and Carns, Donald E. "Singles in the City." *Transaction/Society* 9, no. 4 (February 1972): 43–48.

Stein, Peter J. *Single.* Englewood Cliffs, N.J.: Prentice-Hall, Inc., A Spectrum Book, 1976.

Steiner, Franz. *Taboo*. Baltimore, Md.; Penguin Books, 1956.

Stunkard, Albert J. *The Pain of Obesity*. Palo Alto, Calif.: Bull Publishing Co, 1976.

———. "The Success of TOPS, A Self-Help Group." *Postgraduate Medicine* 51, no. 5 (May 1972): 143–47.

Stunkard, Albert J., and Mendelson, Myer. "Obesity and the Body Image: I. Characteristics of Disturbances in the Body Image of Some Obese Persons." *American Journal of Psychiatry* 123, no. 10 (April 1967): 1296–1300.

Sumner, William Graham. *Folkways: A Study of the Sociological Importance of Usages, Manners, Customs, Mores, and Morals*. New York: New American Library, Mentor Books, 1940.

Sussman, Marvin B. " 'The Calorie Collectors': A Study of Spontaneous Group Formation Collapse, and Reconstruction." *Social Forces* 34, no. 4 (May 1956): 351–56.

Szasz, Thomas. *Ceremonial Chemistry: The Ritual Persecution of Drugs, Addicts, and Pushers*. Garden City, New York: Anchor Press/Doubleday Anchor Books, 1975.

Toch, Hans. *The Social Psychology of Social Movements*. Indianapolis, Ind.: The Bobbs-Merrill Company, 1965.

Tönnies, Ferdinand. *Community & Society,* trans. and edited by Charles P. Loomis. East Lansing, Michigan: The Michigan State University Press, 1957.

Turner, E. S. *Taking the Cure*. London, England: Michael Joseph, Ltd., 1967.

van Gennep, Arnold. *The Rites of Passage,* trans. Monika B. Vizedom and Gabrielle L. Caffee. Chicago: University of Chicago Press, Phoenix Books, 1961.

Wagner, Muriel G. "The Irony of Affluence." *Journal of the American Dietetic Association* 57, no. 4 (October 1970): 311–15.

Wagonfeld, Samuel, and Wolowitz, Howard M. "Obesity and the Self-Help Group: A Look at TOPS." *American Journal of Psychiatry* 125, no. 2 (August 1968): 249–52.

Wamsley, James. "Deserted Spas." *Holiday* 56, no. 3 (April/May 1975): 10–11, 18.

Warner, W. Lloyd. *The Living and the Dead*. Yankee City Series 5. New Haven, Conn.: Yale University Press, 1959.

Watson, Jeanne. "A Formal Analysis of Sociable Interaction." *Sociometry* 21, no. 4 (December 1958): 269–80.

Wax, Murray. "Themes in Cosmetics and Grooming." *American Journal of Sociology* 62, no. 6 (May 1957): 588–93.

Weiss, Robert S. "The Fund of Sociability." In *Sociological Realities: A Guide to the Study of Society*. A Trans-Action Textbook, edited by Irving Louis Horowitz and Mary Symons Strong, with the assistance of George A. Talbot. New York: Harper & Row, Publishers, 1971, pp. 198–205.

———. ed. *Loneliness: The Experience of Emotional and Social Isolation*. Cambridge, Mass.: The MIT Press, 1973.

Wernick, Sarah. "Obesity and Weight Loss in Weight Watchers; A Study of Deviance and Resocialization." Ph. D. dissertation, Columbia University, 1973.

"Where to Take the Waters." *Time Special 1776 Issue* 105, no. 20 (May 1975): 72–73.

Wilkens, Emily. *Secrets from the Super Spas*. New York: Grosset & Dunlap, 1976.

Wilson, Bryan R. *Sects and Society*. Berkeley, Calif.: University of California Press, 1961.

Wirth, Louis. "Urbanism as a Way of Life." *American Journal of Sociology* 44, no. 1 (July 1938): 1–24.

Witkin, H. A.; Dyk, R. B; Faterson, H. F.; Goodenough, D. R.; and Karp, S. A. *Psychological Differentiation; Studies of Development*. New York: John Wiley & Sons, Inc., 1962.

Wohl, Michael, and Goodhart, Robert S. *Modern Nutrition in Health and Disease*. Philadelphia, Pa.: Lea & Febiger, 1971.

Wolfenstein, Martha. "The Emergence of Fun Morality." In *Mass Leisure,* edited by Eric Larrabee and Rolf Meyersohn. Glencoe, Illinois: The Free Press, 1958, pp. 86–96.

Wollersheim, Janet P. "Effectiveness of Group Therapy Based upon Learning Principles in the Treatment of Overweight Women." *Journal of Abnormal Psychology* 76, no. 3, pt. 1 (December 1970): 462–74.

Wyden, Peter. *The Overweight Society.* New York: Pocket Books, Inc., 1966.

Wyden, Peter, and Wyden, Barbara. *How the Doctors Diet.* New York: Trident Press, 1968.

Zusman, Jack. " 'No-Therapy': A Method of Helping Persons with Problems." *Community Mental Health Journal* 5, no. 6 (December 1969): 482–85.

Author
Index

Hafen, Brent Q., 79
Hastorf, Albert H., 34
Hodges, Jr., Harold M., 1–2, 4
Hoffer, Eric, 59
Holt, Herbert, 79
Hughes, Everett C., 24–25, 41, 106, 131–32, 142, 187
Huizinga, Johan, 16–18, 107, 127
Hyman, Herbert H., 5

Irwin, J., 131

Jacoby, Susan, 130
Johnson, Paul F., 81
Johnson, Stephen M., 130
Jordan, Henry A., 79
Jordan, Herbert, 83

Kalb, S. William, 79
Kalisch, Beatrice J., 34
Kaplan, Max, 86–88
Karp, Stephen A., 81
Kelley, Kitty, 83–85
Kenyon, Gerald S., 88
Kiell, Norman, 79
Killilea, Marie, 22–23, 26–27, 35–37, 79, 89–91, 127, 133–34, 179–85
Kinzer, Nora Scott, 4
Kotkov, Benjamin, 79

Lafargue, Paul, 127
Laing, R.D., 11, 137
Lasch, Christopher, 28, 185
Laslett, Barbara, 43, 79
Levine, Jacob, 81
Lévi-Strauss, Claude, 81
Levitz, Leonard S., 79
Lichtenstein, Grace, 30
Liederman, Veronica R., 30–32, 34
Louderback, Llewellyn, 19, 81

Maddox, George L., 30–32, 34
Manning, Peter K., 4–5
Marty, Martin E., 81
Matthews, Victor, 34
Mayer, Jean, 32–34
McCannell, Dean, 85
McKenzie, Roderick D., 1
Mendelson, Myer, 34
Merton, Robert K., 13–14

Messinger, Sheldon I., 21, 79
Mills, C. Wright, 28
Modigliani, Andre, 49
Monello, Lenore F., 34
Montagu, Ashley, 173
Moustakas, Clark E., 9

National Association to Aid Fat Americans, Inc., 81
Neimark, Paul G., 81

O'Dea, Thomas F., 51
Orbach, Susie, 31
Oursler, Fulton, 85

Pardes, Herbert, 81
Park, Robert E., 1
Potter, Robert J., 23, 119, 127
Powdermaker, Hortense, 29
Pruyser, Paul W., 6, 80

Radcliffe-Brown, A.R., 51
Reichman, Stella Jolles, 19, 81
Richardson, Stephen A., 34
Riesman, David, 23, 119, 127, 152
Riezler, Kurt, 16–18, 127
Robertson, Josephine, 127
Rodin, Judith, 34
Roebuck, Julian B., 128–29, 140–41
Room, Robin, 13–14
Rudofsky, Bernard, 29
Russell, Bertrand, 127

Sagarin, Edward, 42–43, 62
Sarton, Edgar, 83
Schachtel, Ernest G., 52
Schachter, Stanley, 34
Scheimann, Eugene, 81
Schilder, Paul, 179
Schur, Edwin, 8, 28
Seeman, Melvin, 15–16, 139
Simmel, Georg, 2–3, 5–6, 23–24, 26, 52–53, 57, 127, 140, 158, 169–70, 179
Singer, Eleanor, 5
Sklar, Kathryn Kish, 127
Slater, Philip E., 81
Smith, Roger W., 62
Sommer, Robert, 175
Spykman, Nicholas J., 81
Starr, Joyce R., 130

Steiner, Franz, 51
Stein, Peter J., 130
Stone, Gregory P., 49
Strauss, Anselm L., 57, 158–59
Stunkard, Albert J., 34, 79
Sumner, William Graham, 5, 61, 110, 179
Sussman, Marvin B., 80
Szasz, Thomas, 19, 31

Toch, Hans, 80
Tönnies, Ferdinand, 6
Turner, E.S., 82–83

van Gennep, Arnold, 48, 56, 159

Wagner, Muriel G., 29
Wagonfeld, Samuel, 80
Wallace, Samuel E., 81, 187

Wamsley, James, 84, 127
Warner, W. Lloyd, 81
Warren, Carol A.B., 43, 79
Watson, Jeanne, 23, 101–3, 119, 127
Wax, Murray, 104, 108
Weiss, Robert S., 9, 16, 139, 153–54
Wernick, Sarah, 80
Westie, Charles, 34
Wilkens, Emily, 82, 84–85
Wilson, Bryan R., 6, 26, 44
Winick, Charles, 79
Wirth, Louis, 2
Witkin, H.A., 81
Wohl, Michael, 33
Wolfenstein, Martha, 123
Wollersheim, Janet P., 80
Wolowitz, Howard M., 80
Wyden, Barbara, 30
Wyden, Peter, 30, 84–85

Zucker, Martine, 4–5
Zusman, Jack, 27

Subject Index

Playful Loners
  health spas, 100–103, 112–16, 126
  in research process in health spas, 191
Playful Withs
  health spas, 100, 102–3, 116–20, 126
  in research process in health spas, 191
Powerlessness, 15, 31
  singles bars, 161–62, 164–65, 177
Primary relationships/secondary rela-
      tionships, 4, 6, 180, 183
  group dieting, 36, 41, 66–67, 73
  health spas, 90, 102–3
  singles bars, 129, 133–34, 175–178
Private public, 10, 13–15, 19
  group dieting, 35, 40, 44, 50, 53,
      62–63, 66–67
  health spas, 87, 89, 99–100, 103,
      110–12, 119–20
  public drinking establishments, 128
  in research processes, 188–94
  singles bars, 133–35, 137, 145, 149–51,
      168–78
Pseudo-gemeinschaft. See also Primary
      relationships/secondary rela-
      tionships
  general, 6
  singles bars, 175
Public. *See* Private/public
Public drinking establishments, houses,
      bars, saloons, taverns
  values and norms, contemporary
      American, 128–29, 176–78
  values and norms, cross-cultural and
      historical, 128–31, 176
Reassurance of worth, 16
  singles bars, 154, 164–68, 177
Reciprocal relationships between re-
      searcher and people studied,
      187–96
Reference group, 5, 26
  group dieting, 44
Regulars, as singles bar patrons, 146,
      156
Relational functions, 16
Repetition compulsion, group dieting, 52
Research strategies, 7, 187, 196
  limitations, 189–90, 192, 195–96
  personal reactions to group dieting,
      188–90
  personal reactions to health spas,
      190–92
  personal reactions to singles bars,
      192–96
  questions about, 78–79, 127, 178
Rituals, 6–7, 24–26, 181
  group dieting, 36–43, 47–57, 66, 72,
      77–78, 80–81
  health spas, 90–91, 104
  in research process in group dieting,
      189

singles bars, 168
Role distance, 9–10, 27–28
  group dieting, 50
  health spas, 115–16, 124
  singles bars, 132, 136–37, 140–42, 157
Role embracement, 9–10, 27–28
  singles bars, 132, 137, 157
Role-playing, group dieting, 69–70

Saloons. *See* Public drinking
      establishments, houses, bars,
      saloons, taverns
Secondary relationships. *See* Primary
      relationships/secondary rela-
      tionships
Secret society, 6, 26, 182
  group dieting, 52–53
  singles bars, 141
Sect, 6, 26
  group dieting, 44, 59
Security, as social motivation for going
      to singles bars, 166–68, 177
Self-absorption, 6, 8–13, 17, 27–28,
      180–81, 185
  group dieting, 34–35, 43, 49, 51, 58
  health spas, 86, 88–91, 98, 100–105,
      107–8, 111–16, 119–21, 126
  in research processes, 187–96
  singles bars, 132–33, 137–39, 153,
      155–56
Self-authentication, self-validation, 1, 3,
      6–7, 19–24, 27, 185
  group dieting, 35–36, 51, 58–59, 67
  health spas, 89–90, 104, 108, 114
  in research processes, 187–96
  singles bars, 133–36, 142, 155, 159–62,
      164–65, 167, 170
Self-consciousness, 10, 16, 180
  group dieting, 35, 49, 58
  health spas, 88, 103, 107–8, 110–12,
      116–17, 123
  singles bars, 132–33, 138–39, 155–56
Self-estrangement, 15–16
  singles bars, 151–52, 166–67, 176–77
Self-help groups. *See* Mutual help
      groups
Self image passim
Self-validation. *See* Self-authentication,
      self-validation
Serious, seriousness, unserious,
      unseriousness, 5, 14, 16–18,
      181
  group dieting, 35, 49, 67
  health spas, 86–89, 99–101, 103–12,
      114–16, 118–27
  public drinking establishments, 129
  in research process in health spas, 191
  singles bars, 133, 140–41, 156, 161,
      176

singles bars, 132–33, 135, 138–39, 142, 162, 171, 173–78

Troubles, 28, 180–85

Uncoupling, unsingling. *See* Coupled, coupling, uncoupling, unsingling

Unembodied self, 11
  singles bars, 132, 137–38

Upkeying, health spas, 123–24

Uplifting ceremonies. *See* Degradation, elevation/uplifting ceremonies

Unserious, unseriousness. *See* Serious, seriousness, unserious, unseriousness

Urban life, general characteristics of, 1–4

Validating oneself. *See* self-authentication, self-validation

With, withness, 15
  health spas, 99–103, 107–112, 114, 116–20, 126
  in research process in health spas, 191
  singles bars, 135–36, 139–40

Work, 5, 12, 14, 17, 182, 184
  group dieting, 35, 57, 59, 76
  health spas, 85–90, 99–101, 103–111, 113, 115, 118–24, 126
  in research process in health spas, 191
  singles bars, 128, 133, 140–41, 146, 150, 152, 155, 162–64, 166